Shaker Baskets

Shaker Baskets

Martha Wetherbee
and
Nathan Taylor

edited by
Mary Lyn Ray

Martha Wetherbee Basket Shop
Sanbornton, N.H.

Design—Todd Smith
Typography—Sant Bani Press
Printing—Murray Printing
Copyright © 1988 by Martha Wetherbee Basket Shop
ISBN: 0-9609384-4-3   HARD COVER VERSION
ISBN: 0-9609384-2-7   SOFT COVER VERSION
Library of Congress Catalogue Card Number: 88-051261

Published by
Martha Wetherbee Basket Shop
Star Route, Box 116
Sanbornton, NH 03269

This book is dedicated to those of you who purchased our baskets, and thus provided the funds for this research project.

Fig. 1

A·C·K·N·O·W·L·E·D·G·M·E·N·T·S

First we want to thank the Shakers themselves, who gave us access to their collections and have helped us all the way: Eldress Bertha Lindsay, Eldress Gertrude Soule and Sister Ethel Hudson at Canterbury, New Hampshire; Sister Mildred R. Barker, Sister Frances A. Carr, Brother Arnold Hadd and Brother Theodore E. Johnson at Sabbathday Lake, Maine.

We want to thank the staff at museums, libraries and other institutions: Bristol Historical Society, Bristol, N.H.; Essex Institute, Salem, Mass.; Fruitlands Museum, Harvard, Mass.; Hancock Shaker Village, Pittsfield, Mass.; Henry Francis du Pont Winterthur Museum, Winterthur, Delaware; Hood Museum of Art, Hanover, N.H.; Kettering Moraine Museum, Dayton, Ohio; League of N.H. Craftsmen, Concord, N.H.; Lower Shaker Village, Enfield, N.H.; New York State Museum, Albany, N.Y.; Ohio Historical Society, Columbus, Ohio; Peterborough Historical Society, Peterborough, N.H.; Shaker Historical Society, Shaker Heights, Ohio; The Shaker Museum, Old Chatham, N.Y.; Shakertown at Pleasant Hill, Pleasant Hill, Ky.; Shakertown at So. Union, So. Union, Ky.; Shaker Village, Inc., Canterbury, N.H.; United Society of Shakers, Sabbathday Lake, Maine; Western Reserve Historical Society, Cleveland, Ohio.

More personally, we want to thank these people—who include artisans, academics, collectors, dealers, business people, professional people and "just friends"—who have helped in so many individual ways: Barbara M. Adams, Bill Allen, Cheryl Anderson, Faith Andrews, Edward Baker, Donna and Jim Bargar, Warna Brickner, Ruth Ann Brod, Jean Burks, George Butler, Edward Cazazza, Ed Clerk, Peter Corey, Jim Cosgrove, Jean Crispen, Dan and Diane Czernowski, Richard and Roberta Dabrowski, Cheri Dorschner, Robert P. Emlen, Julia Fifield, Bill Finney, Marshall Ford, Grace and Robert Giusti, Jerry Grant, Steve Grivois, Cliff and Ann Hall, Douglas H. Hamel, George and Marie Hay, Marjorie Hazelton, Willis and Karel Henry, Wendell and Viola Hess, Carroll Hopf, Avis Howell, Melba Hunt, Bernice Hunter, Steve Kistler, Dean Lahikainen, Maria Larson, Peter Laskovski, Jane Law, Rachel Nash Law, Page Lilly, Sharon and Peter Lips, Hugh McMillan 3rd, Steve and Charlene Mallarick, Tom and Maureen Meyan, Amy Bess Miller, Steve Miller, Betty Morris, Charles R. Muller, John Munro, John Ott, Marius B. Peladeau, Barbie Prokosch, Joe and Nellie Ptaszek, Richard Reed, David Richards, Paul Rocheleau, Robert and Paula Rustick, Vicki Sand, Gregory C. Schwarz, Todd Smith, Roger Sorel, June Sprigg, Richard Starr, Elizabeth Stell, Winola Stokes, Robert Straw, Beatrice Taylor, Dorothy Taylor, Robert and Mary Taylor, Charles ("Bud") Thompson, Frederick and Anne Tolman, Diana and Paul Van Kolken, Rick Vollmer, Walker Weed, Douglas White, Craig Williams, Artelia Wilson and Dean Zimmerman.

Finally, we thank our staff who've kept shop while we've been gone: Roberta Beaupre, Jeannine Frost, Betty Grondin, Eric Taylor, Laura Volker, Joann Vollmer.

Fig. 2

Martha Wetherbee and Nathan Taylor have filled a large gap in the study of Shaker crafts, that needed their particular gifts. All interested in things Shaker owe them much.

Where so many have been willing to take "Shaker" loosely, Martha and Nate have not been satisfied unless they could confirm that there was an intrinsic basis for any attribution. They have discovered the details that identify Shaker work and the reasons for them. In their study of Shaker baskets, they have set a new standard for what Shaker research should be. Their book is a monumental work. It is a pleasure to endorse and introduce it.

Faith Andrews

Fig.3 Back in the 1930s when William Winter was making his classic photographs of Shaker interiors, and Faith and Edward Andrews were beginning to collect and write about Shaker, the monumental architecture and the furniture they found upstaged baskets. Baskets turn up in photographs, but little is said about them because little was known.

The last Shaker basket was made in 1958; but Shaker basketmaking had effectively come to an end by 1900. In a period of some sixty or seventy years, the Shakers had made 150,000—maybe 200,000—baskets. A good half of these were for their own use; and the rest were made for sale. Perhaps 2,000 are extant, allowing for the one here, the one there, those in museums and private collections. On the open market you're lucky if you see one in a year.

Because the Shakers made things well, this attrition seems unnaturally high until you think how fragile a basket is. Baskets that are used eventually crack and break. Few old-looking American baskets you see around are older than the late nineteenth century, and most date from the 1920s-30s. Compared to others, surviving Shaker baskets are unusually old. A high percentage of the baskets the Shakers produced for themselves remained in their communities until families began to sell off what they no longer needed, around 1900-30. Most of these baskets were well preserved until then; but once they were dispersed, their "right use" wasn't understood and they were, many of them, damaged. The fancy baskets made for sale were exposed to potential misuse from the start. Damaged baskets weren't something people kept; and as a result, more than 148,000 Shaker baskets have been thrown out.

We became interested in Shaker basketry in 1974. We had other careers then. We weren't basketmakers; we weren't historians. But a book by Edward Andrews changed that. Flipping through *Community Industries of the Shakers* (1933), we saw that Shaker baskets had a different look; and we wanted to know how they got it.

Only the baskets were left to learn from. No one had taken down the process or the history of the basket industry when there were Shakers who knew. By the 1970s, even outside the Shakers there were few old-timers in the northeast who still made black ash baskets; and their work wasn't like the Shakers'. So we began our research by examining baskets which were said to be Shaker. We took apart baskets that were damaged to see how they had been put together. We collected every scrap we could find in archives where Shaker basketry was mentioned. We became basketmakers, and apprenticed to the Shakers through their baskets. In attempting to make baskets that looked like theirs, we had to learn to make them like theirs. If our handle or our splint or our form didn't match theirs, we didn't get it the way they got theirs. So we kept experimenting; and when finally we got it, and got it easily and efficiently, we knew we got it their way. Through our experience we learned to make meaning of the basketmakers' journals, their formulas, their methods.

As we studied other splint basketry in the northeast, we came to understand the context that Shaker baskets came from. We learned to separate baskets by material, technique and form. We learned to read the "signature" a basket carries, that relates it to others of a type, representing a locale, a shop or a single maker. We began to test existing attributions and provenance against information in the baskets. We began to see what Shaker was; and we also saw that much of what passed for Shaker wasn't.

Here is what we have learned about Shaker baskets.

We knew we would write a book; but we didn't know it would take thirteen years. We found out that you don't just make baskets or research them. You live them. You enter their story, and that story keeps unfolding.

Shaker Baskets

Fig.4 A basket in a Shaker barn, c. 1930.

"In the manufacture [of their baskets] the line of beauty has unconsciously introduced itself."
From the diary of an Englishwoman visiting the Shakers, 1848[1]

In 1947 E.M. Forster went to New York to take a look at the Shakers. He was not moved by wooden chairs hanging on wooden pegs on a wall. "Their simplicity," he said, "is impressive but not interesting." If anything commended these people, he concluded, it was their "hard work," their "good if dull craftsmanship," their honesty and celibacy. "Sometimes in meetings," he observed, "they were seized by the Spirit and shook: otherwise nothing remarkable occurred."[2]

Not everyone thrills to the idea of Shaker. But there is agreement that Shaker craft is "good." A century and a half ago, when it was new *(1)*, anything with the Shaker name had the reputation for being "of the neatest kind, and command[ing] the best of prices."[3] Even while the Shakers' views on religion were ridiculed, their manufactures were highly respected. Their stores attracted a national clientele. Shaker seeds, Shaker bonnets, brooms, baskets and chairs were household words. But times changed. The Shakers became a forgotten phenomenon. Their radical aspirations, their radical achievements went unguessed of a few old-fashioned ladies. Then in 1923 historical accident brought the two people who would do the most to rescue the Shaker name to the Hancock (Mass.) community. "Though we were born and raised within a few miles of the Hancock Shakers, neither of us," Faith and Edward Andrews wrote later, "knew much more about them than the current gossip that they were a peculiar sect. We had never heard that they made their own furniture. No one had ever collected it. No one knew the history of their [industries]."[4]

With the Andrews, the Shaker "discovery" got out. In 1928 *Antiques* published its first article on Shaker furniture. In 1929 *House Beautiful* advised its readers "if you own [something Shaker], preserve it with great care, for it will soon be considered an antique, and a rare one at that. . . . Now is the time to secure any pieces obtainable."[5] Shaker became collectible. It became high art. There was a rediscovery of its severe beauty that linked easily with modern ideas coming out of Europe. It seemed as if the Shakers had prefigured Bauhaus *(2)* design. "The only kind of beauty [the Shakers tolerated] was that springing unsought from what is today called functionalism. . . . Their aim was to make the lines right so that their buildings, their chairs, would be strong and would endure. . . . It is a paradox," Marguerite Melcher wrote in 1941, "which the early Shakers would not have appreciated, that their furniture is now being collected and their buildings admired as contributions to American art, while the principles on which their religion was built have [been discarded as retardetaire]."[6]

The spare line of Shaker is what you notice. But there is something—the word you almost use is hallowed—too. The idea of work as sacrament infused the lives of the Shakers. "You see," said an English writer around 1867, "that the men who till these

1. The Shaker experiment goes back some 200 years. Organized into communities by the end of the eighteenth century, the Shakers had their greatest strength in the nineteenth. Many of the villages were disbanding by the first decades of this century; but others held on. Mt. Lebanon closed in 1947, Hancock in 1960. The two communities continuing today are at Canterbury, N.H. and Sabbathday Lake, Maine.

2. Form answered to use in Shaker design. The same premise was at the core of Bauhaus theory. Founded in 1919 in Weimar, Germany, the Bauhaus began as a school of architecture and applied arts seeking to find new forms, a new style, for modern industrial society. Design— and its product—"must be useful," the Bauhaus taught, "and above all must correspond to the function of the object." – "Function should dictate form, which should never be hidden under superimposed decoration." ±
Concerning itself with industrial method, prefabrication, standardization, economy of line and means, and right use of materials (all ideas the Shakers dealt with), the Bauhaus became the center of new design in Europe in the 1920s; by the 1930s, when it relocated in the United States, the name "Bauhaus" had become synonymous with modern functional style.

The March; Shaker Worship.
Lebanon. Aug. 16. 1856

Fig. 5

Fig.5 What set the Shakers apart from other protestants was their insistence on a celibate and communal life, and their supposed conviction that Christ had made a second appearance in a woman named Ann Lee.

"There was another day prophesied of," the Shakers wrote, "called the second appearance of Christ . . . in which the mystery of God should be finished as he had spoken by his prophets since the world began."[1] In Ann Lee (1736–84), they said, the "mystery" that had been withheld was "finished." An otherwise unextraordinary woman who worked in low jobs in Manchester, England, she preached an apocalyptic message, which she had received in vision: those who would be saved must "give up the world and the flesh." The resulting church took the name of the United Society of Believers in Christ's Second Appearing; but the members were usually called "Shakers" because of the dances they performed in their meetings ("Come life Shaker life," they sang as they danced, "come life eternal. Shake Shake out of me All that is carnal").[2]

"The Shaker Way," Robley Whitson writes in *The Shakers: Two Centuries of Spiritual Reflection,* "begins where other Christians expect the pilgrimage of Faith will one day end: the Second Coming of Christ in Glory." Among the Shakers, he interjects, "for some the emphasis is on the community of Believers, the Church-who-are-Christ; for others, it is on the tension of conversion from a pervading sense of sin and unworthiness to the wonder of discovering a transforming perfection in Christ; for still others, the emphasis is on the person of Ann Lee and the recognition of Christ-come-again through her ministration. But whatever the emphasis . . . Ann Lee herself is *not* an 'incarnation' of Christ. The reality of Christ is indeed experienced in her, but also *equally* in each and every one united in Christ."[3]

Although the Shakers were a people of quiet virtues, who made a doctrine of simplicity, honesty, utility, generosity, kindness and peace, to their more prosaic neighbors they seemed dangerous and queer. "Why this jumpin up and singing? This long weskit bizniss, and this anty-matrimony idee?" the satirist Artemus Ward [Charles Farrar Browne] asks. "My frends," he says, "you air neat and tidy. Your lands is flowing with milk and honey. Your brooms is fine, and your apple sass is honest. . . . You air honest in your dealins. You air quiet and don't distarb nobody. For all this I givs you credit. But your religion is small pertaters, I must say. You mope away your lives here in single retchidness. . . . You wear long weskits and long faces, and lead a gloomy life indeed. . . . The gals among you, sum of which air as slick pieces of caliker as I ever sot eyes on . . . you old heds fool yerselves with the idee that they air fulfilin their mishun here, and air contented. Here you air all pend up by yerselves, talking about the sins of a world you don't know nothin of."[4]

Fig.6 Derisive illustrations like this one were published to express the suspicion many people felt toward the Shakers because of their "odd" views on sex and religion.

fields, who tend these gardens, who bind these vines, who plant these apple-trees, have been drawn into putting their love into the daily task; and you hear with no surprise that these toilers, ploughing and planting in their quaint garb, consider their labor on the soil as a part of their ritual, looking upon the earth as a . . . sphere which they have been called to redeem . . . and restore to God."[7] The same conviction went into their crafts, somehow irradiating them.

The Shakers were not a craft community; their manifesto was social and religious. Yet craft became important to them, as the baskets are clear testimony. They are craft transposed. By excellence. And by a poetry the Shakers lived, a vision they were convinced of, a mystic doubling that let them believe that angels not only dwelled among them but also brought them "gifts of love and blessing," and carried these gifts in baskets.

Because "Shaker" is trailed by a mystique ("There is a charm about genuine Shaker that cannot be put into words," *House Beautiful* intoned in 1929[8]), too often anything suggesting "Shaker" has become Shaker. "Attribution" has been more important than seeing what the Shaker difference is. And sometimes the difference is very subtle; Shaker art is a subtle art. Especially in baskets.

*Fig.*7 From a Shaker drawing, 1848.

A reverence for something in Shaker craft that seems sometimes otherworldly has led to the idea that "Shaker" defies definition. And so the mystery of where Shaker art has come from has perpetuated a mystique.

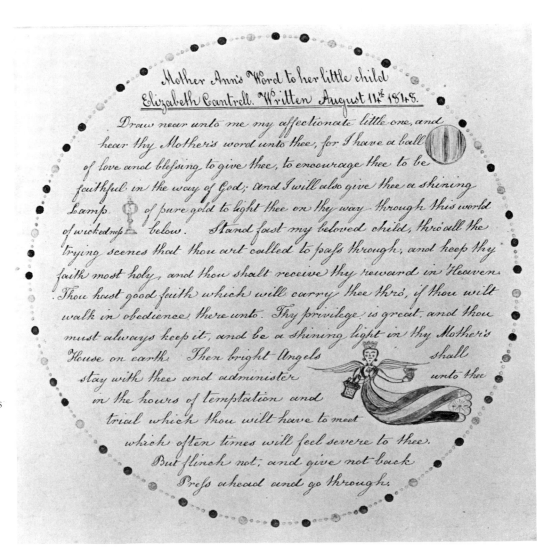

If a basket is not made of black/brown ash, it's not likely Shaker. Ash was the traditional "basket tree" in the areas of New England and New York where the Shakers resided. Ash baskets are the baskets they put their signature on. But other makers also worked in ash. And there lies the confusion: what is Shaker?

Long before white settlers arrived, Indians in the northeast were making split-ash baskets. Sometimes they used other indigenous materials: birch bark, sweet grass, oak, hickory, maple, elm. But where they had a choice, they preferred black/brown ash.

As colonists began to extend a web of settlement inland, the Indians sold them baskets made of ash. And up until 1930/40 they continued to sell and trade very similar baskets. It was a common occurrence for an Indian to come around peddling baskets; others were typically offered in stores. Thousands of these baskets were sold; and thousands are still around. Many of them are light and beautiful, because the Indians made frugal use of their materials. Many of them have a nice spare form. And many of them have been mistaken for Shaker.

As many as eight out of ten baskets attributed to the Shakers are in fact Indian-made; and their origins are easy to see once you know what to look for. If a basket has no carved outer rim—if a simple piece of splint, the width of a carved inner rim, forms the outer "rim"—you're probably looking at an Indian basket. The rim, and also the handle, on this basket will likely be triangular in section, from the cut of the knife (called a crooked knife) which Indians used from an early date on into the eighteenth and nineteenth centuries, and some still use in the present century. Where the handle is notched to accept the rim, the shelf of the notch, for the same reason, will most probably also be triangular in section. The notch is typically "single," with a shelf below but not above the rim.

At the base of the basket where the sides start up, there may be a wide weaver, which is another Indian characteristic. When they started to weave the sides, Indians commonly laid in a wider weaver to help hold the bent uprights in place and thus speed up the weaving process.

Another point to check for is an upright or rib that has been split (to allow for continuous spiral weaving; see *Chapter Five*). A split upright is not unique to Indian work—it became very common in splint basketry; but it was originally an Indian idea and has remained an Indian attribute.

Material in an Indian basket is light, and the splint is typically "split" or pulled apart, giving it a "satin" finish on the outer face. (Less often it is scraped, leaving it somewhat hairy.) Basketforms are almost infinite. Utilitarian types are routinely square bottom-to-square top; square bottom-to-round top; round bottom-to-round top; square bottom-to-ovoid top. Fancy types range from basic square and round forms to more unusual shapes, and in these the splint may be colored or decorated with designs drawn or stamped on.

As you begin to recognize Indian work, you may see some baskets you aren't sure about. They have some Indian attributes but they have a different look. The material is still light; there is still the thin strip of splint as an outside "rim," the wide weaver where the sides start up, the single notch. But the inside rim, which is a carved rim, may seem more round than the "typical" Indian rim; the shelf below the notch, likewise, may appear rounded or squared in section. In some instances even the wide weaver at the bottom may have been deleted, or the thin outer "rim" of splint may have been replaced with a rim carved like the inner rim. These are hybrid baskets made by Indians who, over time, dropped some of their old ways and took up new tools and a new way of making a basket that they learned from the settlers, who had in turn learned from them. These hybrid baskets are those most easily confused with Shaker.

Fig. 8 The basic tools of the white basketmaker were familiar to almost any farmer—tools used for splitting fence, ripping shingles, dressing lumber.

Colonists had come to America knowing the utility of baskets. But the baskets they were accustomed to were, for the most part, made of willow. Willow grew freely in the old world in copse and hedgerow; it could also be cultivated; it came back after harvesting; and it made a strong basket. Splint baskets had been common once in England and in Europe, before trees became scarce. But as the natural forests were depleted, and surviving stands were protected in parks closed to ordinary people, basketmakers substituted willow for splint. And with the use of willow, a different type of basket—and basketcraft—evolved.

Among the many reversals colonists experienced in America was the discovery that they had come to a world dark with trees but devoid, in the northeast, of suitable willow. Baskets they used in the new world would be made of splint. Settlers learned the Indian preference for black ash and borrowed some Indian methods. But instead of using the Indians' tools, they used tools that were already familiar to them, to prepare the splint and shape the handles and rims. Most significantly, they substituted a drawshave (or drawknife) for a crooked knife. As a result the baskets they made look like Indian baskets in some respects but differ in others.

First off, the settlers' baskets tend to be heavier. They can have a grace, but it tends to be a heavy grace. The splint is usually scraped instead of split, leaving it coarser in texture than the Indian's "satin." Because the tools were different, tool marks are different; and rims and handles are rounded or squared in section, as is the shelf of the notch. The notch itself is more often "double" than single, with a shelf above the rim as well as below. Unlike the Indian, the settler did not use a wide starter weaver. Nor did the settler use a thin piece of splint for an outer rim; both rims are carved.

Basketforms correspond to the simpler Indian forms but they are straightforward, made for use. Settlers rarely, if ever, made decorative baskets. If they wanted something fancy, they bought from the Indians. The typical basketmaker was an untutored artisan, often a farmer who made baskets for his own use, and sold or traded some extras. For most, basketmaking was a part-time business that brought in some supplemental income. Some itinerants made a living by stocking up baskets at home and then peddling them in the countryside, as the Indians did. But most makers supplied only themselves or a very local market.

Up to the 1800s, Indian or settler, basketmakers in the northeast were making baskets as they had been made for generations. Their concept of how a basket should be made and what it would be used for had been passed down to them from basketmakers before them, who had used the same simple tools and shaped the same simple forms. What had worked then worked still.

This is the context out of which Shaker baskets evolved.

Material eliminates many baskets as not-Shaker. Black/brown ash is what you want to look for. If a basket is made from another material, be cautious. There are very few utilitarian Shaker baskets known that are not ash. There are a handful of oak and willow baskets associated with the Shakers in western states, but no genre as such has surfaced. There are also some "fancy" baskets made of palm leaf. But the primary material, beginning to end, was ash.

Although the Latin name *fraxinus nigra* translates literally "black ash," in some parts of New England "basket ash" has traditionally been called brown ash; the New York Shakers called it "black." It is the most versatile of the basket trees in the area of the northeast that became New England. It extends west across the United States to Wisconsin, but white oak takes over to the south; the line effectively dividing ash territory from oak crosses close to the lower tier of New York. Oak is stronger and more rigid, but ash has resilience and flex. Ash is easier to work with, easier to bend, easier to clean. Because it is more pliable, it is less apt to break or splinter. And when it has been refined, it has a quality second to none: it is like a satin ribbon that can be pulled, won't snag and will slip tight.

Long before there were settlers or Shakers, Indians in the northeast were making baskets of brown ash. They may have observed how trees that had blown down shattered along their growth rings into hundreds of thin strips of splint. For a time they may have relied on this free splint for their baskets; but it was probably not long before they found that they could force the growth rings to separate by pounding the trees. And for centuries to come, technology as simple as that, along with elementary knife-work, was all that was required to make a basket from a tree.

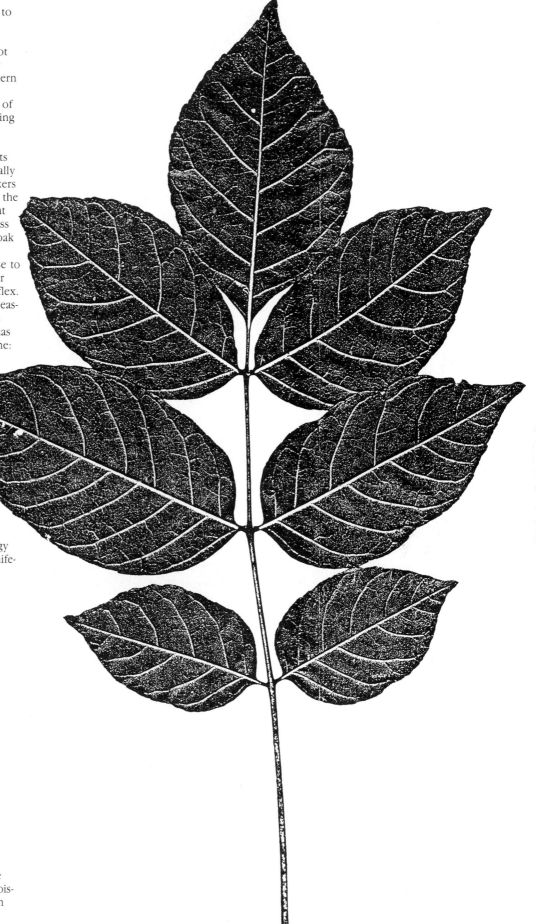

Fig.9 Black/brown ash is most likely to be found in wetland where it can wick up moisture. The swampy habitat that black/brown ash prefers kills out other growth, leaving room for the ash.

Fig.10 Pounding releases the layered growth rings of an ash log.

Fig.11 More often than not, the outer face of splint in an Indian basket has the "satin" finish of split ash. A growth ring (from which the splint is taken) is grainy when it leaves the tree. If, however, the growth ring is split down the middle, it gives splint that's "satin." Split ash has a nice look and finishes easily. The inner surfaces emerge smooth; there's no reason to work them. Only the original outer surfaces need scraping. Splitting is also a frugal method, making splint go twice as far.

10

Fig.12 If a basket has no carved outside rim—if a piece of splint, the width of the inner rim, forms the outer "rim"—you're most likely looking at an Indian basket.

Basketmakers sometimes called this type of rim a "cheat rim." Long before the word was invented, the Indians were "streamlining," altering their routine or method—as here—to make processes simpler, quicker, more efficient. Their idea was to use the least material, the least effort, the least time to get the product they wanted.

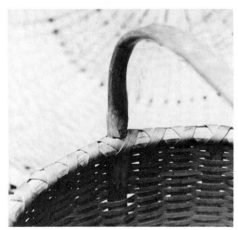

Fig.13 Most Indian baskets have a single notch for the rim in their handles. There is a shelf below, but not above, the rim. Typically, this shelf is triangular in section.

Fig.14 You may, however, come across an Indian basket with a double notch, as in this example.

Fig.15 The Indian's traditional basket tool is called a crooked knife, because the blade comes off the handle at a "crooked" angle (to compensate for the position in which the knife is most comfortably and efficiently held). Material to be worked is placed in the opposite hand and rotated three times. The three resulting cuts account for the pointy look of Indian-carved rims and handles; the lack of leverage in the way the knife is held and pulled toward the chest explains the choppiness of the strokes.

11

Fig.17 The wide starter weaver seen in many Indian baskets is not just decorative. It was laid in to help hold the uprights in place and speed up the weaving process. Without a wide starter, a basketmaker must otherwise invest considerable time in bending the uprights and holding them in position while starting to weave the sides.

Fig.18 Baskets made by Indians who had adopted some of the white man's tools and methods are those most easily confused with Shaker. The shelf of the notch may not be tri-angular. Both rims may be carved. There may be no wide starter weaver. These baskets may trip you, because they tend to look like what you think a Shaker basket should look like.

This carrier has typical Indian rims and material, and typical square form. The notch, however, is rounded as is the handle in section.

Fig.16 Indians commonly split one of the basket ribs or uprights to allow for continuous spiral weaving (for a technical explanation, see *Chapter Five*). A split upright, however, is not unique to Indian work; the majority of basket-makers working in splint have borrowed the idea from them. Almost any country basket you look at will have a split upright.

Fig.19 The squared corners and light material in this basket are Indian attributes. Other details—the drawshaven rims (the outer one, a thick growth ring), the square shelf of the notch, the split upright—are ambiguous.

Fig.21 This basket has typical Indian rims but the shelf below the notch is square (Fig. 20). A cupped bottom is often associated with Shaker basketry, but it is not necessarily indicative of Shaker work. Although some Shaker fancy styles (such as "fruits" and "cat heads"; see *Chapter Three*) have similar form, no Shaker field basket of this design is known.

Fig.22 A country basket of the sort that has passed for Shaker. The patina is rich and warm, making the basket seem old and significant. The work is fair but appears exceptional, because the material is light and has good balance. This is what you see when an Indian didn't use a crooked knife. Rims are thick growth rings, cleaned with a drawshave. The handle is also drawshaven. The double notches have square shelves. Splint, however, has the satin finish of split ash and is light, like Indian splint.

Fig.23 More easily recognized as Indian is this basket with painted decoration.

14

Fig.24 William Bellerose (leaning on his elbow), an Abenaki who later married into the French Canadian community in Manchester, New Hampshire, was foreman over eighteen men in his village around 1900. You can see here the scale of their operation. Long after factories had introduced other methods, they (and other Indians) continued to prepare their splint in the old way—pounding the ash logs to free the growth rings, which they then split (note the vise held between the knees) and trimmed to size. The portable engine possibly ran the saw that was used to cut the logs.

Fig.25 Indians made more baskets than anyone else in the northeast. "Tons of ash logs were stripped into millions of yards of ribbon strips to make the famous Abenaki baskets," the caption under this newspaper photograph read.[5] The volume of Indian sales was never severely challenged until cheap baskets began to be mass-produced in factories around the middle of the nineteenth century; and then the Indians simply developed a new market (which is examined in *Chapter Three*).

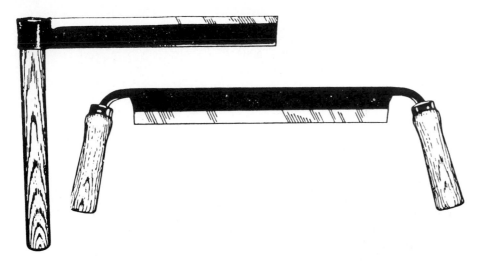

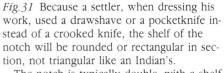

Fig.26 A froe was used to split the wood for handles and rims. A blade with a chisel edge, set at a right angle to the handle, was driven into a log when the blade was struck with a maul. In this way a tree was quartered and reduced to blanks from which handles and rims were made.

Fig.27 A drawshave or drawknife was used to smoothe the splint and to shape rims and handles. Where the Indian used a crooked knife, the settler used a drawknife, sometimes finishing up with a pocketknife.

Fig.28 A shaving horse, a kind of vise, held the material firmly in place while it was being worked with a drawknife.

Fig.29 Both rims on a settler basket are carved and dressed. They will vary in section from semi-round to rectangular; that choice was part of a basketmaker's signature.

Fig.30 Handles, also, are characteristically semi-round to rectangular in section, with ridgy bevels left by a drawshave.

Fig.31 Because a settler, when dressing his work, used a drawshave or a pocketknife instead of a crooked knife, the shelf of the notch will be rounded or rectangular in section, not triangular like an Indian's.

The notch is typically double, with a shelf above as well as below the rim. Designed for hard use, a double notch helped prevent a handle from slipping up and down, and weakening a basket.

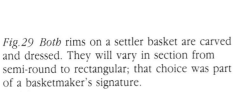

Fig.32 The splint in a settler basket is typically heavier than the Indians'. Usually scraped instead of split, it tends to have a grainier finish. Note how the outer face of the splint in the basket (from ''Center Lovell, Maine / 1907'') is similar in texture to the inner face of the Indian splint shown in Fig. 16.

Figs.33–35 Some straightforward settler baskets.

Fig.36 The shape of this basket is typical of settler forms. The material is oak, which you see in some baskets from the northeast but not in Shaker (with the exception of a very few baskets found in western communities; see Figs. 272–75).

Fig.37 The elemental geometry of rounds and cones makes this an exceptional basket. Here was a country maker who understood design and cared about workmanship. The narrow cut of the splint gives the basket an Indian look; but the weight of the material is heavy, like settler splint, and the rims and handle are drawshaven.

18

Fig.38 Indian or settler, the vernacular basket-maker continued to use the same methods and tools that had been passed down to him. As a result, the basket in this photograph from 1901 is little different from baskets common 150 years before.

"The severity and stripped utility of all Shaker objects . . . was in perfect harmony with machine work. Shaker art [was] molding a new tradition."

John Kouwenhoven, *Made in America*, 1948[1]

In their early years the Shakers made do with whatever furniture, tools, buildings and land were donated. They made do with ordinary baskets that believers brought in when they came to live with them. Attempting to transcend the gratifications of this world to enter the grace of another, the Shakers knew their first work was to clear, till, plant—and worship. They were just surviving.

The Shaker experiment had begun very simply. The first believers, who had broken off from the Quakers, left England and arrived in America in 1774. Because someone told them of some land near Albany, New York, they went there *(1)*. They had no definite plan, except to honor the vision Ann Lee had seen of a new salvation open to whomever would accept their testimony. Their message at first brought few converts; but convinced there was to be "an increase" in their numbers, in 1781 they went east into New England on a tour that kept them from home over two years. Response to their preaching was, for the most part, hostile: they were beat up, jailed, made sport of. But among the crowds who assembled to abuse them, "there were those who heard." By the time the original group returned to New York, they had seeded several congregations, and the idea of separating from "the world" *(2)* had become part of their testimony.

Before the Shakers could achieve their vision of a community, their "Mother," Ann Lee *(3)*, died; and direction of the new society shifted to her followers. As they began to give shape to their faith, they saw proof—long before they applied it to their handwork—of what she had been teaching, that "every force evolves a form."[2] They were, they felt, being led to create "a new order" fusing the spiritual and the temporal *(4)*. Their few collective households swelled, as more and more converts withdrew from the world to openly join with them. Their faith was finding a form. And as they saw they had outgrown—on a spiritual and a practical level—the scale of life they had carried over, they began to think on a new scale.

In 1787 the first community in "gospel order" was gathered at Mt. Lebanon, New York *(5)*. Within a few years believers were dispersed among ten additional communities in the northeast: Watervliet (in New York); Hancock, Harvard, Tyringham and Shirley (in Massachusetts); Enfield (in Connecticut); Canterbury and [New] Enfield (in New Hampshire); Alfred and Sabbathday Lake (in Maine). Within a decade, another seven communities would be added to the west, in Ohio, Indiana and Kentucky. Each village was organized around large "families" where men and women were segregated in male and female "orders," and children were placed in their own order. A typical village was composed of several Shaker families *(6)*, each with their separate (and monumental) dwellinghouse and (in time) shops, barns and mills; a single meeting-

Fig.39 View of the Church Family, Mt. Lebanon in the nineteenth century.

There were eleven different Shaker communities in the northeast. In no two of them did basketmaking develop the same, and in some there was possibly no basketmaking at all. Greatest production was at Mt. Lebanon, which was the "lead" community and the largest.

"It was a subduing sight," a writer for *The New Yorker* described Mt. Lebanon as late as 1947—"a phalanx . . . of big, raw-boned, white clapboard buildings of indeterminate purpose, all rearing up among towering elms and maples."[6]

house was located at the "lead," or Church, family. In each family deacons and deaconesses were appointed to manage shop and domestic matters, and trustees were appointed to oversee financial and legal transactions. At the head of each family were two elders and two eldresses, with those in charge of the Church Family serving additionally as "ministry" for the whole village *(7)*.

Separated from "the world" to gather into visible order and build a place where they could articulate the precepts of their vision, the Shakers made no real distinction between physical and spiritual labor. Pledging to "improve [their] time and Tallents in this life in the way in which [they] might be most useful,"[3] they "labored" in the dance, they labored in the field, they labored in the kitchen. Labor was a kind of sacrament, which they accepted as something to be shared, a holy communion. Each person was to take part *(8)*.

For the Shakers the point of all labor was to get to what was fundamental and so to come to God; and out of this premise a radical idea they called "economy" evolved. "*1. Thrifty management; frugality in the expenditure or consumption of money, materials, etc. 2. management of the resources of a community, with a view to its productivity 3. regulation of the parts or functions of a whole; an organized system or method 4. efficient, sparing or concise use of something 5.* Theol., *a. the divine plan for man b. a method of divine administration*"[4]: the Shakers took the dictionary definition whole and in the concept of "economy" found the integration of the spiritual and the temporal they were seeking. They rejected whatever was "superfluous" *(9)* and made it their task to simplify, pare, improve; to honor right use; to seek right form; to eliminate the unnecessary. *This* is the economy—more than just an economy of line—that shows in their baskets.

The Shakers began making baskets when the baskets they had weren't right for what they needed. These earliest baskets, however, were similar to others in common use. The Shaker basketmakers used the traditional tools of the vernacular basketmaker; they prepared their splint by pounding and stripping ash logs, and used a shaving horse and drawknife to shape handles and rims. All of the early Shakers who made baskets probably shared this stage—producing baskets for shop, barn, garden and dwelling-house using traditional "naive" methods. Some families appear never to have gone beyond; others did.

Any basket made in any community of Shakers is a Shaker basket; but what is generally meant by "Shaker" are baskets that were made at Mt. Lebanon between 1810/20–1900. Yet even while the iconic Shaker basket is usually from Mt. Lebanon, there are other classic baskets made in New Hampshire and Maine, and possibly elsewhere. As you see the differences between these, you see the saga of the Shaker basket is diffuse and complex. In no two communities did basketmaking grow the same way, and in no community is the basket story complete. There is a body of baskets that are unquestionably Shaker; there are manuscript journals and account books regarding certain eras, giving the names of some basketmakers, types of baskets made, production figures. But much has been lost in between. There is no known documentation of basketmaking at Tyringham or Enfield (Conn.). There is varying evidence for Watervliet, Hancock, Harvard, Shirley, Enfield (N.H.), Alfred and Sabbathday Lake *(10)*. The most evidence points to Mt. Lebanon, with Canterbury ranking second.

What *is* clear from extant baskets and all other sources is that it was Mt. Lebanon that put a Shaker signature on black ash basketry, and established the Shakers' reputation in basketwork. It was in New York that certain methods were introduced that changed the traditional concept of basketmaking and began to differentiate Shaker baskets from all others.

At first look, the Mt. Lebanon idea of a basket appears quite similar to an Indian idea of a basket. The baskets are light, because the Shakers made frugal and efficient use of their material. Like the Indians, they made no more work of production than was necessary. The forms are similar to straightforward Indian forms, with the significant exception that the Shakers did not make oval forms. Also, the Shakers did not follow the Indian custom of laying in a wider weaver where the sides start up, or of substituting a piece of splint for a carved outside rim. Otherwise, what identifies these early Mt. Lebanon baskets—what makes them neither Indian nor settler—is an attitude expressed in the way in which handles and rims are finished.

Early on, the Mt. Lebanon makers began using metal files to get the profile they wanted and to remove the marks left by the drawshave. Files were expensive, and not easily obtainable. Few rural basketmakers cared to acquire files or could afford them; nor were they something Indians had. The Shakers' situation was different; they drew on the pooled resources of a whole community. From the start they could experiment with any tool or material that would improve their work so long as it was within the capability of the community to produce or purchase it; and this sets their work apart. Although the idea of file marks seems a small detail, it speaks of perfection, which the Shakers were always "attaining to."

Because files were so uncommon among country basketmakers, there are very few baskets with file marks that are not Shaker. Most basketmakers worked up rims and handles with a drawshave, and that was it. The Shakers kept paring away. And what the Mt. Lebanon makers did with a file they soon learned to refine further. After roughing out handles and rims with a drawshave, they took a spokeshave (which is similar to a drawshave, but with a curved blade that gives a rounded profile) to get the contour smoother. Then they took a file to clean the edges, and finished up with metal scrapers. In a next phase they began using block planes (that carried a curved blade) in place of, or in addition to, a spokeshave. They were after a perfect look, and they were also after system.

"In every department perfect order and neatness prevail," a nineteenth century visitor remarked. "System is everywhere observed, and all operations are carried on with exact economy."[5] Most Shaker converts were accustomed to working with their hands; the brethren were familiar with tools, they were good tinkerers. They brought to the Shaker experience an artisan or shop mentality that they married to an idea of collective labor, "joint economy," "right use." They were keen on the idea of order. ("Order is the creation of beauty," the Shakers said. "It is heaven's first law, and the protection of souls."[6] Making baskets, making chairs, making dinner, making beds, they did things "according to order." They were fascinated by the task of converting to efficient large-scale living (and in their shops, production) that would enable them to "improve."

In a short time the Mt. Lebanon basketmakers were becoming very proficient; but they were not (then, or at any other time) making all the baskets that were needed. The community continued to buy some baskets from outside. "Bargained with an In-

Fig.40a Those appointed as elders and eldresses had usually been selected on the basis of their character, their spirituality, their leadership, their active intelligence and their commitment to the Shaker way. But there was another side to their ministry. Shaker art often had its most profound expression in them. It is not surprising, therefore, that a high percentage of the basketmakers at Mt. Lebanon were also elders and eldresses. Of these, quite a number rose to the level of parent ministry, where they used their influence to enforce a certain purity in basket art.

dian and a squaw for half-a-dozen half bushel baskets," a Mt. Lebanon brother noted, for example, in an 1837 journal.[7] In all departments the Shakers tended to purchase whatever answered their need without contradicting their ethics, if that was better economy.

Most of the baskets made at Mt. Lebanon, up to 1835, were baskets for shop and domestic use scaled to communal needs. These were limited to a few simple forms adapted for multiple uses by varying height, weight and handles. Some small baskets were made during this period but the principal effort went into large forms.

The earliest baskets that we recognize are shop types, square bottom to (typically) round top. Severe but suave, all of them are large, some of them quite large. Made for indoor use, they are medium weight, with side ("ear") handles. In some of these there is little evidence of the cabinet tools the basketmakers were beginning to use. Handles and rims are split out, and dressed only with a drawshave and file. In some, however, there is already unusual sophistication. There is a finesse developing in them that is not duplicated elsewhere.

From the first gathering into formal order in 1787, Mt. Lebanon had been established as the "lead community"; all the separate societies looked to Mt. Lebanon for direction, and came under the jurisdiction of a "parent ministry" resident there. It turns out that a number of believers who served as the parent ministry or as Church Family ministry at Mt. Lebanon were the basketmakers there. This meant they were inclined to be very doctrinaire in seeking what was "right" for Shaker. It also meant they were meticulous practitioners of their craft, "attaining to perfection" and setting a high, high standard. It meant, too, that they were in a position to see things done as they wanted them done.

Overlaying the idea that Shakers were joined "as brothers and sisters in Christ," there was a definite power structure within the Shaker communities; and the elders and eldresses—and beyond them, the parent ministry—were at the top of it. In an effort to validate the power vested in them, the early leaders called them "the elect," made them custodians of "holy laws," and instructed them to keep apart, to have their separate shop, their separate dwelling, their separate table at communal meals. They were, however, to do their share of work within the community: "No one who is able to labor can be permitted to idly live upon the labor of others. All, including ministry, elders and deacons, are required to be employed in some manual occupation, according to their several abilities, when not engaged in their necessary duties."[8] It appears that, far from using their position to excuse themselves from the "joint labor" expected of every member of a Shaker family, the ministry participated fully in the real work of the community. Over the years most, in fact, had projects that were dear to them; and their power, when it was expressed in the "temporal sphere," was most likely to be evidenced in the energies or priorities they assigned to these projects that interested them. The history of Shaker basket art is graphic proof.

John Farrington (1760–1830) was one of the earliest converts to Shaker belief. He "received the faith" from Ann Lee in 1780; he was among those jailed with her. He joined the Shakers at Mt. Lebanon when the community was formed there in 1787 and signed the original membership covenant in 1795. In 1805 he was made an elder of the Church Family and subsequently he was appointed to the parent ministry. He was also a basketmaker. Considerable role accrued to Farrington in the early transitional years in defining and implementing the communal concept that became central to the Shaker experiment. But his particular "manual" interest appears to have been basketmaking—experimenting with new woodworking machinery to facilitate production.

Under Farrington the concept of splint basketry was revolutionized. Abilities at Mt. Lebanon would have improved just with the volume of baskets made and the introduction of improved hand tools. But around 1820 machine tooling was introduced and system began to get very sophisticated, increasing capability even more.

In his manuscript history of the Church Family, written between 1856–60, Isaac Youngs recalled that there were "no essential improvements" in the woodworking trades for some years. "The people were poor at first, inexperienced, and unable to put up costly and well built houses; their tools and conveniences for work were indifferent and inferior . . . . But after the year 1813 there were some important improvements, particularly the buz saw was introduced for streightening and slitting stuff—also matching works came in use: this greatly relieved the workmen of much hard labor. Planing machines were introduced for planing timber and boards, which has been of very great utility. Besides there has been a great increase in the number and quality of tools, and various machines, as mortising, and boring machines, etc. by which work can be done easier, quicker and better."[9] Almost simultaneously with these improvements Farrington was finding applications in basketmaking and dividing the expertise that went into a basket.

In 1816 a triphammer, which the Shakers had built for their blacksmith shop in 1800, was adapted to pound ash logs. The triphammer mechanized the laborious work of freeing the splint from a log and enabled the Shakers to obtain almost unimagined quantities of basket material. The "buz [circular] saw" reduced dramatically the time it took to rip up stock. Between 1823–26 planing machines began to be used to smooth splint to an even thickness. In 1828 a tongue-and-groove machine (the "matching works" Youngs referred to) was set up to run out blanks for rims, as boards were passed over a spinning blade. As a result of these and other innovations—which were for the most part the inventions of a young basketmaker, Daniel Boler, and another young Shaker, Daniel Crosman, who was in charge of the oval box industry—an unprecedented degree of regularity became possible. Splint (which the Shakers called "basket stuff") was always a consistent thickness and cut to a uniform width. Rim stock and handles were tooled until they were perfect and then were shaped on molds to set their lines, so all of a kind would be alike and fit alike. Bodies were, similarly, woven on molds.

A basket in which the system clearly shows is the Mt. Lebanon carrier. Made medium weight and light weight, carriers were for indoor use. Handles are either overhead (running across the width) or "ear" (forming handloops on the sides or ends). In all of these baskets, the corners are square, the sides are straight, the shape is rectangular. Their sure lines give them a classic look; their material has "Shaker" balance. You know they aren't ordinary baskets. But it is in the rims and handles you really see their era in them. The rims are a perfect round tooled to a half-oval (like an egg sliced vertically). Some of the handles are still imperfect (rims were resolved first); but others have the round that's in the rims, a lovely liquid contour on their inner face. Little is marred in these baskets. Over and over and over you see a new signature in the work; and you see it's not the hand of a single maker. The uniformity of shape, the control of line and material could only come from an integrated effort, a collective expertise, and from advanced tooling.

The basketmakers were finding a simple way, a quick way, to get the look they wanted. But by the time they had perfected their product and system, they had made up most of the baskets the families they supplied had a need for. The only call for large new baskets was for an outdoor type to carry and store the harvest from orchards that had been expanded and were beginning to fruit (11). So they made an apple basket, and in it expressed all the clarity, economy and craftsmanship of the New York system. It is clear that the apple basket satisfied the Shakers' sense of what a basket should be. Made for use, it is use made beautiful. It is virtuoso basketwork. A derivative of the shop forms, the apple rises from square to round, with a change that's so subtle it's hard to say where it happens. Shaker line shows in its "tumble-home"—the bow of the sides proceeding from bottom to top (12). There is an optical play in it that Mt. Lebanon was good at. The handle on the apple basket is usually overhead, but ears may be substituted on larger sizes. Rim stock and handles have the now-typical round. On the bottoms of the baskets, flat hardwood strips are applied as reinforcing. These are normally split out and drawshaved, the strips nailed on and their tails woven up the sides. In a very few apples, however, an idea introduced in some carriers—in which strips resawn from material rejected in the manufacture of oval boxes were nailed onto the basket bottoms—is taken a step further. Three quartersawn strips are applied inside and outside the bottom, and riveted on with rivets used in leatherwork.

One other group of utilitarian baskets—cheese baskets—would have been needed in quantity in a Shaker community. These open-weave baskets were lined with a gauze cloth and placed over a basin. Curdled milk was placed in them; and as it sat, the whey dripped through, leaving the curd. This is an innovation said to be Shaker, an improvement on the less efficient method of whey dripping from a single point at the bottom of a suspended cheese bag. In fact, the basket method goes back almost as far as the production of cheese. It is not Shaker; and thus "cheese form" is not sufficient in itself to identify a basket as Shaker. Additional ambiguity stems from the very design of a cheese basket: the weave is a hexagonal pattern requiring a lay-up different from other splint baskets (see *Chapter Five*). It is so generic there is little place in it for a signature. Consequently, the only cheese baskets that can be reliably attributed, in this instance, to Mt. Lebanon are those in which rimwork matches Mt. Lebanon's round.

There are no records for this period; but it is certain that the number of baskets made at Mt. Lebanon was larger by far than production at other communities. Some villages were simply smaller; they didn't have the same need for volume. Families there could almost make do with ordinary baskets bought from Indians or local makers; and they could get large forms from Mt. Lebanon instead of making them themselves. Other communities didn't have the capabilities to tool up for real production, or there wasn't the interest among the leadership who made the decisions.

Although Mt. Lebanon was the parent community, what was done at Mt. Lebanon wasn't automatically reproduced elsewhere. At the start of the Shaker experiment, the outlying collectives looked to Mt. Lebanon for direction in all things; they did things "the Mt. Lebanon way." And so, in the communities where baskets were made, the early basketmakers attempted to copy as closely as they could Mt. Lebanon's lead in basketwork—not only because that was "right order" but also because the New York basketmakers were the top ministry. Before very long, however, the zeal to imitate wore off *(13)*. Certain shared principles of simplicity, economy and utility continued to inform basket craft. And visits from the ministry had some influence, as did baskets they presented as gifts or samples *(14)*. But, for a clutch of reasons, baskets made outside New York are different.

Fig.41 "When you have seen one Shaker settlement," a visitor observed, "you know almost precisely how they all look,—the same arrangement of buildings, the same style of dress and furniture, the same habits of thrift and tidiness.

"Not the least desirable among the nineteen that exist in the United States," she said, "is that in the old, farming town of Canterbury, in New Hampshire. [Three] villages, separated by fields, are on one long street on the crest of a ridge. They come into sight—three clusters of white or straw-colored buildings, with red roofs—as you ascend the last hill. The orchards are for the most part away back, and smooth fields fall towards the south so far as the line of the forest down in the low-lands."[8]

Several people who visited at Canterbury corroborate that baskets were made there at a comparatively early date. One of them, Cyrus Bradley, who had driven up from Concord, New Hampshire, wrote in his diary (1832–37): "The men make churns, pails, boxes, powderhorns, baskets, brushes, tobacco pipes, combs [and brooms]."[9]

At Canterbury basketmakers started out following Mt. Lebanon's example. But when Mt. Lebanon began to innovate, and developed a new look linked to a system Canterbury couldn't replicate, the New Hampshire Shakers went on their own. They didn't disregard New York's new sophistication, but they went at it in a more elementary way.

Among the several forms made at Canterbury, there is a singular basket in which you can see a signature evolve. Unique to Canterbury, the chip basket was originally designed for one use—to contain kindling and small stovewood; and it was produced by the hundreds for that one use. Form was rectangular (a good "Shaker" form from Mt. Lebanon) and the basket was often lined with leather or ticking or other material to prevent bark or dirt from sifting through. Handles were of two types: a unique overhead handle running the length of the basket, or side ("ear") handles attached at either end. Skates, or wooden runners, were sometimes lashed to the bottom so a basket could stand clear of winter slush.

The earliest chip baskets were made with little system; each one was the work of an individual maker who took it from start to finish. These baskets were woven without a mold; and handles and rims were dressed with a knife or drawshave, which sometimes gives them a choppy look. Yet even while form and line are typically off, the parts fit together because body, rims and handle were made one at a time, to fit. In chip baskets that came later, some handles and rims do not fit well. A handle that is always one size is forced to work on baskets that vary in size, suggesting that basketmakers in a naive phase were attempting to divide operations before they had a successful system. Woodworkers, it appears, were turning out standardized handles before the basketmakers had standardized bodies. When body molds and handles were coordinated, basketwork began to mature. Keeping the base within a range of sizes, the basketmakers wove the sides to differing heights and used differing weights of splint. Among the earliest chip types there had been some intentional variations on the norm. But with the use of new molds, the inherent utility of the rectangular form was more easily released; and the chip basket was converted to a generic basket for shop, laundry and dwelling.

There is a finesse you can see developing in these baskets, along with incipient system. It is not the tooled finesse of Mt. Lebanon, or even an optical finesse. It comes instead from an understanding of how wood works, and you see it in the rims and handles. The early basketmakers had to struggle to get a straight and uniform look. They had to pare the wood on a shavehorse, and work it and work it. In this era they learned to slice into the end grain of a long riven blank or bolt, find the path of the grain down the length, and then just rack it to split the grain apart. Getting straight stuff took only a few strokes instead of a lot of labor: the basketmakers popped out blanks that required little additional dressing. They started rims with a bar that in cross-section was a cube and then simply took a bevel off the edges. They started handles with a bar that was rectangular in section and did the same. What you see is the *blank*, a certain squareness—not the Mt. Lebanon round and not the tooling. What you see is expertise expressed in simple art. A blank, a bevel, grain that runs true. Rims and handles from Canterbury don't have the forced look of Mt. Lebanon work; it's a there-you-have-it look. But it's a signature with its own sophistication.

Canterbury basketmakers were less inclined than those in New York to discard traditional basketforms for severe "Shaker" design. For example, the most common vernacular basket was the round-bottom, round-top. Too unsystematic perhaps to satisfy Mt. Lebanon (the lay-up of a round bottom is not so efficient as that of a square bottom), it was central to Canterbury's repertoire (from which Mt. Lebanon's square-to-round forms are absent). A great variety of round-bottom, round-top baskets are associated with Canterbury. There is no single design they all follow; but two recurring tumblehomes help to group them. One type has a flat bottom, a flat start-up and straight, angled sides. The other has a raised or kicked-up bottom, a rounded start-up and straight, non-flaring sides.

Among the flat bottoms with angled sides there are some naive-looking examples that appear to date from the same early period as chip baskets of similar workmanship. But there is not a range of these in which to trace the development that is in the chip types. There is instead a basket here, a basket there; and the majority are so like other country baskets that, without a Canterbury history, they would not suggest a Shaker origin.

Some of the Canterbury rounds with raised bottom, round start-up and straight sides *are,* however, signature baskets. These are baskets in which the facility that emerged in the chip baskets came to full flower. These are, also, the only Shaker baskets known that are made of white ash. Black/brown ash was the Shakers' preferred basket wood. But historically it has been in shortest supply. Mt. Lebanon's basketmakers, who were more doctrinaire, stuck with black ash even when it was hard to come by, and they had to go a great distance to find any that was good. The Canterbury basketmakers were less rigid and found that they could use white ash. White ash is less pliable than black ash. When it dries it is stiff and difficult to work. But it is strong and holds a shape well. It would be very hard to use in small baskets but it can be used for larger types, such as these exemplary ones from Canterbury.

The white-ash round bottoms are straightforward: they have a directness in getting from here to there. The materials have balance, the lines are clean; they have the sureness that marks classic work. But it is, again, the rims and handles that identify them best. You see in them the same work that's in the late chip forms. Little cubes, little bars, control. They are made from blanks popped out of a bolt and dressed with a bevel. They are strangely delicate, straight and square. An era ends in these baskets, and it ends strong. They are the epitome of Canterbury art.

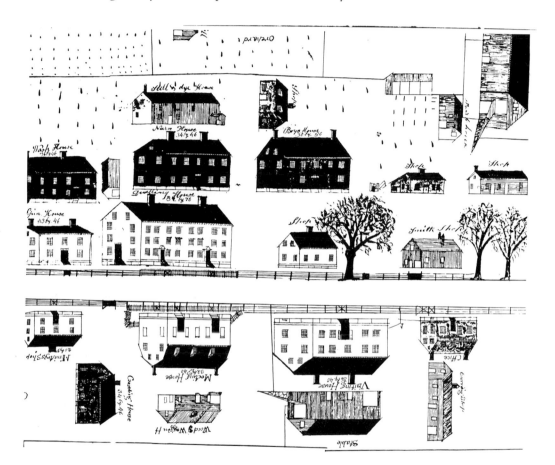

Fig.41a View of Alfred, 1845.

One other surviving group of utility baskets are Maine-made Shaker. In some respects the most elusive to identify, these are the most country of all Shaker baskets, and the most Indian. They are the least like New York's. In the attributes that make them Shaker, the correspondence you see is between Canterbury and Maine, rather than Mt. Lebanon and Maine. They retain a naivete in form and line; but there is some good joinery in them and an understanding of making baskets to take use.

There is no record of basketmaking in Maine until late in the nineteenth century. But there are early baskets with an Alfred history that show evidence of Shaker manufacture. Prominent among these are square and rectangular forms. A basket with squared corners was, primarily, made only by the Shakers and the Indians; and these in Maine, despite some Indian influence, are not Indian-made. Handles and rims look like those at Canterbury; details of joinery are close to Canterbury's; material is dressed with a drawshave, and sometimes files. The baskets don't, however, duplicate New Hampshire work. One of their most distinguishing characteristics is a thick piece of splint lashed onto the bottom of many—but by no means all—Alfred baskets. This is usually joined to form a rectangular foot on squared bottoms (or a ring on round bottoms). Indians added a similar foot on their baskets, but no other Shakers did. Another peculiarity of Maine work is a twill (also Indian in origin) spiraling up through the body of some baskets.

The Maine basketmakers made the forms that their small agricultural families needed, and as a consequence there are many round-bottom, round-top baskets in storage at Sabbathday Lake. Many are coarse by Shaker standard, made for use more than aesthetic. Tumblehomes are similar to Canterbury's, and dissimilar: there is no consistent signature. As is the case at Canterbury, many of these would not suggest they might be Shaker if they turned up somewhere else.

In almost all Maine baskets, there is considerable variance in construction detail. No single way of doing things was followed, and it appears that here there was not the divided expertise found at Canterbury and Mt. Lebanon. It seems that several basketmakers were at work, and each took a basket start to finish, making his own rims and handles in his preferred way. All the makers shared an idea, for example, of what a bushel basket should be; but they had different methods for achieving it. When system is not sophisticated, there is no rule. And that is what you see in Maine . . . some very Shaker attitudes, some Indian and some plain country.

Around 1830–40 the idea of handcraft was becoming disassociated from the production of many common goods as America became industrialized. At several factories in the northeast *(15)* systems similar to what the Shakers had originated were set up to turn out a new kind of cheap utilitarian basket. Unlike the Shakers, who saw system as a way to simplify and improve, the factory operators were not seeking a better product. They were primarily after a product to sell at a profit. In these factories the basketmaker became a businessman.

Basket bodies were woven on molds to ensure they would all be alike. Rims and handles were sawn from flat stock and steam bent, and then nailed on instead of lashed. To speed up production more, uprights and weavers were often cut wide—sometimes as wide as 3". Other shortcuts followed. Up until this time splint was obtained by pounding a log to free the annual growth rings. Now a log could be sawn into boards, and shaved in thin strips with a hand or machine planer called a "filling cutter" (referring to the weavers that "filled" the sides of a basket). The resulting splint was like veneer. It became brittle and splintered with age, and it did not bend easily. As a result, basketforms had to be redesigned around the limitations of the inferior material.

Between 1875–1925 there were so many factory baskets on the market that prices were pushed down and down *(16)*, and quality had to be continually cheapened in order to compete. By 1925–40 there were very few traditional basketmakers in the northeast. Baskets became an anomaly in a world of paper bags, cardboard cartons and plastic, and the art of split ash was virtually forgotten. When we began to research Shaker baskets in 1974, we had to learn by going to the baskets themselves.

It was startling to discover the Shaker system. It has been recognized for a long time that the principles the Shakers lived by—simplicity, economy, honesty, order— informed the integrity of their work. It has been less apparent how the idea of system grew out of that discipline to affect their craft procedure and craft form, and tooling made it possible to achieve the clarity and uniformity and standard of workmanship that set "Shaker" apart.

Because art has been abused so often by system—especially where machine tool has displaced hand tool—it has come to seem that where there is system, there can't be art. But if you look at a Shaker basket, you see abuse isn't something inherent in system but how system is used.

1. It is thought that the pilgrim Shakers earned a living however they could for several years after their arrival in America; their earliest history is lost. What is documented is that by 1776 they had purchased a farm outside Albany, in Watervliet, around which they regathered and eventually drew in new converts. When the Shakers began to gather formally into "families," in 1787, believers made Mt. Lebanon, New York, not Watervliet, the center of the church.

2. The concept of "the world" is central to Shaker belief; "you cannot live in the world and be saved," they professed. An early visitor at Canterbury explained the terminology the Shakers used. "They speak of themselves as the 'Brethren' or as the 'Believers,' never as Shakers. They speak of all other people as the 'world's people.' 'In the world,' 'according to the customs of the world,' are phrases in frequent use among them."[1]

"I don't know how we started using the name [Shakers] ourselves," a sister at Mt. Lebanon remarked in 1947. "It wasn't anything to be ashamed of, so I guess we just got into the habit."[2] By investing the name Shaker with respect, they put their hecklers in their place and—typically—released from something negative something positive.

3. Shakers honored Ann Lee their founder and mother of their church as "Mother Ann." They referred to themselves as her "children." It was their belief that it was necessary to become simple like a child in order to come to God, and to express obedience to the church (or its ministry) as to a parent.

In calling Ann Lee "Mother Ann," the Shakers also acknowledged their belief in a male-female duality in the universe. Ann Lee, they said, had restored "the female line" corresponding to "the male line" represented by Christ, which had been ruptured "since Adam and Eve had sinned." By extension of their belief, the Shakers granted women equal role and rights with men. At a time when women "in the world" could not vote or own property and legally were regarded as the possession of men, the Shakers practiced simple equality of the sexes.

4. "Temporal," to the Shakers, meant all that is of this world; "spiritual" meant of the eternal. The fusion of the two was what, more than anything else, rendered their life transcendant.

5. Originally New Lebanon, the name of the community was changed to Mt. Lebanon in 1861.

6. There were three classes of membership.[3]

First was a "novitiate" order, sometimes called a "back" or "gathering" order. Novitiates [for all their other simplicities, the Shakers liked to borrow high-church terminology in defining who they were] continued to live in their own families and to manage their own affairs. They attended meetings for worship and called themselves Shakers, but they were not controlled by the church "either with regard to their property, children or families."

A second class was made up of believers who, "being under no embarrassments to hinder them from uniting together," chose "to enjoy the benefits of that situation." They joined openly in the communal experiment, contributing their services to the church and agreeing to claim no financial compensation for their labor. (Whatever property they contributed could, however, be returned if they decided to leave.) Within each community there were usually several "families" (most often designated as North, South, Center, Second, East, etc.) who represented this large class.

A third class of membership was reserved for "those persons who had proved their faith and manner of life in the Society" and were "prepared to enter fully, freely and voluntarily into a united and consecrated interest." ("Happy for me," Hervey Elkins wrote at Enfield, N.H., "my lot was cast in the Senior Order . . . where the temporal and spiritual privileges are in their highest development; and of course, where the most rigorous discipline is imposed."[4]) Members at this level made up the Church Family, to whom other families deferred. Collectively they were the most "advanced" of all the membership; and among them there was often an additional distinction of First and Second Order, with members of the First Order being those who "had travelled furthest in their faith."

Children were admitted to the community with their parents. Some also came as orphans, and others were placed with the Shakers by parents or relatives who were unable to raise them at home. Assigned to a "children's order" that was separate from parents and under the supervision of adult caretakers, they were from an early age trained to the Shaker life. While some who entered as children later left because they were curious about the attractions of "the world," others continued among the Shakers to become some of the great leaders of the church, and the great artists.

7. Two or more communities in close proximity customarily formed a "bishopric" under the oversight of a shared ministry. This had particular significance for basketmaking at Watervliet, which was joined in a bishopric with Mt. Lebanon. This kind of linking may have had similar significance for other communities; but no record remains.

8. By distributing the work fairly among the membership, the Shakers also meant to make it as easy and pleasant as possible. "Mortifying the soul" was something they might require in their spiritual "labor" but not in physical labor.

9. "Superfluous" (meaning "more than sufficient; unnecessary, or needless") is a word that comes up often in Shaker testimony. Believers were attempting to pare their lives and their motives to what was essential, in order to release what was true and discard what was "superfluous." The elimination of things superfluous was thus implied in another common phrase, "attaining to perfection."

10. There are several holes in the story. Many baskets, for example, ended up at Hancock; but there are none that are attributable there for any valid reason, nor is there any written record that baskets were made there prior to 1900. It appears that the Church Family at Mt. Lebanon was making utility baskets for all the families at Mt. Lebanon and may have been supplying Hancock and Watervliet as well (and even communities in eastern Massachusetts).

Because the lead ministry (several of whom were also the lead basketmakers) resided alternately at Mt. Lebanon and Watervliet, it is probable that any baskets made at Watervliet were close to identical to those made at Mt. Lebanon. The few manuscript records that have surfaced do not indicate any great volume of production there (269 baskets, for example, were said to have been made in 1842; 200 in 1844).[5] However, an early accession card at the Western Reserve Historical Society suggests that at both Watervliet and Mt. Lebanon "thousands of baskets were made each year for sale and a good provision for home use." Furthermore, Daniel Boler, who had charge of the Mt. Lebanon basket shop for some sixty years, was said to have "got out the splints for that society [as] for Mt. Lebanon."[6] In the end it is not insignificant that Mary Dahm, the last Shaker to make "New York" baskets, had resided at Watervliet since she was a child and had moved to Mt. Lebanon only in 1938, long after basket production had come to a stop there: she must have learned how to make the baskets at Watervliet.

After the Civil War, Shaker membership was falling off and a time came when one person could keep up with a community's basket needs. This may have been the case at Shirley where, in 1876, William Dean Howells observed Abraham Whitney, then in his nineties: "At his great age he still works every day at basketmaking, in which he is very skillful and conscientious."[7] It may be that Whitney came late to basketry; there is no record of basketmaking at Shirley. Or it may be he was a basketmaker much of his life, and Shirley's production was so small it escaped mention. What is known is that Whitney was a singing master before he joined the Shakers and achieved early prominence with them in matters of music.[8] Around 1821–22 he was sent by the ministry to Canterbury to give singing lessons—so he could have been introduced to basketmaking there. If this was the case, his work probably incorporated Canterbury attributes; it could account for some of the "odd" Canterbury that turns up. But no baskets have been recovered that can be traced to Whitney or to Shirley.

Basketmaking in Ohio, Indiana and Kentucky is still another story. Although few mid-western baskets are presently known that are distinctly "Shaker," just as furniture and architecture in the communities to the west reflect what was local there, baskets made there also express the local vernacular. Black ash was not available; white oak grew there instead, and some willow. Some western forms were similar to eastern forms; but in general, developments in basketmaking in the northeast were not applicable to materials in the west.

32

11. Most Shaker villages began with a farm donated to the church by an early convert, so that usually an orchard was already in place. These orchards the Shakers developed and expanded dramatically. The communities became as well known for the quality of their trees, their apple sauce, cider and dried fruit as for their chairs and baskets. Apples were also a staple of the Shaker diet. As the membership grew and their landholdings increased, the Shakers kept setting out new orchards, through the first half of the nineteenth century. This was especially the case at Mt. Lebanon, which had the largest membership of all the communities and was located in a region even now still fertile with active orchards.

12. "Tumblehome" is a boatbuilder's term used to describe "the shape of the topsides [the portion of the boat above the low-water line] where they begin to slope inward toward the centerline as they go up toward the sheer [the upward curve of the hull at the main deck]."[9] We have borrowed and adapted the term to mean the contour of a basket, seen in profile, from the bottom up.

13. While order and system served to unify the Shaker membership, there were, from the start, disparities between various communities (as well as among the families of a single community). To achieve necessary unity, the Shakers instituted numerous codes; but initially the covenants they lived by were not written out. An idea of order was internalized. It was not until 1821, some thirty years after believers had gathered into communities , that specific rules were published, as the "Millennial Laws." It would appear that these were sent out because there was a general falling off from "the Mt. Lebanon way." The laws were reissued and made even stricter in 1845; but later they were revised and relaxed.

Because the Millennial Laws were so singularly specific about what was and was not permitted, they have acquired an importance they did not, in fact, carry. Their period of influence was limited and even then their severity was, perhaps, not fully implemented. They comprise an interesting document; but they should not be taken as the sole index to Shaker life.

14. There were regular visits of the Mt. Lebanon ministry to the outlying communities, and reciprocal visits to Mt. Lebanon.

"We often received specimens of the various kinds of manufactures as samples, made in the most substantial and perfect manner," a Canterbury Shaker recollected in later years. The New Hampshire ministry, on visits to Mt. Lebanon, she said, would also "obtain some article to take home as a model."[10]

In this way many baskets traveled from Mt. Lebanon to other communities.

15. Amzie Childs, for example, was operating a basket factory in Peterborough, N.H. which continues in production. In Bellows Falls, Vermont, Sidney Gage and Co. were also manufacturing baskets on a large scale. And at Dantown, Connecticut, some forty families formed a basket business that by 1880 had doubled to involve eighty families.

16. Around 1900 a dozen market baskets made by Sidney Gage and Co. cost $2.00.[11] A single market basket made by Charles Sprague, a traditional basketmaker in Effingham, N.H., sold for $1.25 at the same time.[12]

Fig.42 The Shaker difference begins to show in shop storage baskets. These were made on molds, square bottom to (typically) round top, and were finished with ear handles.

This example is very large—three or four bushels. The "Z" may indicate that it was intended for use in the saw mill. It was designed for heavy use (the rims are lashed with cowhide; the bottom is reinforced with hardwood strips) but it wasn't made heavy, which is the essence of Shaker design.

Fig.43 The characteristic shape of a shop basket is just legible in the dark entry of the Chair Shop, South Family, Mt. Lebanon.

Fig.44 Some of the shop baskets were
stopped short on the mold, leaving the throat
square (because they were still in the square
form of the mold). Others that go taller usually
have round throats, but some of those are also
finished square.

In this view of the herb room at Hancock,
the large basket is a two-bushel shop basket
made at Mt. Lebanon. The squatter basket
marked ''J.A.'' was woven on a one-bushel
mold and made low. On the table, lids to Indian baskets are used as trays for drying herbs.
It is not uncommon for these lids to have
been separated, and by themselves to go un-
recognized for what they are. The round-
bottom basket hanging from the ceiling is from
Canterbury.

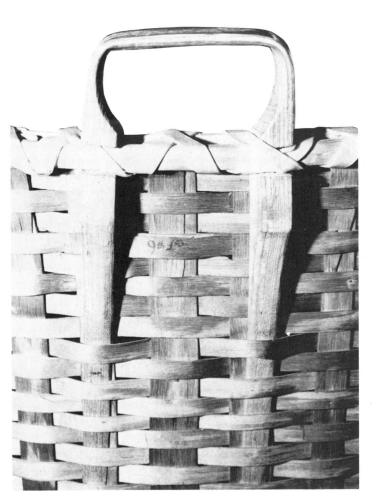

Fig.45 Along with other Mt. Lebanon utility baskets, shop baskets are ordinarily double lashed; and handles have a double notch.

Handles and rims on shop baskets typically come from rectangular blanks with edges (outer, on rims; inner, on handles) rounded off. This is the work of a drawshave and file, in some instances maybe a spokeshave. Contour is not perfect but there is a sense of line in it, and grain runs true. Already expertise in the Mt. Lebanon shop was divided: one person wove a body, another made up the rims and handles.

Fig.46 A shop basket with single lashing: there are exceptions to the rule of double lashing.

The hatch lines under the grip of the handle are the mark of a file. The Shakers weren't satisfied with ordinary standards. They wanted a cleaner look, a look that was more uniform. And so, from a very early date, they began using a file to refine the shape of handles and rims, and to remove shave marks left by a drawknife.

Because files were something the typical basketmaker didn't use, there are very few baskets that show file marks that are not Shaker. File marks alone are not enough to make a basket Shaker; but they are a strong clue to consider Shaker attribution, if other characteristics are present.

The ratio of weavers to uprights is something you want to look at in a basket. The norm in country basketwork is 1½:1, 2:1 up to 3:1. The norm in Indian and Shaker work is 2:1 up to 4:1 or sometimes 5:1, with the average 3:1. (The weight of Shaker material follows similar ratios; a weaver is typically ½ to ¾ the weight of an upright.)

There isn't really a big difference in ratios between the Shakers' shop baskets and other country baskets. It is in later baskets the difference is significant. Nor is there exact uniformity in the shop basket splint. Weavers are usually even in width, but a couple of narrow uprights may be interspersed among wider ones.

Fig.47

1 Rims are uniform in weight and shape
2 Characteristic softness in grip of ear handles; cleaned with a file
3 Double lashing
4 Width of uprights adjusted at corners to fit material to mold
5 Tails inside
6 Uprights turned down alternately inside, outside
7 Tails outside
8 Blocking is heavy below the rim, slight above
9 Handle is smoothly worked, doesn't look chipped-away

10 Split upright
11 Uniformity of material speaks of Shaker system that was developing
12 Ratio of weaver to uprights approximately 1½:1
13 Outside rim matches inside rim exactly. There are some irregularities in the rims which later on the basketmakers wouldn't tolerate in work they made for sale, but there is an excellence in them that already surpasses most other New England baskets and most other (i.e., non-New York) Shaker baskets.
14 Both baskets marked "C.B." in paint

Fig.48 The shop basket had many uses. It was a versatile form with a broad flat bottom and a square and ample volume. Made medium weight, it was intended as an indoor basket. Here one is used in the laundry at Mt. Lebanon.

Fig.49 Three of these barn baskets (left and center) found at Hancock are typical Mt. Lebanon shop types. The origins of the others are not known. They may be Shaker, but they do not match up to any baskets that can be attributed.

Fig.50 Another basket off the shop mold, used here to gather trimmings in the sisters' sewing room.

At Mt. Lebanon the basketmakers were able to take advantage of modern machinery introduced around 1815–25. Some of the most progressive people of their day, in the years when the Industrial Revolution was just breaking, the Shakers were thinking in terms of mass production, and tooling up for it.

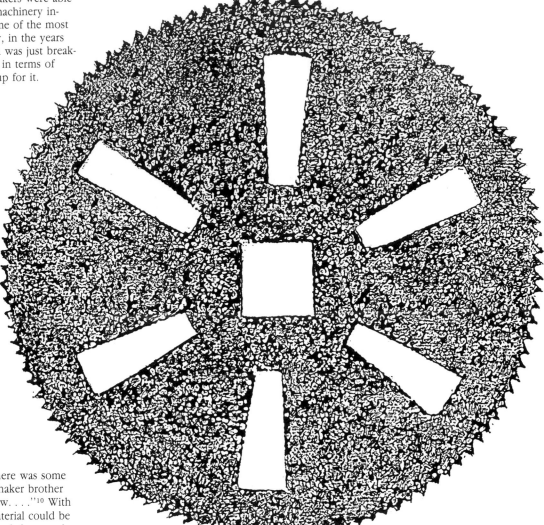

Fig.51 "After the year 1813 there was some important improvements," a Shaker brother wrote, "particularly the buz saw. . . ."[10] With the spinning circular blade, material could be sawn quickly and accurately; and shop work was eased. In 1821 *Nile's Weekly Register,* published in Baltimore, visited the New York Shakers and reported that "for cutting stuff for window sash, grooving floor plank, gauging clap-boards, etc. with one man and a boy to attend it," their circular saw would "perform the labor of thirty men."[11]

The journalist actually was observing a circular saw and a rotary planer. Functioning like a router, a new tongue-and-groove machine dressed the edge of a board and cut a profile into it as it passed across a spinning blade. Now blanks could be ripped up on the circular saw, then shaped for rims and sliced off to length.

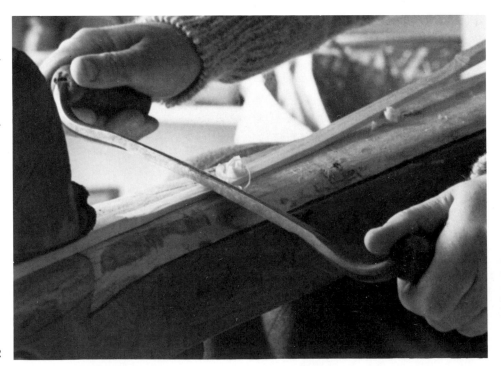

Fig.52

40

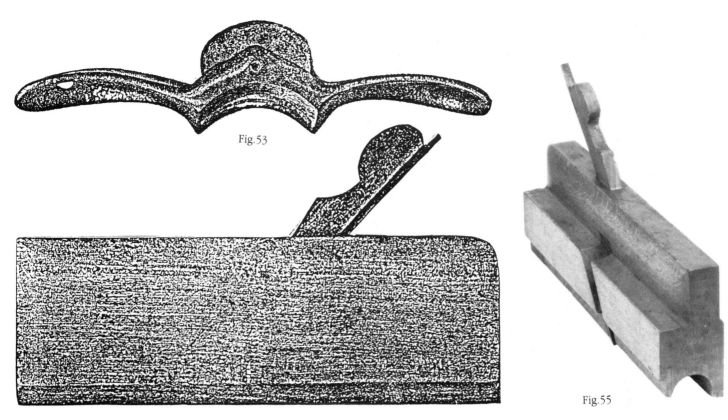

Fig.53

Fig.55

Fig.54

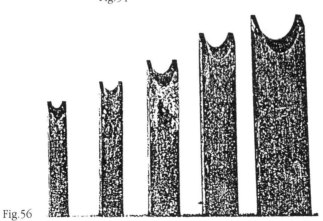

Fig.56

Fig.52–57 Initially the Shakers, like most traditional basketmakers, used a drawknife (Fig. 52) to dress rims and handles—to pare the blanks they made them from, and take a chamfer off the edges. Then they finished with a file (Fig. 57). After a while they began to follow the drawshave with a spokeshave (Fig. 53), using a file and scraper to finish. A block plane (Figs. 54–56) took them into another phase. With it, they got an exact cut each time, so there was very little variance in the line. With each tool they refined the contour a little more, and then finished with a file. Most other basketmakers were satisfied with what they got with a drawknife.

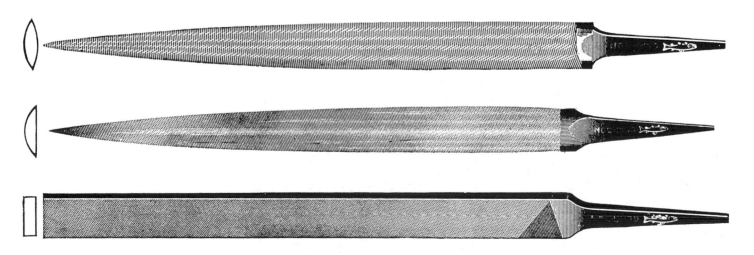

Fig.57

Fig.58 In 1800 the Shakers had set up a triphammer in their blacksmith shop, which in 1816 they adapted to pound ash logs. This eliminated much of the labor in freeing splint from a log and enabled them to obtain great quatities of basket material.

"This day the trip hammer is ready," Isaac Youngs wrote in his journal on September 14, 1816. The following month he noted that "Ebenezer [Bishop] and Jonathan Wood return home with their ash timber [for baskets]"; on October 21 the brothers "go to work at the trip hammer."[12]

Fig.59 Slitting knives were used to trim splint to a standard width. The width of the cut was adjusted by respacing the knives.

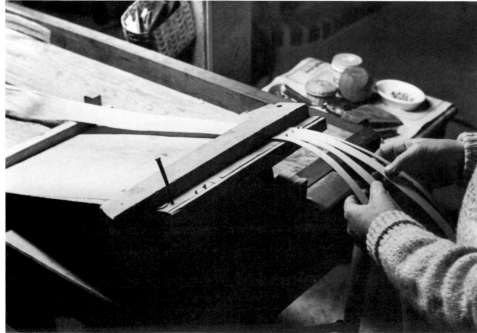

Fig.60 Power planers, another new idea, were adjusted to work up splint. As early as 1828 Henry DeWitt, a Mt. Lebanon brother, notes in his journal, "I planed basket stuff at the [shop] today."[13] In the 1860s Elisha Blakeman, a Mt. Lebanon elder, is routinely "plaining and getting out basket splint."[14] And in 1873 Elder Henry Blinn, from Canterbury, visiting at Mt. Lebanon, is taken to see "the machine for planing the thin strips of wood, of which they make baskets. Passing through a set of rollers," he writes, "it leaves the machine highly polished."[15]

"Rolling out" seems to have been a synonymous term for planing ("Elisha Blakeman assists Andrew Fortier roll out basket stuff") but just how it was done is not known.[16] This and other basket shop machinery has been lost, probably in the fire that destroyed the shop in 1875.

By machine planing the splint, it was possible not only to get a nice finish on it but also to control the thickness of it, so that it was even and exact and easily graded by gauge or weight.

The shop planer was probably a larger and more sophisticated version of this table model. A knife scrapes the splint as rollers hold the splint against the blade. This small (and virtually unused) planer may have been made for someone in another community where there wasn't the volume of basketwork.

Fig.61 In the new Shaker system, basket bodies, rims and handles were shaped over wooden molds. As a result, all baskets of a type were standardized. This uniformity of itself would have pleased the Shakers' sense of "right order"; but it also meant that bodies and parts could be made in stages, in volume, by different people. When the parts were assembled, they fit—perfectly.

Fig.62 One of the Shaker classics is the large rectangular carrier made at Mt. Lebanon. This is a basket in which the New York system really shows. You see the mold. You see the splint. You see the tooling, the control. Squared and straight, here is art in line meeting line.

Fig.63 A carrier (foreground) and two shop baskets, used for laundry.

44

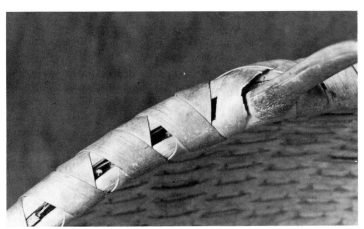

Figs.64,65 Details, Shaker square rim.

The squareness in the carrier is a partial signature. Squared-bottom, squared-top baskets are usually either Indian or Shaker. Country basketmakers didn't normally make them because of their difficulty. There was a skill required to achieve their squareness that their simple lines mask—a knowledge in bending the basketwood to keep the lines clean and prevent them from cracking or splitting. This was extra work that cost the ordinary basketmaker time. With the Indians the problem was minimized by using thin, pliable rims. With Shakers time was a different commodity. "Do all your work," Mother Ann had said, "as if you were to live for a thousand years, and as if you were to die tomorrow."[17]

Fig.66 Detail, Indian square rim.

Figs.67,68 In baskets of this era, rims and handles are what you especially want to look at. More than anything else, they identify Mt. Lebanon work. Rims are tooled to a round that is elongated to half-oval; in section they look like an egg sliced vertically. Very often there is a ledge at the top and bottom of the rim, because the strip was cut off further from its outer face than the block plane or power plane tooled it. Look for the ledge. The plane was used just to "set" the shape on the blank that the rim would be cut from.

Fig.69 Handles on Mt. Lebanon carriers are either "ear" or overhead (across the width). The overhead handles are normally "bonnet" types—imitating the line of a Shaker bonnet where it frames the face. To get this bend in them, the handlemaker had to begin by cutting a blank that ran true, wood with no flaws and straight grain. Then he cut away the bar, to relieve it, and made it beautiful by paring it to a round with a contour blade. Where the handle attaches to the body, the blocking was left in the wood so it could be notched out to accept the rim. The joinery in this era begins to be liquid and nice, as flats melt into rounds.

Fig.70 In this detail of a handle, note again the file marks.

Fig.71 Amenities associated with Shaker work show in flat hardwood runners or strips applied to the bottoms of many of the carriers. These are made of thin maple resawn from materials rejected in the manufacture of oval boxes, then nailed on with the same copper tacks you see in the boxes.

There was no one way these strips were applied; they occur in several different configurations.

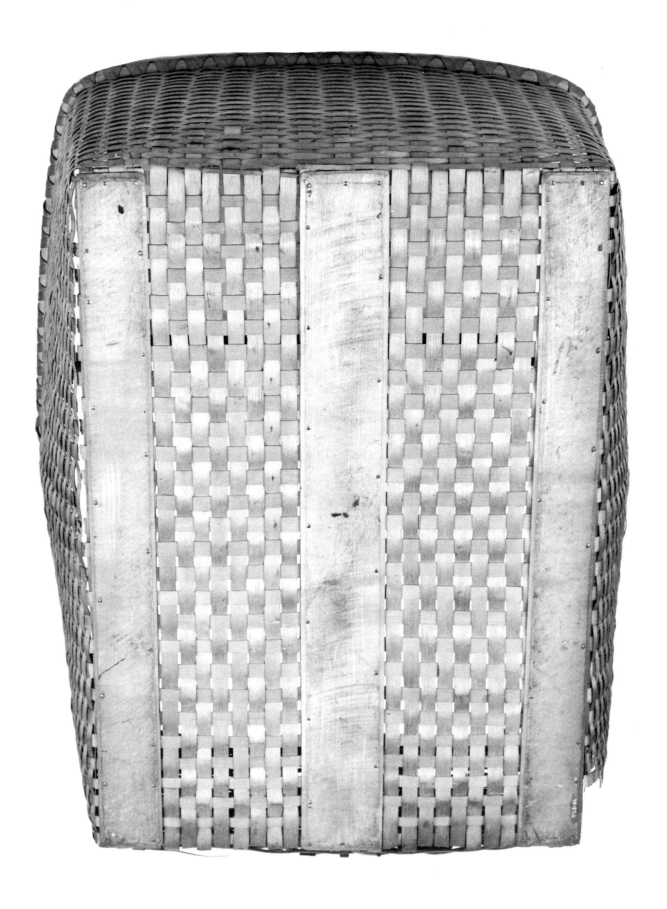

Fig.72 This basket reminiscent of the stacked "C.B." shop baskets (Fig. 47), suggests where the Mt Lebanon basketmakers came from to arrive at the classic carriers.

The splint in these New York baskets was typically split and then planed, removing the hairs from the inside face. Most other Shaker baskets made for utilitarian use, and most settler baskets, have a scraped look inside and outside. Indian work is typically satin outside, scraped inside.

1 Overhead handle may be bow or bonnet type

2 Notch, tail: this is what you see in Mt. Lebanon's mature rim and handle work

3 Block tends to be heavy. Note tail is on the inside.

4 Round contour above notch

5 Square blocking, with flat cut on side

6 Nice crisp edge here

7 Round here

8 Rims are made with the same tool used to shape rims in Fig.62 but they are not so refined. There are places where the wood ripped out. The idea is here, but the method isn't fully resolved.

9 End of weaver is visible here (explained in *Chapter Five*)

Fig.73 Another transitional carrier, filled with coils of original splint from the Mt. Lebanon basket shop. Rims have a nice round; the handle is flat, the work of a drawshave. Lashing is single.

Fig.74 A low-sided carrier, partially lined with leather. This basket probably dates just prior to the mature work. Rims and handles aren't quite resolved.

Figs.75,76 At the opposite end of the range, there is a group of carriers—of which this is one—that are extremely square, extremely fine, with what had become the standard rims and handles. Identical in size, these carriers are wider than the norm in relation to their width. At the ends narrow uprights alternate with regular uprights—a characteristic unique to them (and their width) that contributes to their delicate look. On the bottom they are reinforced, like other large carriers, with thin strips of quartersawn maple, nailed on with copper tacks.

49

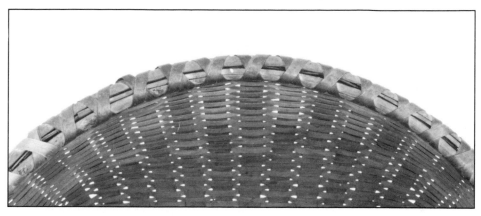

Fig. 77 If you see this lovely liquid work, look for Mt. Lebanon.

Fig. 78 Detail, rim overlap.

The notch on Mt. Lebanon baskets of this era is usually articulated in this way. Below the rim the shelf of the notch is square, the lateral cuts of the blocking are flat, and the tail is pared with a flat cut. Above the rim the blocking has a rounded contour. The handle blank appears to thicken at the notch; but in fact it is just relieved less there than in the upper span.

Fig. 79 Here in the apple basket is the utilitarian art Mt. Lebanon basketwork aspired to. The sculpted form rises from square to round with such control in the shaping it is hard to tell where the change occurs.

The form is similar to that of the early shop types, but system has been refined. Rims and handles are like those on the classic carriers. Note how the ''tumblehome''—the bow of the sides proceeding from bottom to top— identifies this basket. And note how sharply the handle is bent; that extremity is also a signature.

Among the Shakers no one was hiding what they knew; they weren't competing for sales and thus having to conceal the secrets that gave them the edge in production. To this, add a divided expertise and you begin to understand their achievement.

The farmer who was a basketmaker just made what worked; he didn't go on and on with what he could do. The Shakers did.

Fig.80 Many, many apple baskets were made. You can see they came out of a system. Sizes shown here were the most common, but they also went smaller and larger.

All of these baskets have the signature form, the splint, the lines, the tooling. But the basket top right seems somehow more studied, finer, more controlled. It is little surprise that it is inscribed on the bottom "Ministry 1858" — corroborating the idea that the ministry, the elite of the elite, were also the most disciplined of the basketmakers.

Fig.81 The same baskets, bottom up. The strips reinforcing the bottoms were prepared from thick splint cleaned with a drawshave and chamfered on the edge. At the corners they were relieved where they overlapped; then at the tips they were carved down until they were the thickness of normal splint and were woven up the sides on top of the corner uprights. Across the bottom, they were nailed on.

Figs.82–84 Almost everything about the apple basket is here done ultra ultra.

Fig.82

1 Note the sharp turn here

2 The severity of this bend was achieved by relieving the inside of the handle at the turn, which correspondingly gives a heavier look to the grip

3 This crisp edge is something the Shakers got really nice; it is accentuated by the wood being so flat on top and so controlled in the contour underneath

4 Width does not taper as the handle approaches the rim, resulting in a flatter contour than you see in handles of another type where there is a significant taper

5 A typical notch for this era, except for being a little meatier above the rim

6 Characteristic flat cut here

7 Handle rises in line with the body

8 Turndowns on outside to strengthen at stresspoint

9 Last weavers at top tapered to finish the body and level the top

10 Lashing repaired; aligned with original lashing (note shadowing). Splint used in the repair was not stained to give it the appearance of age, as with time it will acquire the right color.

11 Material was machine planed but it wasn't taken to a satin finish; some texture remains. Good splint was apparently in limited supply when this basket was made. The material wasn't thick enough to plane down to satin.

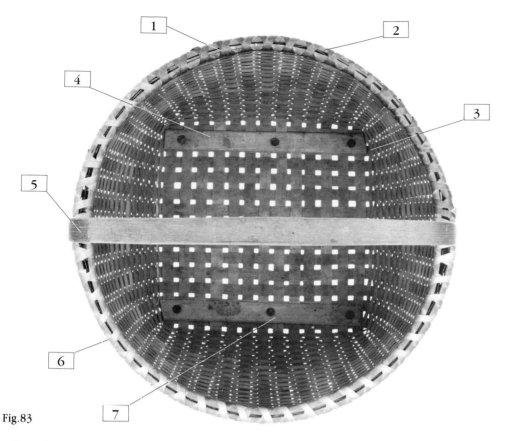

Fig.83

1 Note finesse where rim tips lap

2 Rims on this basket are exquisitely tooled. Note absence of ledge
because radius of contour knife was probably designed for a basket *this size*.

3 Bevels

4 Maple strips to reinforce bottom, applied inside and outside and then riveted together

5 The sharp, sharp bend in the handle has resulted in a stress crack.
Still, the wood is strong because it is under compression on the
underside.

6 Double lashing

7 Rivet from the outside peened over on inside, around a washer

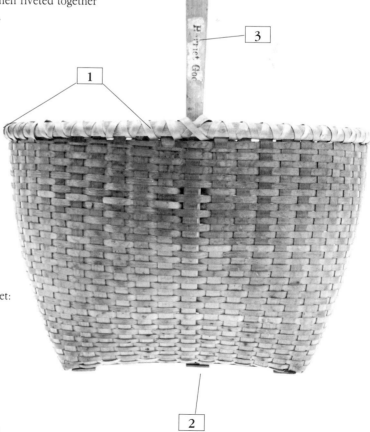

Fig.84

1 There are two tumblehomes to consider in a square-to-round basket:
the profile of the corner splint, and the profile of the center splint
which the tail of the handle runs down

2 The middle strip of the three strips attached to the bottom is off
center. This looks like a mistake but it was in fact a consequence
of design and construction. Because the handle, which must be
centered, must run down an upright, the middle strip has to be
off center in order to be riveted through the "holes" in the bottom
left between the uprights. If it were centered, it would have to
perforate the splint.

3 Paper label pasted on handle. Harriet Goodwin was an Eldress and
a basketmaker

53

Fig.85 Not all apple baskets were for apples. By varying the weight and width of the splint, and the height they wove the body on a mold, the Shakers made up several variants of a basket using the same mold.

Fig.87 Everything in this variant of an apple basket speaks of the Mt. Lebanon system — splint, rims, handles, feet, form, control.

Fig.86 Apples were also made extra heavy and oversize. This example, however, is more coarse than others; most apple derivatives, whatever size, show the same "hand."

Fig.88 The apple basket was not designed as a picking basket (a swing handle was more suitable for that purpose); it was a carrying and storage basket. The Shakers used swing handles (see *Chapter Four*) but it appears they bought them from other makers instead of making them.

Fig.89 This apple basket with muted red vertical stripes has a hand-twisted rope with hoist attached. It may be an anomaly adapted for picking, or something rigged up in a storeroom.

Figs.90,91 Another adaptation is this apple basket made for hard use and lined with leather. The handle on this basket is a bucket handle, pinned with a bucket pin—making a swing handle out of an apple basket. A square of leather from a drive belt was used as a spacer to set the handle out away from the rim, so it would clear it.

This makeover is proof in itself that apple baskets were not made with swing handles; it also indicates that Mt. Lebanon didn't make picking baskets with swing handles. There are many swing handle baskets that are assumed to have been made there. But if Mt. Lebanon had been turning them out, someone in the community would not have gone to this length to make one unique one. There are simply no production swing handles that can conclusively be attributed to the Shakers.

Fig.92 Two "Shaker" elements reinforce the provenance of these cheese baskets, which came from Mt. Lebanon: the contour of the rims, and the exceptional joinery in the ring that makes the foot, which is notched into the angle at each "corner," forming a miter. (This detail recurs in some Shaker rimwork.)

Cheese baskets are so generic there is almost nothing to go on to say who made them. Even the Shakers made them many ways, and the only ones—a dozen or so known—that can be reliably attributed to Mt. Lebanon are those that have rims matching the classic rims and this same mitered joinery in the foot. Made outside the system, because they incorporate a different weave and a different lay-up, the cheese baskets were also the single type not typically made on a mold.

Fig.93 A cheese basket with a rim that suggests Shaker work. But there's nothing else to go on. This basket also came from Mt. Lebanon; and there's no reason to think it isn't Shaker. But stripped of its history, it would be just another anonymous basket.

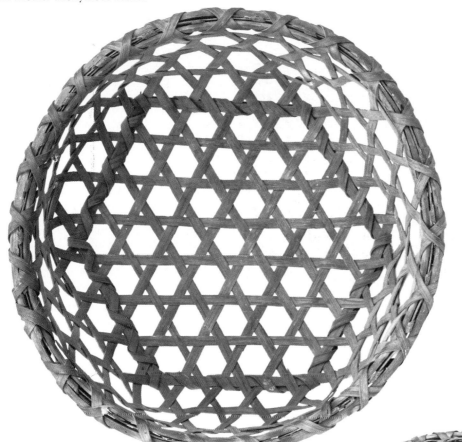

Fig.96 When we began to research Shaker basketry, the cheese basket was the one basket that we were told was definitely Shaker. The one basket that is the least distinguishably Shaker was, ironically, the one to which the idea of Shaker had been attached.

This particular cheese basket has long been attributed to the Shakers. Like many others, it would have to be eliminated just on the basis of hair, knurls and lack of uniformity in the material, which the Shakers would not have accepted. But the splint "rims" and wrapped handles are additional clues that it is Indian.

Fig.94 This example is set on a cheese ladder, which distributes the weight of the wet cheese over a wooden sink. This basket, like the two preceding, came from Mt. Lebanon; without that history, there would be nothing distinctive to suggest it might be Shaker.

Fig.95 Another cheese basket "from" Mt. Lebanon. The foot is similar to those in Fig. 92 but the angles are not mitered.

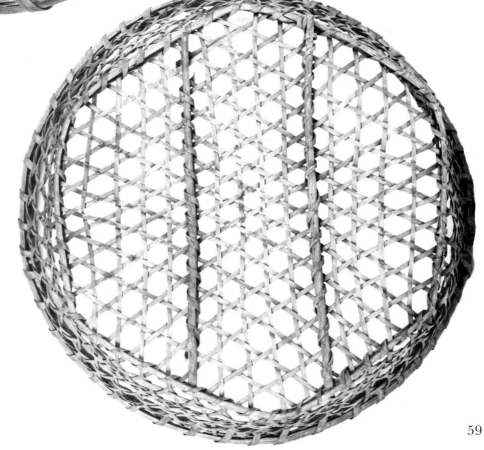

59

Figs.97,98 A singular basket made only at Canterbury survives in sufficient numbers to see in it how expertise evolved outside New York.

The chip basket was designed to hold kindling and small stovewood. Form is rectangular, with straight sides and square corners, a good "Shaker" form from Mt. Lebanon. It is typically double notched and single lashed. Often a basket is lined with leather or ticking or other material ("there is no dirt in heaven," Mother Ann had counselled). Hardwood skates may, additionally, be lashed onto the bottom, so a basket could stand clear of a snowy walk.

Some of the chip baskets have ear handles; but others have a unique overhead handle that runs lengthwise, allowing the weight to be more easily balanced and carried closer to the body. Another characteristic of the handle, which you see in almost all Canterbury work, is that it is lower in relation to the height of the body than handles on other Shaker baskets.

Fig.99 In this chip basket lined with leather, a pine board used as a divider is fixed in place with wrought iron ears hooked over the rims and screwed to the top of the board. The inner rim is a heavy growth ring which you sometimes find in Canterbury work.

Fig.100 At Canterbury it would have been common to see chip baskets set out on the doorsteps.

This early example is lined with a seed bag and marked "C.H.H." for "Church Family." Not technically sophisticated, this basket may well have been one of the first chips. The handle is a typical country handle. In section it is a flat-oval; and notch, blocking and relieving above the notch are all indicative of country method. What *isn't* typical are the square corners on the basket, the handle that runs longways, and the crossed strips (in place of skates) that reinforce the bottom.

Fig.101 Although similar to the Mt. Lebanon carrier, the chip is a different basket. Nothing from Mt. Lebanon turns up lined, with skates, with a longways handle. There is some pictorial evidence (as in this wood-cut view of a "retiring room" at Watervliet) that other communities used baskets to hold stovewood; but none of the baskets depicted are designed like Canterbury's chip.

The longways handle is so practical it shouldn't have been unique to Canterbury basketmakers. Even common carpenters understood that it gave better balance, and put handles on their toolboxes longways.

Fig.102 At Mt. Lebanon, simple woodboxes with "basket" handles took the place, to some degree, of Canterbury's chips. But the handles on these did not have the advantage of Canterbury's design.

61

Figs.103–4 An early chip which, except for its square form and longways handle, is pretty much typical of country basketwork. The body was made on a mold; but the handle, like the rims, was just split out and cleaned with a drawshave. There is nothing studied about it.

Figs.105–6 Another early chip. This is crude and ignorant work. Material is on the light side; and that, and the lack of experience, has made the basket cave at the top. If the up-rights had been heavier and closer together, the voids between them would not have pulled in; weight would have given some control the maker needed. The handle, which is off center, appears to have been carved with a pocketknife rather than a drawknife. In several places it's hacked around; you have to wonder what was going on. Full of knots and knurls, the raw piece itself would have been thrown out by an experienced maker before he attempted to make a handle out of it. Design-wise, the handle is upside down and back-wards, forced to fit a basket it's not sized for. It is clear the basketmaker didn't know what he was doing.

If you saw this basket by itself, you wouldn't think "Shaker." But if you examine other baskets you know are Canterbury, you see this basket has some of the same charac-teristics. Overall dimensions have the chip concept in them. The lashing is, typically, sin-gle. The handle, typically, runs longways. Look especially at Figs. 107–8 and then look again at this handle.

Figs.107–8 Here is a very similar handle on a basket easy to believe (and document) as a Canterbury chip. You see this same handle on other Canterbury baskets of this era. From the preceding basket it would appear that the Can-terbury basketmakers had been attempting to divide operations before they had a system; by the time this basket was made, they had learned that handles cannot be standardized before there is body standardization. With the maturing of the shop, the baskets begin to car-ry a Shaker look.

Figs.109–10 On this basket the handles are ear rather than overhead; but that is not their significant difference. What is important is that they were made a new way—from a simple blank. Rims were made similarly, giving both a cubey look that is a Canterbury signature.

Earlier basketmakers had to work to get the look they wanted; they had to work to follow the grain in getting out handles and rims. And the way they went at it usually gave irregular stuff, which led to irregularity in basketwork. In this period the Canterbury basketmakers learned that with a few strokes of a knife they could slice into the end grain of a bolt, find the path of the grain down its length, and then just rack it apart. Getting straight stuff took only a few strokes, instead of a lot of labor.

This method was known to some rural

basketmakers; you see evidence of it in the straight grain of rims and handles that obviously came easy and ran true. And it was the same method the Mt. Lebanon shop had used. But most country basketmakers didn't get this sophisticated. Most weren't concerned with really understanding how wood worked. Most of them wedged out blanks much larger than what they would cut a handle or rim down to. There was no straightness inherent in these blanks, and there was a lot of waste—of effort and material—in the method.

The Shakers, by contrast, addressed themselves to the easiest, most efficient, most economical way of getting what they wanted— which required an understanding of wood, the right use of material. They learned to let the wood split where it wanted, and to have the confidence it would be right. This is Shaker economy.

Figs.111–12 When you see this squared form, this cubey rim, this handle; you see Canterbury. Just as the tooled round identifies an era at Mt. Lebanon, this cubism identifies an era at Canterbury, c. 1840–50. A blank, bevelled; grain that runs true. This is Canterbury's expertise. A simple expertise. Mt. Lebanon had other concerns; but Canterbury was satisfied with a straightforward art.

By the time this light lean basket was made, the square chip form had been adapted for other uses. This basket grew out of the chip concept but it is different from the chip.

Fig.113 Two carriers, which came from the chip design, can be seen in this photograph of Canterbury sisters making feather dusters.

Fig. 115 Laundry, Canterbury Shaker Village.

Fig. 114 Signature Canterbury chip basket handle.

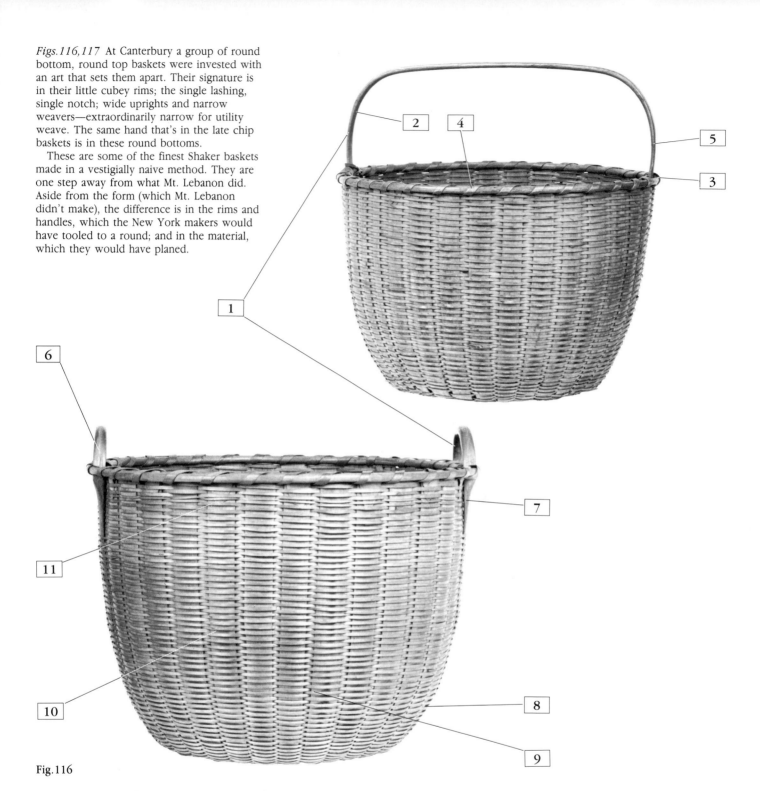

Figs.116,117 At Canterbury a group of round bottom, round top baskets were invested with an art that sets them apart. Their signature is in their little cubey rims; the single lashing, single notch; wide uprights and narrow weavers—extraordinarily narrow for utility weave. The same hand that's in the late chip baskets is in these round bottoms.

These are some of the finest Shaker baskets made in a vestigially naive method. They are one step away from what Mt. Lebanon did. Aside from the form (which Mt. Lebanon didn't make), the difference is in the rims and handles, which the New York makers would have tooled to a round; and in the material, which they would have planed.

Fig.116

1 These two baskets are typical of the two sizes these Canterbury rounds were made in, and suggest the size break at which handles went from overhead to ear

2 Rise of the handle is lower than the norm in Mt. Lebanon work

3 Cubey rims characteristic of these baskets

4 Single lashing

5 Very thin wood; handle blank was wider and thinner than Mt. Lebanon's

6 Handles have a round, soft look compared to most

7 Tail becomes very thin very quickly

8 Characteristic tumblehome

9 White ash

10 Ratio of weavers to uprights is 4:1, 5:1

11 Uprights turned down outside as well as inside

64

These Canterbury round bottoms are made of white ash, which no other Shakers used. White ash is less pliable than black/brown ash. When it dries it is difficult to work. But it is strong and holds its shape well. More importantly, white ash was easily available, whereas black ash was in limited supply.

Although these baskets are extraordinary, there is nothing about the design of them that is different from ordinary round bottoms. The difference is in the material and the control.

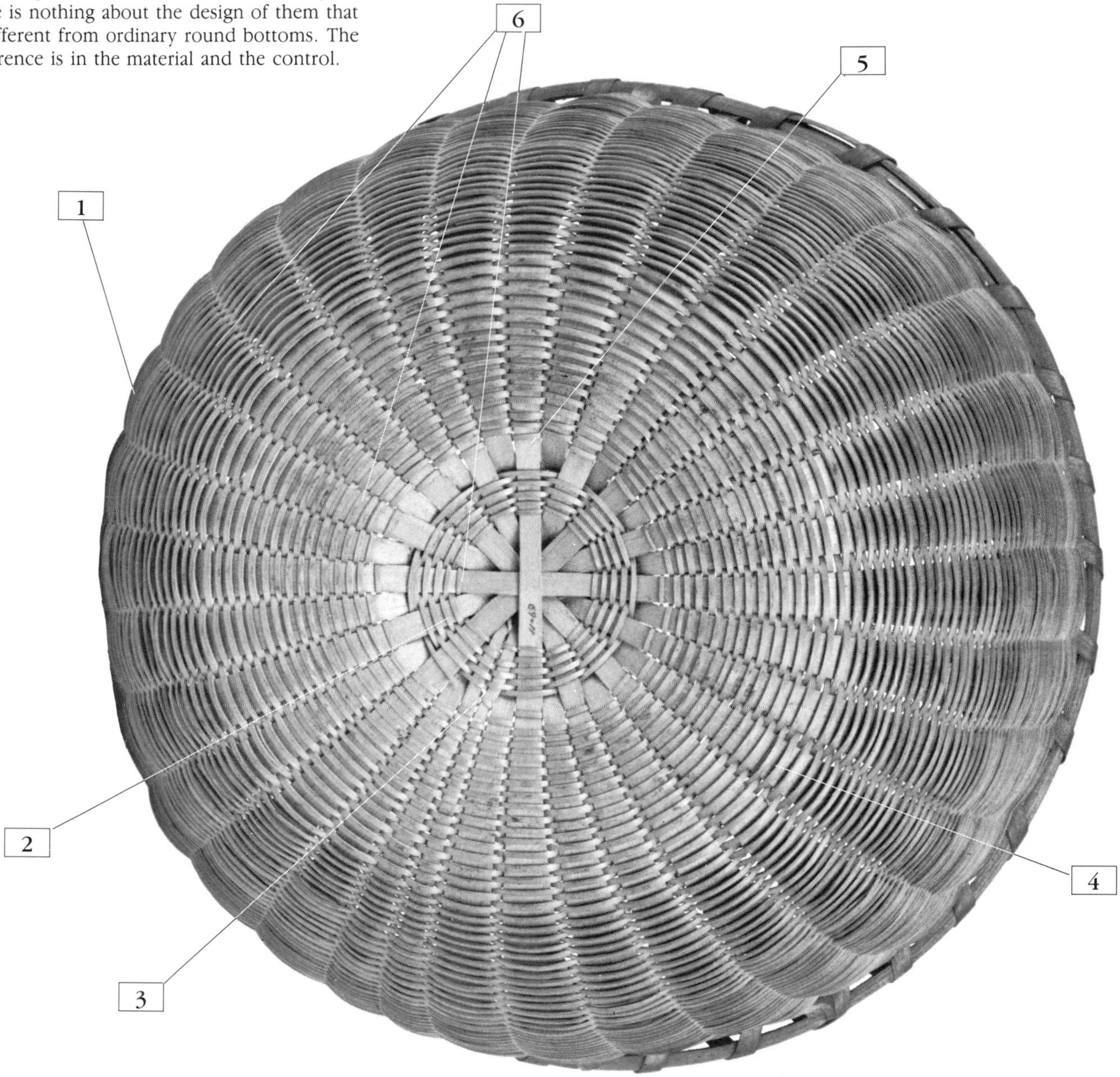

Fig.117

1 The uniformity of the splint, the weight of the material and the quality of it are registered in the perfect "pumpkin" shape and these smooth, smooth scallops

2 Double-bottom construction (explained in *Chapter Five*)

3 Split upright

4 Uprights tapered to give a tight weave throughout the basket

5 Taper in upright stops here, so the rib crosses the center without additional taper in width

6 Weight of material increases incrementally; adjusted to get a refined look using heaviest possible splint at each stage

Fig.118 Canterbury's bonnet handle differs from Mt. Lebanon's in that it is, on the whole, thinner and lighter. As at Mt. Lebanon, a file was used to give the handle contour and to soften the lines; but other tooling was not introduced. Because the initial blank is thinner, the blocking at the notch is also thinner. The tail, which again is thin, is squared at the tip.

In details such as this, you see Mt. Lebanon's sophistication. The New York makers forced their materials into forms they didn't always want to take. Like them, their baskets were doctrinaire. Canterbury was more simplistic: theirs is a uniformity without the severity.

The Canterbury handle is single notched. The tails go deep into the basket to compensate for the notch, but they don't necessarily go far enough. If the notch were double or the tails went all the way down to the bottom, when excessive weight was put in the basket the handle would not push down. But with a single notch, the handle slips up and down if the tails don't reach the bottom; and when that happens, weavers split—as seen here.

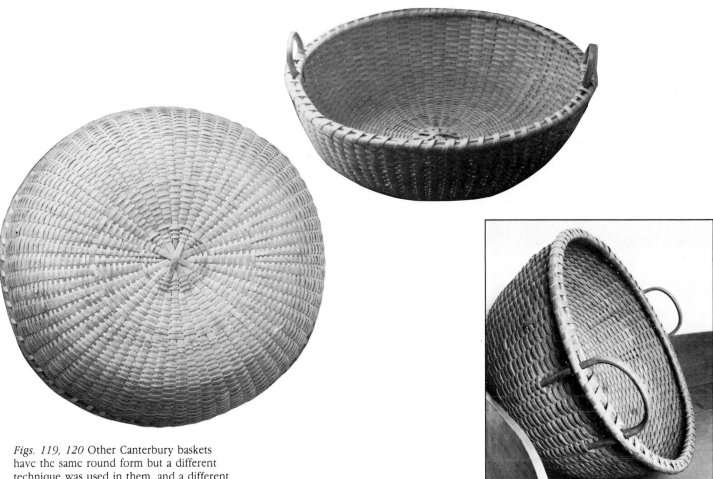

Figs. 119, 120 Other Canterbury baskets
have the same round form but a different
technique was used in them, and a different
aesthetic, identifying them as the work of a
different maker.

Notice there is less taper in the uprights.
Instead, they are split; and this alters the ratio of weavers to uprights so it is nearer 2:1
instead of 4:1 as in the white ash round bottoms. The heavy look of these baskets, however, is deceptive. The material is lighter,
usually, than that in the "similar" white ash
work.

Fig.121 Rims and handles on these baskets are
also cubey, but they are heavier, meatier.

Fig.122 Not all Canterbury baskets were signature baskets. There are numerous hybrids in
square and round forms. System was not so
developed as at Mt. Lebanon, and as a result
baskets were made in a variety of ways. Many
of these, if they were not associated with Canterbury, would pass for generic country baskets. There isn't enough "Shaker" in them to
make them identifiable.

In rounds, especially, there is a range of
tumblehomes. In addition to those that start
round and then finish in straight sides (as in
the white ash baskets, and the earred baskets
with split uprights), there is another that is
common, which starts flat and has straight, angled sides. Several variants turn up; this is one.

67

Fig.123 Another sizable group of round bottoms are late ones, used as apple baskets, which have rims and handles that match closely those on the distinctive white ash round bottoms. Some of these have woven bottoms and others have plank or plated bottoms (discussed in *Chapter Four*).

Figs.124–26 Photographs from Canterbury c. 1920 give some idea of how many of these late round-bottom baskets were in use there. Filled from the orchard, they also indicate the importance of the apple crop. As at Mt. Lebanon, apples were made into sauce (Fig. 129) and cider; others were dried, and still others went into pies. It is understandable that the apple turns up in the Shaker's emblematic drawings as a "gift of blessing."

Fig.127 Sisters set off for the orchard. The truck is loaded with late Canterbury apple baskets. The swing-handle held by the sister who sits on the running board is a factory basket.

Fig.129

Fig.128 The same Canterbury baskets, used here for sorting corn.

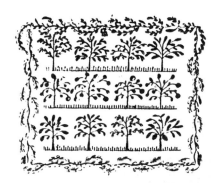

Fig.130 Detail from a Shaker drawing.

Fig.131 Of all known Shaker baskets, Maine baskets are the most difficult to identify by production technique. They are the most country, the most Indian and the least like New York's. However, there are some design elements to go on; and the most conspicuous of these is an applied foot on the bottom of many (but not all) of these baskets.

This foot occurs in many configurations. A thick piece of splint, which is stood on edge, is lashed onto the bottom. Similar rings turn up in Indian work but not in other Shaker work.

In this group of baskets, note especially the example at the far right. The foot here is squared at the corners, with a mitered notch

cut out of the corner to relieve the sharp bend. This detail recurs in rimwork on some Maine baskets and in the feet on some Mt. Lebanon cheese baskets (see Fig. 92). Note, also, in the example second from the left, that wear was on the lashing—suggesting that, over time, some baskets may have lost their feet.

Fig.132 Another peculiarity of Maine work is a twilled chain spiralling up through the body of some utility baskets. (For a technical description of twilling, see *Chapter Five*).

Fig.133 For all the marginality in Maine work, there is still a strong allegiance to the Shaker idea of what a basket should be. Country technique was never fully displaced here, and system was never well established; but considering how "country" Maine baskets remained, it is significant that production is about equally weighted between Shaker square forms (which most naive basketmakers didn't bother with) and rounds.

Many of these baskets in the laundry at Sabbathday Lake are very similar to Canterbury's in size, rimwork and handle manufacture. (The idea of the longways handle, however, was not adopted here.) *The* attribute that distinguishes these from Canterbury work is, often, the applied foot (as seen here on the basket in the right foreground).

Fig.134 Rims and handles in Maine are typically dressed with a drawshave, sometimes a file. But you don't see Mt. Lebanon tooling or even the nice, nice blanks used in the sophisticated Canterbury work.

Fig.135 Baskets for wet wash, in the laundry at Sabbathday Lake.

In the Maine shop expertise was not divided as it was in New York or even in New Hampshire. While the Maine basketmakers respected a Shaker idea of right form and right use, they did not stick to a single prototype. Each, it appears, took a basket from start to finish, and followed his own leadings in various details. Thus the very similar round baskets shown here present two different tumblehomes, two different styles of handles.

The round handle on the basket at top right is especially unusual, even though round handles are characteristic of some Maine work. In this same basket, the tail of the lashing is run diagonally down through the weavers, which is something you see in several Maine baskets but not in other Shaker ones.

71

Fig.136 The round-bottom, round-top form with low sides made an excellent gathering basket. The design is very practical. Things can be heaped or put in loosely; and the baskets stack compactly when stored.

Fig.138 A typical Maine basket. Separated from Sabbathday Lake, where it has been stored in an attic, this basket—and many others there—would elude attribution. They are generic country round bottoms, with too little (except sometimes a coiled foot or a decorative twill) to identify them.

Fig.137 With taller sides, rounds also made serviceable shop baskets. This one is filled with strips of curled poplar (discussed in *Chapter Three*), which will be straightened and processed and made into woven poplar boxes.

Note the tumblehome in this basket. Many of Maine's round baskets have tumblehomes similar to Canterbury's. But there is group—of which this is one—that have a different contour, in which the sides bow out and back in. Less a design decision than a consequence of the top rows of weaving caving as the bodies were finished, this bow nonetheless gives these baskets a tumblehome you don't see in other known Shaker work (although it is very common in country basketry).

72

Fig.139 This cheese basket has been bleached white with use. The design—which avoids traditional "cheese weave" by simply laying the splint in a normal pattern and leaving it loose—is something common to country baskets but not seen in other Shaker work.

Fig.140 Many Maine baskets made for indoor use have a heavy outdoor look. In that respect, this smallish basket with a drum-shape body is typical. The handles, however, are odd, even in the context of Maine's inconsistencies.

Fig.141 Another Maine round bottom, made for use. Despite the similarity in shape to some Canterbury baskets (see Fig. 122), there is nothing here to make you think "Shaker."

Fig.142 The baskets in this photograph of a Maine farmer c. 1901 are very similar to some baskets at Sabbathday Lake (and Canterbury). They are all common country work.

Figs. 143–45 The Shakers had the first mechanized basket shop in America. Seeing a smart idea, factory operators took the Shaker concept and began making production baskets by the 1840s. But they differed sharply from the Shakers in what they were after: a cheap product made with efficiency which they could sell at a profit.

PICKING BASKET

No. 71

The standard oak picking basket. Made with swing bail or stiff bail; plain or with protecting straps running from rim to rim.

Capacity	Plain Fall Bail Per Doz.	Stiff Bail Per Doz.	Strapped Fall Bail Per Doz.	Stiff Bail Per Doz.
1/4 bushel	$ 7.50	$ 7.75	$ 8.25	$ 8.50
1/2 bushel	8.25	8.50	9.25	9.50
3/4 bushel	10.50	10.75	11.25	11.50

We also make these baskets in extra quality all ash or with bamboo filling. Add $2.00 to list price.

STRAWBERRY PICKING BASKET

No. 72

An ash basket designed to hold quart berry baskets.

No.	Size	Per Doz.
72-1	13 1/2 x 13 1/2 x 4 (for 4 quart baskets)	$6.00
72-2	20 x 13 x 4 (for 6 quart baskets)	7.00
72-3	24 x 13 x 4 (for 8 quart baskets)	8.00

For iron over bail, add $2.00 to list price.

16

Fig. 146 A basketmaker uses a hand-guided plane to skim "filler cut" off a bolt of wood. The resulting material had a brittleness that was absent in pounded ash. The nature of this "new" material meant that baskets had to be redesigned to compensate for its deficiencies.

Fig. 147 Typical factory baskets. Rims are characteristically nailed on instead of lashed. Splint is filling cut. Weavers and uprights are wide and thick, giving the baskets the look of bent wood.

Some of the first factory baskets looked very much like traditional splint utility baskets; but as procedures were altered to eliminate extra handwork and save time and material, the baskets acquired a different look.

TRADE

MARK

We beg to call your attention to accompanying price list and solicit your order for our goods.

We have been engaged in the manufacture of these goods for more than fifty years and have every facility for their manufacture. We aim to produce the best baskets that can be made and our prices are low.

We deliver our goods F. O. B. at Bellows Falls, Vt.

Orders by mail will be promptly and accurately filled.

Oblong baskets for factory use made to order.

SIDNEY GAGE & CO'S BASKET MANUFACTORY.
ESTABLISHED IN 1842.

Round Clothes Baskets.
No. 3.   No. 2.   No. 1.
Price per doz. $3.75. $4.12. $4.50.

Figs. 148–50 Two of the major basket shops were in Peterborough, New Hampshire: the Peterboro Basket Co. (Figs. 143–45) and the Needham Basket Co. (Figs. 152–53). Another large operation—Sidney Gage & Co.—was at Bellows Falls, Vermont.

Fig.151 A wagonload of baskets made at the Needham Basket Company (Figs. 152, 153).

Figs.152,153

H. B. NEEDHAM BASKET CO.

—MANUFACTURERS OF—

OAK AND ASH BASKETS

of every description. Also, a general line of

Bamboo, Oxford, and Diamond Market Baskets.

SPECIALTIES.

Factory,	Laundry,	Wood,	Coal,	Covered Lunch,
Bakers',				Butchers',
Market,	Farm,	Clothes,	Fish,	Corn.

PETERBORO,   NEW HAMPSHIRE.

Fig.154 Around 1835 basket sales began to
produce a significant income at Mt. Lebanon,
and production shifted from utility types to a
"fancy" line. By the end of the century the
Church Family had made over 71,000 baskets
for sale.

"Finished making baskets. Have made 500 for sale 40–50 for home use 125 palm leaf baskets."

From a Shaker journal, Mt. Lebanon, 1836[1]

From their first acceptance of a new faith, the Shakers separated their aspirations from the world, but they never attempted to fully remove themselves from it. They bought and sold "outside," and saw no contradiction in it so long as they didn't compromise their ethics. As early as 1795 the ministry were advising that "all things made for sale ought to be well done, and suitable for their use"[2]—indicating that even when the communities were barely formed, already they anticipated developing some sale lines.

"If this were the old days," a Shaker at Mt. Lebanon remarked just before the community closed in 1947, "we wouldn't even be able to hear ourselves think (1). These buildings were about the busiest workshops you ever saw. . . . I couldn't begin to tell you how many different trades were carried on in these shops. The North Family [where she then lived] did weaving, dyeing, tailoring, hatmaking, shoemaking, broom-making, soapmaking, blacksmithing, metalwork, carpentry, woodworking, seed drying, and goodness knows what else. Practically every family did a good deal more than just take care of their own needs. The different families in a village used to make things for each other. They all made things to sell to the world, too. [Our] specialties were brooms and packaged seeds."[3]

The history of Shaker baskets divides around production "for home use" and production "for sale." Although sales may have begun spottily (2), Mt. Lebanon's basket business became a major industry. Before the close of the century the Church Family had made some 71,244 baskets for sale. There was some sale production at other communities in the northeast but nothing to equal what was made at Mt. Lebanon.

Records from Mt. Lebanon that have been recovered (3) begin in 1839. Initial totals fluctuate each year between 300–700, then around 1850 they pick up (1050 baskets were made that year). In the two decades following, production doubled and doubled again; typical totals are close to 4000. Then in 1875 the figures drop: only 772 baskets were made that year. A fire burned through some eight or nine Church Family buildings and destroyed the basket shop, basket molds, stock and inventory (4). For three years no baskets were made; then in 1879, 277 are reported. For the six years following production was erratic. After another break, the business was closed out. The last of the line were made in 1892 (427) and 1897 (364).

Several circumstances coincided at Mt. Lebanon in the 1830s to bring about the new direction in basketmaking, beginning with the improvement in production system. Then in 1833 John Farrington died and Daniel Boler took over the basket shop. Boler had been trained by Farrington since he was a boy (5); and with Daniel Crosman (6), another of Farrington's young Shakers, he had rigged up much of the power machinery that facilitated basketmaking. From the 1830s, when Mt. Lebanon accounts begin, Boler's name recurs over and over, identifying him as *the* central figure in the Shaker basket story. The basket business follows his life and falls quiet with his death, in 1892. Take away Boler and there probably would be no basket industry.

John Farrington had brought basketmaking on line. When he died, he left an original system. But the system had served its initial purpose. Mt. Lebanon was supplied with baskets. Membership also was peaking; it appeared there would be no call for any additional volume for "home use." In order to utilize their tooling and expertise, the Church Family began to concentrate on making baskets for sale.

It would not have been feasible for the Shakers to manufacture their large baskets on a commercial basis. They consumed too much material to be cost effective and were an inconvenient size to make in multiples. But more importantly, the market for traditional utility baskets was being eroded by the new factory-made baskets. Cheaper and quicker to make than traditional types, these factory-made baskets were produced in a quantity and at a price that took away even the Indians' dominance of the utility market. However, the Indian basketmaker still held a hegemony with small, light-weight, "fancy" baskets, as these were difficult to make with factory methods. Indians therefore capitalized on their remaining market, selling baskets for souvenir or "fancy" use.

Under Daniel Boler, Shaker production also shifted to fancy types. The Shakers had the capability to compete with Indian sales, and a market was there. The idea of vacationing and daytripping was just taking hold. "Going to the Shakers" was quite the thing. People made an outing of it—some from intellectual curiosity, some to make fun, some to enjoy the "different world" of the Shakers. But for whatever reason, a Shaker village was a tourist stop. Indian basketmakers could easily undersell the Shakers, who were not known for low prices; in a Shaker shop, a basket could cost as much as a chair. But people bought the Shakers' baskets. ("I did not go into their shop," a visitor at Canterbury in 1834 wrote in her diary. "The others found their articles high but purchased some baskets. . ."[4]). It may have been some sense of obligation to support the Shakers that made their guests buy; but more likely it was the simple idea of souvenir—and the cachet that "Shaker" carried *(7)*.

A line of "fancy baskets" seems at odds with Shaker testimony. The meaning of fancy has, however, changed since the nineteenth century. While it implied nicety, it did not necessarily translate as decorative or decorated. Fancy, instead, was understood to mean "of superior grade, extrafine, choice; complex or intricately made; better than average; suitable for select patronage."[5] Interestingly, the Shakers themselves used "fancy" in reference to sale items—"toilet boxes, sewing boxes, drawer boxes" and other articles—they made from poplar; in their accounts they almost always specify "splint" (with no mention of "fancy") when they mean baskets made of black ash. For some time they had also been making baskets of palm leaf, on the same molds and in the same fancy styles as some splint baskets *(8)*. These several sale lines are often confused, particularly because poplar items look something like baskets, and the Shakers called them "baskets," although technically they are not *(9)*.

Fancy goods and baskets gave the Shakers a sale line which was quite in vogue among "the world." Initial sales at Mt. Lebanon were possibly limited to the "Office" store in the Trustees building, and to some local outlets. But in a short time the

Fig. 155 More than a century before Dinah Shore sang "See the U.S.A. in your Chevrolet" and the automobile made travel something facile, tourists were already out to see the sights. And the Shakers were a prime attraction. Crowds of people came on Sundays to watch them at worship, and others came midweek. Few slipped by the sales shop.

"The Shakers are visited annually by thousands of strangers, who take great interest in their unusual manner of living and worship. Visitors are received into the Society's various workshops and gardens throughout the week."[18]

Advertising brochure (*Columbia Hall, Lebanon Springs, N.Y.*), 1902

"We return to the guest parlor. The office door opposite is open, and tempts you in; the room back is the shop. Wooden ware, feather brushes and pens, whips, baskets of various kinds, seines, bags . . ., cakes of wax and maple sugar, bottles of perfumes, essences and medicines, fancy work, and the coarser articles of their manufacture, with a few Shaker publications—are offered for sale. [You] buy till you have pockets and hands full, and begin to find change scarce."[19]

The *Illustrated News,* 1853

"Lately [we] went to the Shakers in winter . . . The good sisters led the way into the shop, saying that they did not keep it warmed in winter, so few strangers came that way. We entered the room, which was perfumed with extracts and wood-work. It was all in confusion; but there were the nests of boxes, and the delicate baskets, and the white tablemats, and the yellow silk-winders, and the floormats, and rocking-chairs . . ."[20]

Harper's, 1860

81

Church Family had an extensive marketing program for wholesale and retail sales. Close to home (probably the radius of Hudson, N.Y. and Pittsfield, Mass.) they made a circuit of a trade route where they solicited orders and delivered them ("Nathan Williams took Sara Ann Lewis and Mary Hazard *(10)* on a trading excursion," a sister writes, "to put off their small baskets and other store wares"[6]). Additional baskets were sent to accounts all across the country. Shipments went regularly to New York City, Albany and Philadelphia; other wholesale accounts were in Pittsburgh, Chicago, Washington, D.C., New York state (Niagara Falls, Saratoga, Poughkeepsie, Stratford), Massachusetts (Lenox, Springfield, Chicopee), Connecticut (New Haven, Bridgeport, Winsted), Michigan (Saginaw City), Nevada (Virginia City), California (Sacramento, San Jose, Judson Gates) and Nottingham, England *(11)*.[7]

Seeing how the Indians marketed their baskets at resort hotels, the entrepreneuring Shakers also displayed their baskets and fancy goods where affluent guests came for the summer. ("Edward Fowler, Mary Hazard and Tabitha Lapsley go to Saratoga Springs to vend some of the sisters' manufactures, sale wares, baskets, fans," a Church sister writes in 1861.[8]) The routine that developed was apparently quite effective. On into 1874, the year before the fire almost destroyed the Mt. Lebanon business, in mid-August "Sara Ann Lewis, Tabatha L. and Andrew Fortier [start] for Martha's Vineyard to sell dry goods, baskets."[9] And well after the basket business closed, the Shaker women continued to make seasonal trips to the grand hotels to sell their handmade items.

With the shift to fancy types, basketmaking had become something the sisters could do. Up until this time, basketmaking had been men's work. Despite the equal ranking they gave to male and female *(12)*, the Shakers retained a conventional idea of what was women's work and what was men's; and among "white English" basketmaking had traditionally been men's work. The Shaker system developed at Mt. Lebanon changed this by breaking production down into stages, and separating the more physical tasks from lighter tasks. The brothers in the basket shop continued to make utility baskets and to prepare the splint and make up all rims and handles. By the mid-1830s, however, the sisters were weaving the fancy baskets, applying those handles and rims, and finishing them off. They also took over sales *(13)*.

Isaac Youngs, in his history of the Church Family, notes under "Sisters' Work": "For many years the sisters did not follow any particular branch of business for sale. Tho they did a little in the fore part of this century [he is writing around 1855–60], particularly in making linen diaper [a fine-textured linen with a diamond pattern woven in] of a very excellent quality which sold readily. But about the year 1813 they began by little to make baskets for sale. Since which they have increased greatly in that line, and have manufactured various kinds of articles, such as men's palm leaf hats, women's bonnets, baskets a great variety, carriage, chair, pin & needle cushions."[10] It was natural for the women, who were skilled on the loom in intricate textile patterns, to transfer their skills to basket art.

Altogether there were some fifty-one sisters who, at one time or another, were basketmakers—some only briefly and some for a period of five, ten, twelve years. Five women, however, were the regulars, for twenty-five years or more *(14)*: Julia Ann Scott, Elizabeth Cantrell, Ann Maria Graves, Augusta Stone and Cornelia French. It is they, with the help of several "hands" borrowed each year from other departments, who carried a business that produced over 70,000 baskets. In some years only these five sisters were making baskets; in no year were there more than thirteen. And yet they were turning out 3000–4000 baskets a year. The Shaker system was about production as well as perfection.

Basketry was seasonal work. ("We now . . . commence our winter work of making baskets,"[11] the sisters begin a journal.) They usually started in November or December and finished up in April or May. During the year the Shakers moved from job to job; they were usually proficient in several employments, and their system of "joint labor" was predicated on rotation between assignments. ("Each member has her allotted work," a visitor among the Shakers observed, "and in most cases there is rotation enough to relieve the life from monotony; for, after a certain number of weeks *(15)*, she takes her turn at something different."[12]) Switching off to laundry or garden or kitchen or herb room was usually a pleasant shift in the calendar. But there were two years when the sisters in the basket shop had to prematurely leave off making baskets and help out elsewhere in the village. "The winter past," a deaconess writes in 1869, "there has been more constant failures in the Shop occasioned by sickness than I have known for 20 years. We finish sometime in August, not having finished [the baskets] as is usual before this begins. The amount made is 2,228."[13] The next year continues irregular, even though they begin punctually on November 1. "Having begun early we make considerable many Baskets. In March and April we have much sickness in the family. The hands were taken off to work in the kitchen. Not much work done in the Shop these two months. Finish all that we can do this season, May 7th. The amount made 1,966."[14]

The brethren's basketwork was also seasonal. "Roll and break the basket stuff," Andrew Fortier *(16)* starts up his diary in November 1869[15]. "Take apart all my Basket Splints," he writes in the weeks following. "To Hancock Shakers to get black ash . . . Down the Tory wood & cut 2 Black Ash trees . . . Elder Daniel B & I go to Hancock Depot and Cut 4 Black Ash trees . . . Work at basket timber, cold." December continues the same: "Roll Basket timber and Draw it to the Blacksmith Shop [where the triphammer was located that pounded the logs] . . . Elder D Bowler & I hamer out the rest of the Basket timber . . . Take splints apart."

In the fall the brethren went to look for basket trees, often having to go a great distance to find any. Then they prepared the splint ("plaining and getting out basket splint," Elisha Blakeman *(17)*, an elder assisting in the basket shop, writes routinely[16]) and delivered it to the sisters, who stored it on "scaffels" *(18)*. During the winter months the brethren worked up rims and handles. (When spring came, in 1878, Andrew Fortier wrote with quiet Shaker ceremony: "May 4. In the swamp after cowslips. PM in the Shop making the last of the Rims for this year. good news."[17])

Among both the sisters and the brothers, the reliance on Boler is clear from the manuscript record. A typical situation is acknowledged in a sister's journal: "We have just finished 10 Doz. [baskets] which are to go immediately to N.Y. . . . These have filled our time and used all the stuff we could get in Br. Daniel's absence. He has come home and has so arranged matters that we have a pretty good supply on hand."[18] A brother similarly remarks: "I go off to plain out some ash splints . . . With good luck Daniel Boler comes and does it off quick."[19]

Boler made beautiful baskets but he appears to have taken as his job the preparation of splint which he gave over to others to weave up. In 1835 an eldress notes that "Daniel Boler prepares [the sisters'] timber for them. He took it," she continues, "when Elder Br John [Farrington] left it, has had it two years."[20] Entries in other diaries and ledgers fill out the story. 1846: "E. Daniel Boler went after timbers for basket stuff."[21] 1862: "Elder Daniel B . . . after basket stuff."[22] 1873: "Elder Daniel at Basket Stuff . . . Elder Daniel planing basket stuff . . . Elder Daniel fixing his basket knives . . . Elder Daniel planing basket stuff . . . Elder Daniel working at stuff."[23] 1881: "Elder Daniel works at blacksmith shop repairing the trip hammer for pounding basket stuff."[24] 1890: "Elder Daniel making stuff for seats and baskets." 1892: " Elder Daniel mending baskets."[25] Boler also continued to improve on tooling. In 1864 he set up a new planing machine "for planing basket stuff." In 1866 he was working on a machine for "getting out basket stuff, instead of pounding it out." In 1872 he introduced an "improved" planer.[26] There were likely other ideas he tried, but they are not recorded.

Under Boler sale production received the attention of the lead Shakers that utility production had received under Farrington. To the end of the nineteenth century, it appears that—besides Boler—most of the ministry made baskets. A number of visitors at Mt. Lebanon describe finding them at basketwork. ("Ministers, elders and deacons," Charles Nordhoff wrote, "all without exception, are industriously employed in some manual occupation, except in the time taken up in the necessary duties of their respective callings. So carefully is this rule observed that even the supreme heads of the Shaker church—the four who constitute the [lead] ministry at Mt. Lebanon, Daniel Boler, Giles Avery (19), Ann Taylor and Polly Reed—labor at basketmaking in the intervals of their travels and ministrations and have a separate little 'shop' for this purpose near the church."[27]) It may not be just coincidence that the ministry made baskets instead of, say, seating chairs. "A Man can Show his religion as much in measureing onions as he can in singing glory [hallelujah]," a Hancock brother attested[28]; but how a basket sang.

Basketmaking was an art kept in the Church Family from the start; and it appears it was limited even to the "First Order." In the several ledgers and account books for the business there is nothing to suggest that members as close as the Church Family "Second Order" were making baskets (20). The sisters there "furnished" baskets (with needlework and toiletry accessories) and did various kinds of sale work; but the basketmakers who worked in splint were all members of the First Order. These were the most "Shaker" of the Shakers. Many of them had come in as children. All of them had "proved their faith." Consider how many of the carpenters, cabinetmakers, joiners, oval box makers, weavers, etc. whose work is classic Shaker lived in the First Order (21), and you see some correlations. They had a close communion with each other and with something spiritual. And in the 1830s, 40s, 50s this was translated into visions, dances, drawings, tables, chests, boxes, clocks, cloth—and baskets. A sister has suggested that the songs of this period were not "just songs but deep feelings from the soul."[29] Neither was craft just craft.

Right around the time the basket business began to develop, believers everywhere were seized with a sense of profound revival, and "an atmosphere of intense expectation was created."[30] A purge was on to restore more spiritual motivation, such as had animated the society in the Shakers' early days. There was a showering of spiritual gifts (22), together with admonitions and instructions from departed spirits. A renewal, moving and mystic, was at work, and it continued some ten years.

The special mood that pervaded the basket shop becomes apparent when you read the names in Daniel Patterson's lists of those who "received" inspired songs or were "instruments" for the emblematic drawings.[31] Twenty or more of the seventy believers at Mt. Lebanon to whom "gift" songs are attributed were basketmakers; and at least two of the basketmakers were among the artists who drew the beautiful spiritual drawings *(23)*. And all were affected. "The attention to spiritual gifts [was] by no means confined to the place and time of worship," Isaac Youngs reflected. "The people were full of faith and zeal, and . . . mixed spiritual and temporal things together. Meetings were held occasionally at any time of day; religious exercises could be going on in one part of the house, and hand labor in another."[32] Among those who made baskets, certainly the pattern of the dances, all members singing, weaving in and out in concentric circles converting to spirals and squares, mingled in their subconscious minds with the patterns of the baskets they wove *(24)*. Virtually everything they were after, everything they did, was impelled by a commitment to bring their faith into form. Think of them paring and paring and paring a mold to get the body right, shaving a handle to get the contour right. When you know their context, you look at the clarity of line in the severest basket and the intricate, radiant weave of a twilled top with a new recognition of a sense of vision among the basketmakers and those around them. "Here are pretty little baskets, filled with love," they sang in meeting, "and I've brought them to you on my silver wings, says Mother's little dove."[33] You can see they believed it.

Mt. Lebanon's fancy baskets carry over some vernacular conventions and some Indian ideas; but they are subtly different from all other American baskets. System, and the Shakers' attitude toward system, shows in them. When the sisters wove the baskets, they were essentially working up kits. Brothers who understood the ways of wood had been to the swamps and found the trees, pulled the splint and planed it, cut it and graded it; a cabinetmaker had shaped the molds; a joiner had tooled the rims and bent the handles. The sisters' job was to weave the bodies even and tight, and apply the handles and rims. No one else approached basketmaking this way. Theirs was a system where each person did just one part, but gave all their art to that part.

Traditional basketmakers used the most rudimentary system, if any at all. The basketmaker selected the trees, prepared the splint, wove a basket, made its rims and handle(s), finished it off and started on another. Indians may have worked in multiples, and certainly they streamlined where they could: their aim was to produce a saleable basket as quickly as they could. They did good work because they respected their craft, but they weren't after a perfect look. Factory operators combined, in some ways, the Indian concept and the Shaker system; they eliminated a lot of handwork but they cheapened material and process, to get a product that "would do." Only the Shakers sought perfection. And that is what you see in the sale line. The ultralight and even splint, "satin" on both sides. The tooling in the rims and handles. Perfect shape, perfect line. The cleanness of the work. The symmetry and balance. These were production baskets; but they show production could be art.

Form and detail in the fancy baskets are nascent in some of what came before. Rims and handles are the same as those on apple baskets and some carriers. Shapes are still basic shapes (with rounds added). But tumblehome is showier in the fancy line; it was part of the sales aesthetic. Tumblehome helped to sell a basket, especially where the Shakers were competing with Indian sales. For almost every fancy form the Shakers

Fig.155a Some twenty styles were offered for sale in the fancy line, in a range of sizes for each style. The baskets illustrated in the pages following are those that can be positively identified by a mold, manuscript reference or other documentation.

made, there is an Indian form similar to it. During this period the Indians went off in some new directions. (Bulbous forms were woven on molds. Color was used freely, and splint was often decorated. Fancy curlicues were incorporated in some weaves, and spiralling chains and herringbone patterns in others.) But the Indians continued to make plain, undecorated baskets as well. And these are easily confused with Shaker.

Between 1835 and 1855 the sisters established their sale line. In the *Memorandum of Baskets etc. Kept by the Basket Makers*, which lists some twenty styles (in several sizes), there is nothing to suggest that other models were added after this time. There were some refinements in pattern and method; but the styles named at the outset *(25)* in 1855 carry through to the end of the ledger in 1875. Even twilling, which *looks* late-Victorian, was common by 1855, as it was cited in the subheading ("also directions for weaving, twilling and proceeding with the work").

Basket formulas helped to ensure standardization and may have been introduced even by 1830. Accounts in the *Memorandum* which give annual production figures are prefaced by several pages of directions specifying the number of uprights, the width of weavers, weaving method, rim length and lashing for each style. The formulas are spare; it took us long experience to decode them ("No. 1 Spoon. 13 short 7 long stand [ribs or uprights] laid loose filled with fine fill, bound with narrow bind. Cov 6 short 13 long fine fill filled with super fine"[34]). If this was all you knew, you couldn't make a basket. It becomes obvious that the sisters carried a lot in their heads: the formulas are really only codifications or clarifications of what was understood. Also understood were allowances for differences in material. The basket weaver fit the material to the molds and fit the idea of a basket to material on hand. As a result, it is not uncommon to find variations in the ratios of weavers to uprights among several baskets of the same type. Throughout the fancy line, rims and handles are tooled alike

Fig.155b The Shakers and the Indians were often competing for the same customer.

Indians knew where the sales were. They went to where the tourists were. (Here a basketmaker displays her work near the Flume, in New Hampshire's White Mountains.)

Indian designs included many bulbous forms with shoulders and necks. Color was used for decoration. Fancy curlicues were incorporated in some weaves, as was a lot of twilling. However, the Indians continued to make plain undecorated baskets, in many of the same forms and the same range of sizes as the Shakers'. These are easily confused if you look only at basketforms.

and made alike; bodies show they came off the same molds: all the baskets share a look. But within the uniformities, there are little adjustments of form and scale.

The squared-bottom, round-top "fruit" was among the first fancy baskets the Shakers offered for sale. While clearly related to Mt. Lebanon apple and shop baskets, it is a different basket; and the difference speaks to distinctions the Shakers made between "home use" and "sale" production. As were most of the fancy styles, fruits were woven both high and low on the mold. Handles are either overhead or ear. Very similar to the fruit is a smaller basket whimsically called a "cat head." The peaked corners of the bottom form "cat ears," and the basket turned upside down looks like a round little cat head. Many cat head molds exist, but few baskets have survived. A smaller version of the cat head is the "kitten head." Again, molds exist (many of them quite miniature) but very few baskets.

Among the fancy types there are few squared forms. But one of these—the "knife" basket—was the most popular of all the Mt. Lebanon line; more were made than any other style, and more have survived. The knife is a carrier which possibly takes its name from its shape, as the sides appear to have been knifed off. All knife types have rectangular bottoms; sides are straight, rising perpendicular or with a slight flare from the base. Handles vary; some are overhead, some ear. Many knife baskets were lidded with a double hinged lid twilled in a pattern unique to the Shakers. (Almost every basket in the sale line was offered "covered" or "uncovered" but, aside from knives, there are few examples with lids extant.) Knife forms turn up in a range of sizes, and weights. This was a basket made not only for sale but also for "home use," with materials scaled up and down to answer the purpose the basket was made for. Some of the larger examples, which the Shakers reserved for themselves, are woven of comparatively heavy splint and reinforced on the bottom with strips like those attached to shop baskets, the large rectangular carriers and apple baskets.

The "box" basket is another squared form, designed to be lidded. Like a flat pillow, each face of the square (sometimes a rectangle) bows or bulges below the rim, giving the basket a compressed and cushiony look. The separate tray-like lid slips down over the rim of the "box."

One other known form with a rectangular bottom is the "spoon" basket, which may take its name from a tumblehome resembling the bowl of a spoon. One of two Mt. Lebanon fancy types with an oval top (the other is a furnishing basket called a "boat"), the spoon was made in large numbers, as is evident from sales records and from pricks in surviving molds. No example, however, has been found.

Round-bottom, round-top forms—which the Mt. Lebanon basketmakers had not previously made for their own use—were popular fancy forms, and (along with low-sided fruits) sold well as dressing table baskets or sewing and handwork baskets (sometimes simply called "round work" baskets). Some of the round-bottomed forms have straight angled sides; these were called "tubs." Others, with a rounding tumblehome, were called "saucers." Any that have handles usually have ears; but many were originally lidded, without handles. A "quadrifoil" twill, resembling a four-leaf clover, is incorporated in the base of all Mt. Lebanon round-bottoms. Unique to the New York Shakers, the quadrifoil gives these a special signature.

Another style of toilet or work basket was created in an openwork or "hexagon" weave, which was a fancy version of utilitarian cheese basket weave. Baskets of this type were loosely referred to as "hexagons," even though in form they are typically round. (The weave pattern produced a six-sided base which could easily be worked up into round or ovoid sides.) Some of these baskets are made entirely of hexagon weave. Others have partially "open" bases and solid sides. Hexagon fancy baskets were not an idea unique to the Shakers; the Indians made many similar ones. But the idea of combining openwork bottoms with solid, filled sides was something only the Shakers did.

In addition to these preceding types, the Shakers (and Indians) also made thousands of hexagon "boats" and furnishing baskets as accessories for toilet and work baskets. The boats are oblong-to-oval in shape, and intended to be attached inside another basket, usually at the rim. Almost any basket in the sale line was available "furnished" or "unfurnished." Most of the furnishing was done by sisters in the Second Order who equipped the baskets, typically, with cushions and/or boats, along with an emery, sewing wax and needlecase (usually made of poplar). A variety of cushions were also made for separate sale; and several of the cushion forms were inserted in splint bottoms, ranging from kitten heads to low fruits to saucers.

In virtually all the communities, after mid-century the Shakers' removal from the world was losing its appeal. "Much depression of spirit has been felt, and struggling through dark and gloomy prospects," Isaac Youngs confided in 1856, "on account of apostacies, lifelessness and backslidings of unfaithful members, and the scanty ingathering from without"[35] (26). Fewer and fewer males were attracted to join with the Shakers, and many former believers—especially among the brethren—left. Of necessity the productive base of the community shifted to the sisters. They needed a source of support that was not male-intensive, something they could do with the help of a few brothers or hired men. Baskets and other fancy work saved them. Even at Mt. Lebanon, it was the sisters who provided a stop against failure as the community adjusted to a new scale of life. Outside New York at least one community that had not previously made baskets experimented with basketmaking to generate extra income (27). And at Canterbury and Alfred, where there were established basket shops, a variety of sale types were made. But as helpful as this production was to each village, the volume was negligible compared to Mt. Lebanon's. When Elder Henry Blinn from Canterbury visited Mt. Lebanon in 1873, he was quite impressed with the business there, suggesting he had seen nothing like it elsewhere. "We went to the Ministry Shop," he wrote, "where we met Elder Daniel Boler and Elder Giles B. Avery. Before leaving this place, Elder Daniel Boler shows us the machine for plaining the strips of wood, of which they make baskets. Passing through a set of rollers it leaves the machine highly polished. Much of the basketwood is prepared in this shop. It forms quite a branch of business for the Family and several hands are engaged at it, most of the year."[36]

Despite the expertise Canterbury had acquired in making baskets, the fancy types attributed there don't come up to New York's. The basketmakers—sisters now—didn't have the same hand, the same experience or the same advantage. In their designs you see a close correspondence to Mt. Lebanon models; but palm leaf, for example, is often substituted for ash uprights, and rims are made of cane. Canterbury was trying to get the look without the system or the supplies. Some of the work is very fine, but it is not the *perfect* work of the Mt. Lebanon basketmakers.

Meanwhile, something very different was going on at Alfred. Maine baskets had traditionally been the most irregular of all Shaker work; but suddenly, in the late nineteenth century, Maine fancy work looks exactly like New York's. In the summer of 1879 Harriet Goodwin (1823–1903), a Mt. Lebanon eldress and one of the original basketmakers there, was sent to Alfred to reside. With her, Mt. Lebanon standards were transferred to Maine; and under her tutelage, Maine Shakers began making fancy baskets Mt. Lebanon's way. To facilitate their work, splint was shipped to them from the Mt. Lebanon shop. ("Elder Daniel preparing splint for Maine," a brother at Mt. Lebanon wrote around 1880. "Elder Daniel packing stuff to send to Alfred, Maine," he notes on another occasion.[37]) But despite the best splint and the best instruction and a volley of molds, the Maine Shakers still lacked a system; they especially lacked experience in working up rims and handles. As time went on, their baskets were made with just a slip of a handle, sometimes tied on with ribbon, and bodies were finished without rims.

By this time other types of "fancy" sale work were beginning to take precedence over baskets in all the sisters' shops; and, except at Mt. Lebanon, basketmaking was virtually dropped. Of the many factors that were involved, a lack of splint was the most critical. Even at Mt. Lebanon good splint was giving out. Black ash, which was never abundant, became harder and harder to find. As early as the 1860s Andrew Fortier (who, with Daniel Boler, was largely responsible for scouting trees for the Mt. Lebanon shop) remarks repeatedly in his journal on the scarcity of ash. "Elder Daniel B & I to Hancock Swamp to look for Black Ash timber. A narow chance," he writes typically, "for Black Ash any Where within 40 miles."[38] Fortier had to look further and further afield to find basket trees, and what he found was often unsatisfactory. Then in 1875 the fire that burned the Mt. Lebanon basket shop also consumed precious stock, and basket production stopped. It recovered a while, then wavered. On

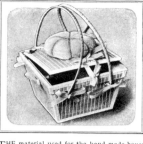

The Christmas
Ladies' Home Journal

DECEMBER 1908   FIFTEEN CENTS

What the Shakers Make for Christmas

By Marion Wire

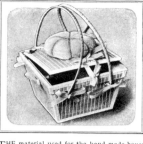

SOME time ago THE JOURNAL published an article telling of the origin and progress of this little world of people at Mount Lebanon, New York, known as the Shakers. Their industries, their agricultural pursuits and domestic arts were then, as they are now, carried on with a methodical exactness and earnestness of purpose characteristic of their principles and belief. There is, too, among the women a delightfully feminine feeling for the dainty little articles so dear to the hearts of all women, and this page shows some of their lighter handiwork.

This style of Shaker bonnet, which is made of flowered organdy in many varieties of color, is so becoming that it is a general favorite for outdoor wear in the summertime. The flaring brim is stiffened with light-weight canvas.

THE material used for the hand-made boxes and trays illustrated is the wood of the black poplar tree. It is cut into strips so thin and fine as to be almost threadlike in quality. White cotton thread is used in the weaving. The foundation of these boxes is of cardboard, and the bindings are of white paper. The little fittings and the linings are of soft silk or satin in pale blue, pink or buff, with ribbon trimmings to match. These woven novelties vary from sewing-boxes to jewel-cases.

An exact reproduction of the Shaker costume is shown in this little doll. Her winter cloak protects her as completely as does that of her grown-up sister.

One of the smallest of the novelties is this daisy emery. The flower is in yellow velvet and white flannel, with the stem in leaf-green satin ribbon—all pleasingly suggestive of a real flower.

Our doll again, dressed in a typical Shaker dress of mohair with silk kerchief. The bonnet is for summer, in straw and lawn.

Fig.155c "We say that Shakerism can't be told; it must be lived," one of the last believers at Mt. Lebanon informed a reporter when the community was closing in 1947. "Still, you can learn a lot about it just from [our] barn."[21] The same could be said about the baskets. Everything the Shakers believed was expressed in them. The practical and the spiritual were fused in their aesthetic, and the art of the individual was transcended in their collective system.

This collage from the 1908 Christmas issue of *Ladies' Home Journal* indicates how the economy of the community had shifted. Most of the old industries had closed down. Oval boxes with bail handles, like the one lower left, "were made in various sizes years ago by some of the Shaker brothers," the correspondent wrote; "but few of them are in existence at the present time." All the items shown here—with the exception of the drop-handle oval box (or "carrier") and the tub basket, incorrectly identified as "woven of strips of black poplar wood"—were articles the sisters could make without real reliance on the brothers.

When the "joint interest" failed, the "joint labor," the joint art failed also.

EVEN in their conception of these delicately-made articles the element of usefulness and practical value manifests itself in the production of such homely things as dusters. Shown above is one made of lamb's-wool, which is particularly desirable to use in dusting polished furniture. The handle is of yellow wood, and there is a mixture of dyed wool—yellow —mixed with the white. The broom-cover tells its own story, does it not? It is made of Canton flannel, covering the broom, and tied with tape strings securely around the handle so there is no possible chance for it to slip off at the critical moment of demolishing a cobweb.

Most important among their products for women is the Shaker cloak, which is so well known for its qualities of good material and comfort. The lighter shades are used for evening wraps.

THE handy basket illustrated above is also woven of strips of black poplar wood, and is charming in its simplicity of design. The absence of trimming is rather pleasing than otherwise. The wooden basket shown in the lower left-hand corner bears the mark of a true craftsman in design and make. These baskets, for fruits or flowers, were made in various sizes years ago by some of the Shaker brothers, and but few of them are in existence at the present time.

And so these varied occupations keep the people of this little world bright, happy and healthy. Their days are full of interest. A visit to the delightful country of their home, and to be made a welcome guest in their houses, is indeed a pleasure.

This handy spool-stand justly claims the admiration of all home sewers. It is a typical Shaker novelty. Sometimes the cushion is made in different colors, but the design is always the same.

again, off again, by the 1890s it had almost ceased.

In the last years the shop was run by the veterans Julia Ann Scott, Ann Maria Graves, Cornelia French, Mary Hazard and Augusta Stone, who had been making baskets for at least forty years. Cornelia French was primarily occupied in weaving the twilled quadrifoil bottoms, which were often finished off by Mary Hazard. Julia Ann Scott's job was "to bind the whole unit." Ann Maria Graves concentrated on tubs and ball baskets. There was apparently insufficient splint to engage other "hands." Eldress Augusta Stone worked "through the year on cloaks."[39]

This was the year that Boler died.

Five years lapsed and then in 1897 there was a last attempt to revive the business. "An effort is being made," a sister wrote, "to start up the basket business left by Daniel Boler. Shades of Elder Daniel Boler hover over us, peace to his ashes."[40] 364 baskets were made that year. But the lack of quality material, if nothing else, thwarted their efforts. "Cornelia has been working on baskets the past six weeks, to considerable disadvantage with unsuitable stuff," the diarist wrote.

The basket industry had died with Boler. But the expertise expired only with the deaths of the last sisters. In 1904 Ann Maria Graves was still weaving a few special baskets. Cornelia French kept on ten years more. In 1947 Harriet Bullard, who had been eldress at Mt. Lebanon, moved to Hancock when Mt. Lebanon closed; she was accompanied by Mary Dahm, a Watervliet sister who had relocated to Mt. Lebanon. While at Hancock Harriet Bullard worked on baskets; but a fire there destroyed the shop and her work. Mary Dahm became the Shaker to close out their art. In 1958 she made a small lidded basket in hexagon weave, with no rim or handle. "This is the first basket of this type I ever made," she wrote, "and it is not quite perfect."[41]

The Shakers' faith was a progressive faith, and their art was also. They were always improving.

1. *"[W]e wouldn't . . . be able to hear ourselves think"*: the sister probably slips up here. Shaker industry was systematic and serene. *"Do all your work as if you had a thousand years to live, and as if you were to die tomorrow,"* Mother Ann had counselled.[1] Visitors repeatedly comment on the absence of hurry and noise. What they heard was stillness. *"Every building, whatever its use,"* one writer observed, *"has something of the air of a chapel . . . . A white sheen is on everything; a happy quiet reigns around . . . . Mount Lebanon strikes you as a place where it is always Sunday."*[2]

Shaker shops were very different from mills on the outside.

2. It appears that Mt. Lebanon began selling some baskets around 1815. Andrews sets the date at 1809[3]; a Shaker sister records it as 1816[4]; Isaac Youngs, the Mt. Lebanon historian, puts it *"about the year 1813"*[5]. Some documented baskets (see Chapter Six) carry a date c. 1816–17. However, it was not until around 1835 that a basket business *really* developed.

3. There are several ledgers that help to reconstruct the scale of the business and the structure of it. The most significant of these are *"A Memorandum of Baskets etc, Kept by the Basket Makers. Also directions for weaving twilling & proceeding with the work"* (1855–75) at Winterthur; *"Journal Kept by the Deaconesses at the [Church] Office"* (1830–71) also at Winterthur; *"Journal of Expenses and Incomes Kept by the Sisters"* (1864–71, 1875) at Williams College Library.

As incomplete as the record is, it is unusual, in terms of other Shaker industries, to have this much manuscript data to go on.

4. The fire occurred on February 6, 1875. Beginning in the sisters' shop (where basketmaking was centered), it consumed at least seven other buildings, including the dwelling house, the ministry's dwelling and a barn. The Berkshire *Evening Eagle* reported that *"though eight miles away, and beyond a great mountain, the smoke of the conflagration was plainly seen from [our] streets, and even before the news of the disaster reached us, people were watching the thick clouds roll up over the western range, and had concluded that a large fire, and probably a disastrous one, was raging in that vicinity."*[6] The fire company that went to assist observed that *"hundreds of excited men were darting about, slipping over the ice and plunging through the snow; the flames were rolling high from burning buildings, and huge masses, bunches of fire— they [could] hardly be called 'sparks'—were being blown great distances in the air by the strong bitter wind that swept over the unfortunate settlement."*

Several basketmakers figure in accounts of the fire, and Daniel Crosman was *"quite seriously hurt by falling from a roof,"* while *"Elder Daniel Boler was badly burned and nearly lost his life from suffocation in trying to save property."*[7]

Almost everything, it was reported, *"was burned and melted in the awful heat."*[8] Considering the scale of the fire, it is astonishing that any Church Family records, any furnishings, any tools survive from the decades prior to 1875.

5. Daniel Boler was born in Kentucky in 1804. When he was four years old, his father joined the Shakers at So. Union (Kentucky) and brought Daniel along with him. Taking to the Shaker life, they remained for several years and then resettled at the Pleasant Hill community. In 1814 they journeyed east to unite with the parent society at Mt. Lebanon. Daniel was then ten years old. By 1833 Boler was an elder in the Church Family. In 1852 he was appointed to the parent ministry, and from 1859 until his death in 1892, he served as senior elder over all the Shaker membership.

"Elder Daniel passed a useful life," a brother eulogized when Boler died, *"But few—very few—of the denizens of this earthly sphere have ever passed through it, from the cradle to the grave, leaving such a gracious record. He was not of the world for when only ten years of age he was called out of the world, as Jesus was called out of it when young. To the public generally he was not a great and showy man. His name was not blazoned forth by the press, nor . . . orators; yet he was the senior elder of seventeen [Shaker] societies."*[9]

Boler was thoroughly a Shaker. From other testimonials it appears that he went about his life with a certain rectitude, and expected rectitude in return. He was convinced the Shaker way was the right way, and he gave all his gifts to it. He was, spiritually, an old-school Shaker; the faith he had been taught was the faith of the first generation. But he was also a pragmatist. Early in his service as senior elder, he helped to rethink and rewrite the unduly restrictive *"Millennial Laws."* While enforcing *"right"* attitude and form where attitude and form really mattered, the new code introduced considerable margin for individual discretion, in laying out *"[essential] orders,"* *"conditional orders"* and *"counsels."*[10] Boler brought a similarly open mind to managing the basket business. Under him the switch was made from production *"for home use"* to production *"for sale,"* and an aggressive marketing program was implemented.

6. Through the years Daniel Crosman (1810–85) often worked alongside Boler, in the ministry and in the shop. He was born in Vermont and entered the Church Family at Mt. Lebanon when he was twelve. For almost forty years he was in charge of the oval box business. He was also an elder, and his name surfaces in several accounts of spiritual *"labor."*

7. Early on the Shakers made a name they could trade on. *"Over all the United States [manufactures] furnished by any settlement of Shakers bear a premium, in the market, above the ordinary price of similar articles from other establishments,"* an English traveler observed in 1841.[11] There was a tendency, however, for the world to regard Shakers—as a believer in Maine has put it—*"only as a chair."* In 1876 William Dean Howells, editor of the *Atlantic Monthly, wrote with some poignancy: "It was our fortune to spend six weeks of last summer in the neighborhood of the people called Shakers—who are chiefly known to the world-outside by their apple-sauce, by their garden seeds so punctual in coming up when planted, by the brooms so well made that they sweep clean long after the ordinary new broom of proverb has retired upon its reputation, by the quaintness of their dress, and by the fame of their religious dances. It is well,"* he said, *"to have one's name such a synonym for honesty that anything called by it may be bought and sold with perfect confidence, and it is surely no harm to be noted for dressing out of the present fashion, or for dancing before the Lord. But when our summer had come to an end, and we had learned to know the Shakers for so many other qualities, we grew almost to resent their superficial renown among men. We saw in them a sect simple, sincere, and fervently persuaded of the truth of their doctrine, striving for the realization of a heavenly ideal upon earth."*[12]

8. The palm leaf came in bales from Cuba. The Shakers initially purchased palm leaf to make bonnets for their own use. Then when they saw there was a market in them, they also made them to sell. The palm leaf (and later, straw) bonnets were sold in such quantities that in nineteenth-century America *"a Shaker"* (sometimes *"shaker"*) came to mean a bonnet for plain wear.[13] In *"Anne,"* a story serialized in Harper's in 1881, the heroine is admonished: *"Is that all the bonnet you have? It is far too fine. I will buy you a Shaker at the store."*[14]

Palm leaf was to some degree interchangeable with splint and suitable therefore for small fancy baskets.

9. Poplarwork is sometimes called basketry but technically it is not. It is the product of an entirely different process. Because it is very brittle, poplar cannot be bent like splint into basketforms.

Poplar (or *"popple,"* as it is called in New England) is a bane to the tree farmer. It is a low-grade hardwood virtually useless except, when absolutely dry, as stovewood to get a quick fire going; in furniture making it has sometimes been used for secondary applications, such as drawer bottoms. In a woodlot poplar grows rapidly, shading out better trees; when it is mature, it tends to break and litter the forest. But the Shakers, trained to *"right use,"* found a productive harvest for it.

Tree trunks were cut into manageable lengths (about 24") and then split. Thin strips of wood were then planed off, straightened and dried. From these shavings narrow strips 1/8" to 1/16" wide were obtained. These strips were woven into poplar *"cloth"* on special looms warped with cotton thread. Patterns were stamped or drawn on the resulting *"cloth"* which the sisters then cut, backed with cardboard and assembled in boxes of various shapes.

10. Office sisters or deaconesses (and their male counter-parts among the brethren) were appointed by the ministry to handle sales and other business. *"All trade and traffic, buying and selling, changing and swapping, must be done by them or by their immediate knowledge and consent,"* the community was instructed.[15] Within the semi-closed Shaker society, generally it was only they who went out *"to vend manu-factures."* Their

assignment to the Office did not mean, however, that they were considered less spiritual than other members; it usually meant simply that they had a good head for business. Many, many of the Shakers' songs—which she "gathered from the Tree of songs"[16]—are, for example, attributed to Mary Hazard.

11. These accounts were, many of them, probably "fancy goods stores." These newly fashionable boutiques were proliferating in American cities as early as 1800–15; with the patronage of the carriage trade, by mid-century they were also springing up around spas and scenic attractions. Drawing a clientele who appreciated "craft and quality for the lady," fancy goods stores provided an extension of their market the Shakers capitalized on.

12. The Shaker experiment was structured on an idea of equality, not synonymity. In all departments, "men and women were separate but equal," Beverly Gordon writes in Shaker Textile Arts. "Although their work was different, their respective jobs were considered equally important. Leadership, both temporal and spiritual, was shared; there was always an eldress for every elder, a deaconess for every deacon. Women supervised women, and men supervised men."[17] Only in the late years, when the number of females was disproportionate to the number of males, was this balance broken.

13. Virtually all the records of the basket business were kept by the sisters in the Church Family. There are no records on the brothers' side corresponding to those kept by the sisters. Nor are there any records known for the period prior to sale production, when the brethren were making vast numbers of baskets "for home use" and supplying other families besides the Church.

It is uncertain when the women began to make baskets, as continuous records begin only in 1839. But the manuscript clip that opens this chapter reveals that by 1836 basketmaking had become one of their occupations. It also reveals that already the volume of sale baskets far outnumbered baskets "for home use" and shows that, at this date, the sisters were making "palm leaf baskets" in addition to splint baskets.

14. At least two decades of basketmaking predate the annual listing of basketmakers, which begins in 1855. As yet the first sisters identified as basketmakers are Prudence Morrill, Eliza Ann Taylor, Elizett Bates, Matilda Reed, Mariah Lapsley, Harriet Goodwin and Elizabeth Sidle; the year is 1835.[18] On a list of Church Family occupations dated 1840, Elizabeth Bates, Matilda Reed, Harriet Goodwin and Elizabeth Sidle are named as basketmakers.[19] By 1850, judging from another list, basketmaking had shifted to these: Julia Ann Scott, Elizabeth Cantrell, Ann Maria Graves and Miranda Barber.[20] In 1855, when names are given for the first time annually[21], Augusta Stone and Cornelia French turn up.

15. Turns in the kitchen and laundry probably ran six weeks, but craftwork—such as basketry—spanned a period of months.

16. On a page entitled "Business Occupations of Brethren, First Order"[22] compiled in 1875, "ministries, horses, blankets, hats etc." follows Andrew Fortier's name. The journal quoted here covers the years 1867–75, during which period Fortier split his time primarily between basket work, Office work and "fixing about garden."

17. About the time that Boler was named to the parent ministry, Elisha Blakeman was appointed an Office deacon for the Church Family. A sometime schoolteacher, inventor, broommaker, basketmaker, joiner and printer, he was appointed an elder in 1861. After six years he stepped down from that position in order to serve as caretaker of the boys. This diary, which begins then, in 1867, is almost concurrent with Fortier's; it closes in 1872, when Blakeman—who was fifty-three and had lived with the Shakers since he was ten—left to marry.

18. Scaffolding is an excellent way of storing lengths of splint. In 1828 Henry DeWitt notes in his journal that he has made "scaffel in the brick shop cellar to lay basket stuff on."[23] In 1840 he is employed in making additional platforms "for the basketmakers."[24] Peripherally involved in basketmaking over the years, DeWitt came to Mt. Lebanon in 1813, when he was eight, and died there in 1855.

19. For thirty years Boler and Avery served together in the ministry. When Avery died in 1890, a Shaker coming to pay respect "found our aged father, Elder Daniel Boler, somewhat depressed under the great loss he sustains in parting with a loving and helpful soul companion."[25]

Giles Avery was born in Connecticut and came to Mt. Lebanon in 1821, when he was six. "At twenty-five years of age," he wrote in his Auto-biography, "I was appointed to the Order of Elders . . . . My manual employment was the repairing of buildings, digging cellars for foundations, stone masonry, sawing stone for a new dwelling, plumbing, carpentering and plastering. I had some experience at cabinetwork and wagon making, and even made wooden dippers. I took an interest in orcharding, trimmed and grafted many hundreds of old apple trees; and prepared cisterns for holding liquid manure for fertilising. I mention these things," he says, "to show . . . that members of a community should be willing to turn a hand in any direction in order to render up their best service in building up and sustaining the cause."[26]

20. A single notation in a "Journal of Domestic Events" kept by the deaconesses of the Church Family, Second Order indicates that in 1844 "Abigail C. goes to the North Family to learn them how to make baskets".[27] Because there is no other mention of "Abigail" as a basketmaker, and no other source even suggests that sisters in the Second Order made splint baskets—while there is considerable documentation that they were proficient in palm leaf and poplar work it—seems most likely that the sister in question was instructing the North Family in poplar, not splint. More significantly, nothing seems to have come of this: there is no additional allusion to basketmaking at Mt. Lebanon outside the Church Family, or the First Order.

21. See June Sprigg, Shaker Design (New York: Whitney Museum of American Art, 1986). These were the children of the Shaker idea, a second generation, who came of age in the 1830s–40s. Many of them—the great basketmakers, the great cabinetmakers, etc.—had entered the Shaker life as young children and had grown up in it. The only way they knew was the Shaker way; the only standard they knew was the Shaker standard. It is understandable that the years between 1830–50 were the era of classic craftform. By practicing perfection, they came close to it.

22. The idea of spiritual gift informs the whole of Shaker experience; gifts represent the working of God. Because the Shakers' faith was in progressive revelation, gifts were especially important in discovering leadings of the spirit. There were gifts of attitude (humility, love, etc.), of instruction (these could impinge on any spiritual or domestic matter—"I have a gift to . . . ." was a common preface for introducing a new idea), and of vision (expressed in song, dance and drawing).

"Never murmur because you think your gifts are not so great, or are more mortifying than some others. Remember, God in his wisdom will deal out to everyone what they most need. In whatever way your gifts come, whether by [dreams], visions or inspiration, never, never murmur. If you are faithful, you will have all that you need to help you on your way," a believer in Maine was instructed to inform the community "for" Father James.

"I warn you," the writer continues, "never to keep back any gift given to you; but go to your Elders and offer up whatever you have. You may often times think it is small and not worth the trouble of telling them, as you call it. But you know not the worth of the precious crums which are bestowed upon you. Perhaps someone will be suffering for that gift which you do not offer up; but, as it were, throw away."[28]

23. Miranda Barber (1819–71) whose name appears among the basketmakers in 1850. She had come to Mt. Lebanon in 1828, when she was nine. When the revival began (1837), she was one of the prominent "instruments." Pages and pages of emblematic drawings, some of the most magically persuasive of all the drawings known, are hers.[29] The vision she drew, and sometimes transcribed in song, was real around her. Something of it must have infected the basketmakers. In one of her loveliest drawings, dated 1848 (see Fig. 7), an angel brings to Elizabeth Cantrell, a young basketmaker, a cup of blessing; on her arm she carries a holy basket, as if to say, "See. This is what you make."

When the revival had passed, Miranda returned to "common weaving." In the 1860s she served as a deaconess, and she continued to "receive" some charming songs.[30] Her name does not show again among the basketmakers. But she had already made her gift there. She

93

had reminded the shop sisters that what they did was, maybe, hallowed.

At least one other basketmaker was also an "instrument" for the drawings: Polly Reed (1818–81), an eldress in the First Order who later served in the parent ministry with Daniel Boler.

As Daniel Patterson writes, Polly Reed's "gifts were many[31]"—in music, [basketry], needlework, scholarship and love. A colleague said "she was a great worker with her hands"; and the watercolors attributed to her confirm it.[32] Many of these, Patterson suggests, imitate the stitchery patterns and applique she was especially skilled at. But more intimate is a detail in one drawing—for Mary Hazard, who sometimes made baskets—of a little blue basket filled with "balls of love."[33]

24. There are numerous testimonies from believers about the influence the dance had over them. "When I saw the twinkling light emerging from [the] windows, and caught, by the radiation of the chandeliers of the sanctuary, the glimpse of human forms, gliding like shadows, or sprites of an angelic nature in divine service, I sighed," Hervey Elkins confided, "to go thither and learn the mysteries of that devotion. . . . The frequent meetings, prolonged every evening [during the period he writes of, in the 1840s] until eleven o'clock at night, and often later; the tender and sweet voices of the instruments; their countenances beaming with purity and devotion . . . .; their bodies oscillating in graceful undulations; the pious ceremonies; the belief that these were dictated by the angels and prophets of God; the rapid conversion of the minds of my comrades," all this, he said, "undoubtedly [had] some influence in thus enrapturing . . . my mind."[34]

25. These are the names the sisters called the baskets in the fancy line (in order of entry in the ledger): Large Work, Cap, Knife,* Box, Spoon,* Sugar Bowl, Hexigon, Round, Cat Head, Kitten Head, Saucer,* Tub, Fruit,* Demijon (also, Crocha demijon), Flask, Small Hexigon for cushions, Cushion, Card, Ball (also, Knitting).

Initially these appear to be idiomatic names the Shakers made up; but some (such as "Cap" and "Card") have been found to have been in contemporary usage, and it may be that all of them were common names.

Directions exist for all the types listed above; these directions, however, are so sketchy that the baskets cannot be reconstructed without knowledge of the system behind them. Only a few molds (those marked *) are inscribed with a basket name. But unsigned molds are, for the most part, easily linked with their name, leaving only the Cap, Card, Demijon and Flask uncertain.

Two additional "baskets" not mentioned in this ledger appear on wholesale orders[35]— "quadrifoil" and "bellows." These are not anywhere specified as splint or poplar, but most probably they were poplar boxes. Quadrifoil twilling was incorporated, for example, in tub baskets but these were still called "tubs"; whereas a quadrifoil-shaped poplar box is elsewhere called a "quadrifoil." A poplar "bellows" style has also been identified, made with a silk gusset.

There is no record of what the Shakers called their utilitarian baskets. Markings (see Chapter Four) identified what purpose a "home use" basket was intended for. A name was clearly more critical in the sale line, where customers had to order baskets by name.

26. Some "depression of spirit" is corroborated by entries in the sisters' accounts: under "Expenses" are amounts "Given to the females that turn back"; "To Backsliders"; "Money Given to Apostates collectively"; "Given to Apostates (females)."[36] What is especially telling of a certain deterioration of belief is the fact that these were not casual Shakers; they were members who had progressed to the Church Order, and left.

27. "Rosie, Alice, Scottie and Fannie are about to commence on baskets," a Harvard sister writes in her diary for Jan. 30, 1884. "Preparing for cutting the ice," she says, "I help the girls make baskets, some do quite well." Along in February she notes: "The girls on baskets, we are mending." There is no further mention of baskets.[37]

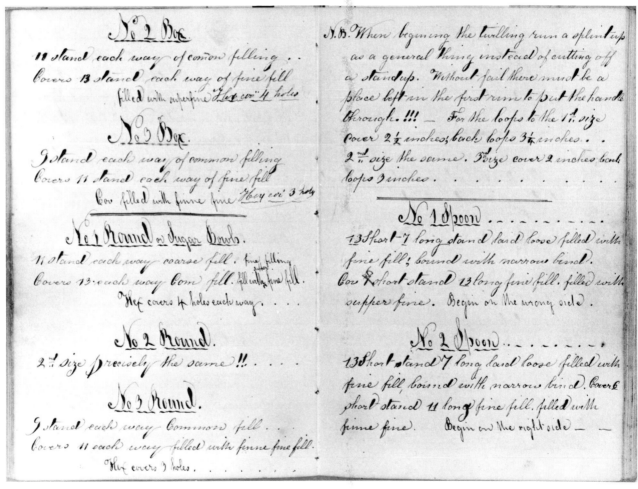

No 2 Box

11 stand each way of common filling . .
Covers 13 stand each way of fine fill
     filled with superfine. Cover 4 holes

No 3 Box.

9 stand each way of common filling
Covers 11 stand each way of fine fill
     Cov filled with finne fine. Cover 3 holes

No 1 Round or Sugar Bowl.

11 stand each way coarse fill. fine filling
Covers 13. each way Com fill. filled with fine fill.
     Wef covers 4 holes each way. . . .

No 2 Round.

2nd size precisely the same !! . . . .

No 3 Round.

9 stand each way Common fill . . .
Covers 11 each way filled with finne fine fill
     Wef covers 3 holes. . . . . .

N.B. When begining the twilling run a splint up
as a general thing instead of cutting off
a stand up. Without fail there must be a
place left in the first rim to put the handle
through. !!! — For the loops to the 1st size
Cover 2½ inches; back loops 3¼ inches. . .
2nd size the same. 3rd size cover 2 inches back
loops 3 inches. . . . .

No 1 Spoon . . . .

13 Short - 7 long stand stand loose filled with
fine fill; bound with narrow bind.
Cov 8 short stand 13 long fine fill. filled with
supper fine. Begin on the wrong side .

No 2 Spoon . . . .

13 Short stand 7 long stand loose filled with
fine fill, bound with narrow bind. Cover 6
short stand 11 long fine fill. filled with
finne fine. Begin on the right side — —

Fig. 155d Instructions for weaving from basketmakers' journal, now at Winterthur. (see
Fig. 176).

95

Fig.156 In addition to the baskets the Shakers sold to guests as souvenirs, a great volume went to wholesale accounts all across the country.

Because few of the wholesale orders were for splint baskets alone (most include other items made or merchandised by the Church Family sisters: poplar boxes, palm leaf baskets, tablemats, nests of oval boxes, bail boxes, woven splint and feather fans, workstands, pincushions, applesauce, maple sugar, sugared nuts, emeries, waxes, needlecases), the commercial accounts were, many of them, probably "fancy goods stores"—new boutiques proliferating in American cities as early as 1800–15. With the patronage of the carriage trade, by mid-century fancy goods stores were also springing up wherever scenic attractions or a spa ensured a clientele. This probably explains why repeat orders were sent out not only to places such as New York City, Philadelphia and Chicago, but also to Niagara Falls, Saratoga Springs and Lenox (Mass.).

Fig.157 Poplar box. At the same time they were developing a sale line of splint baskets, the Mt. Lebanon Shakers were offering "palm leaf baskets" and, later, woven poplar boxes which they also called "baskets."

Although few are known to survive, the palm leaf baskets were apparently identical in design to some of the splint ones, with palm leaf simply substituted for splint. However, the items made of poplar are *not* baskets. Because poplar (or "popple," as it is called in New England) is very brittle, it could not be bent like ash splint in basket forms. Instead, strips were woven on special looms into "cloth" which was cut up and assembled into myriad box shapes (Fig. 159).

Fig.158 Poplar items advertised by Mt. Lebanon.

Possibly all of the communities in the northeast engaged in poplarwork. But Maine and New Hampshire, along with New York, were especially proficient at it (see Fig. 252).

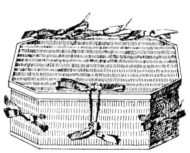

OCTAGON WORK BOX. $1.90   OBLONG WORK BOX. $1.75   SQUARE WORK BOX. $1.00   SILK-LINED WORK BOX. $2.50

Fig.159 There was a time in the early nineteenth century when production in splint and palm leaf appears to have been about equal at Mt. Lebanon. (In 1841, for example, the sisters in the Church Family made 308 splint baskets against 300 palm leaf.) Then splint basketry picked up; and palm leaf, which was imported from Cuba, became hard to come by during the Civil War.

Around 1860 when "popplework" had come into production, annual figures for splint were about double the figures for poplar. But from 1869, there was a new development. In that year "splint baskets of various sizes" totaled 2223; "Popple Baskets, Chests, Boxes, etc. wove and made," 1122. The year following popple gained (2090 splint, 1523 popple) and by 1871 took the lead (1286 splint, 1736 popple).[22]

Fig.160 The girls under the sisters' care learned "the Shaker way" while they were still young. Helping the sisters at basketry, poplarwork and straw, they began with the simplest tasks and graduated to more complex ones.

Under the brethren, the boys were also introduced to the mysteries of basketcraft by assisting in "setting" the bottoms of utility baskets, filling bottoms, turning down tops and helping to "pick splint."[23]

Fig.161 One of the novelties of the Shaker system was regular rotation between assignments. No one spent year in, year out, doing the same thing. A sister might, for example, give several weeks in the kitchen or the laundry and then switch to herb room or basket shop.

"A continual change of experienced help for the young and insufficient is no great advantage to this business," a sister commented in her journal one year when "hands" usually assigned to the basket shop for the winter were needed elsewhere in the village, and the basketmakers had to make do with whomever they got.[24]

Fig.162 Basketwork was, for the most part, winter work. Mid-fall, brethren who knew the woods would scout the swamps for suitable black/brown ash. Then they cut the trees and pounded the logs to get the splint, which they planed in the shop, cut to width and delivered to the sisters. Then they began making handles and rims. Beginning sometime in November or December, the sisters spent the winter making up the baskets, ending around the first of May.

Fig.163 "The sisters finished making a large lot of fine baskets [and] set off in a company to the office, but the wind," Bro. Isaac Youngs recalled with merriment, "as if to have a little diversion, dashed away the baskets as they lay loosely piled in large baskets, and the way they flew about the door yard and in the road was to make one laugh, tho' it might excite a little pity too—to see the sisters chase them about for fear of some harm to the baskets—but however it all ended well."[25]

The sisters in this photograph carry between them one of the square-bottom, round-top shop forms that could easily have held "a large lot of fine baskets."

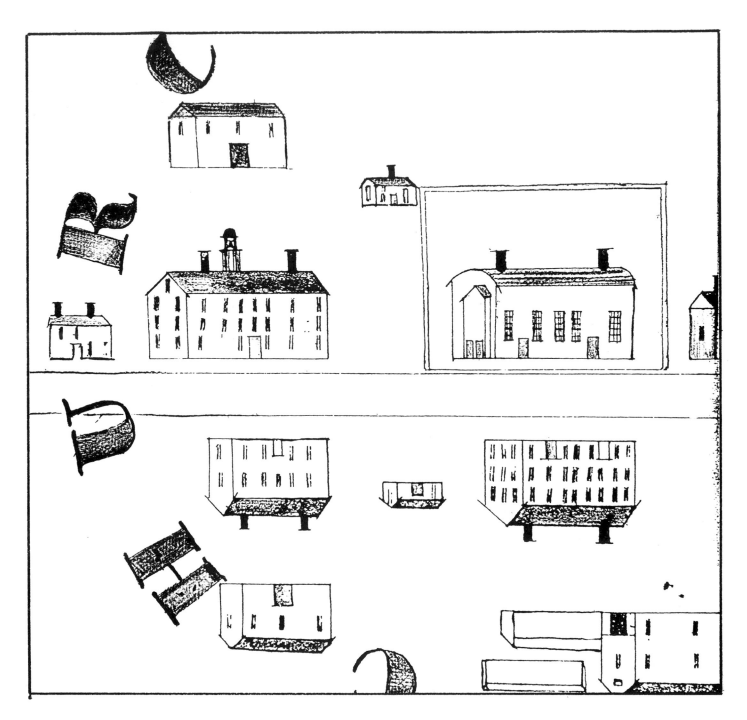

Fig.164 It is important to keep in mind where Mt. Lebanon's baskets came from. They were made solely by the First Order of the Church Family, the most "Shaker" of the Shakers.

"Families should be of different classes, or grades, as to order, government and arrangement in things spiritual and temporal," the Shaker covenant began. "The Church or center family should be composed of such members as are free from any involvements with those without, and such as are prepared by a previous privilege in families that are back (where those who come, over the age of thirteen, should be first proved) to advance into a further degree of gospel order, in a forward family, and a closer spiritual work of purification."[26]

Figs.165,166 During the era when the basket business was developing—when form and standard were being set—there was a great spiritual renewal occuring in all the Shaker communities, inspiring believers to pare their lives and everything they did to "right order." This was felt especially by the church at Mt. Lebanon.

These two "tokens of blessing" were addressed to Daniel Boler. During the period of revival, spiritual "valentines" were exchanged by members of the Church Family, reinforcing their sense of consecration. These little slips carry an immediacy still, and reveal how close, how real, they felt a spiritual sphere.

Fig.167 In their great and passionate dances the basketmakers wove in and out, as they wove the splint to form the baskets, forming circles, spirals, squares. The same fervor was invested in both.

"[How] solemn and joyful to see the brethren and sisters advancing," Isaac Youngs confided. "O how happy they look, how beautiful. Surely said I to myself, how mean are all earthly joys, how trifling are all the little trials which we have to pass through in finding such spiritual comforts, such reviving glories which the gospel opens to our souls."[27]

Fig.168 Diagram of a dance.

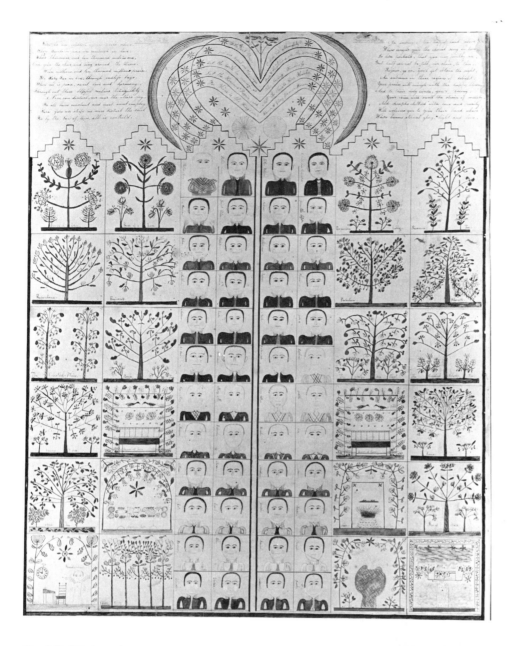

Figs.169,170 Something moving and mystic was at work. The radiant weave of a quadrifoil twill answers the interlacing arc of light seen in a vision.

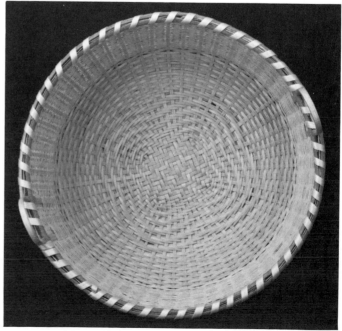

Fig.171 The Shakers weren't opposed to mass production; but production at the expense of quality was against their beliefs. The fancy baskets are production baskets that show production could be art.

When the sisters wove the baskets, they were essentially working up kits. When the shell of a basket was completed, it was removed from the mold, and rims and handle(s) were attached to it.

No 1 Knife . . . .
19 long stand 21 short the last long stand
each side turn under filled with coarse fill.
Cover 13 short coarse filling 16 long coarse fill.
filled with common fill. Bind 2nd bundle

Fig.172 Molds gave control to the work that could not be gotten freeform, and made it possible to achieve extreme and exact lines. Molds also meant that design could be replicated. They ensured that bodies, handles and rims for each basket type would all be alike, and would fit right when assembled. Many basketmakers used body molds, but few had jigs for rims and handles, as the Shakers did.

More than anything else, molds are what made the Shaker system sophisticated.

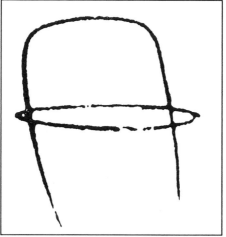

Fig.173 The contour that was tooled in the rims and handles of all the fancy baskets—ranging from a half-round to a half-oval—is so uniform that the uniformity itself becomes a signature. The work is perfect. The lines flow. There are no tool marks left on the wood (except on the tails). Rim and handle components in the fancy baskets don't all have the same profile, as different knives were used from time to time to shape them; but each round or oval shows the same control and the same aesthetic. Introduced in Mt. Lebanon's late utility work and designed into the sale baskets using the same tooling and system, this control and this contour occur in no other production splint basketry.

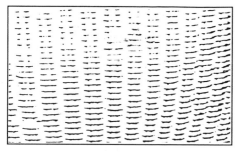

Fig.174 Splint for the fancy baskets was pounded on a triphammer, planed to standard thicknesses, then cut to standard widths and graded by color. The planer gave the splint a polished look, "satin" on both sides. But the quality began with the tree itself. Just any tree wouldn't do, and many were rejected. Supply was a constant problem; by the 1850s, if not earlier, there was a scarcity of usable ash.

The Shakers preferred splint from the sap (cambium) layers because it was white, and was also more flexible than that from the inner layers. Browner/darker layers were typically bleached to make them white. The Shakers were competing for sales on several points, and one of their advantages was a white satiny look their clientele liked. Today, dark color or patina, implying age, enhances the value of a basket. But for the Shakers, whiteness sold.

Fig.175 Handle blanks from Mt. Lebanon.

The Shaker system separated tasks that went into making a basket and got a collective expertise. The person who went to the woods and selected the trees was the person who had the best understanding of them. The person who made the rims and handles was the person best at that. And so the person who graded and prepared the splint, shaped the molds, wove the bodies, applied the rims, shipped the orders . . .

Fig.176 Width of splint was selected according to formulas copied out in a ledger. By measuring extant work, we have found that widths of the weavers were standardized in increments of 32nds of an inch. What the basketmakers referred to as "coarse fill" was cut 3/16"; "common" was 1/8"; "fine" was 3/32"; "superfine" was 1/16"; and "finne fine" was 1/32.

"I can go no further," a Shaker brother professed, "without [a measuring stick] for positive exactness is required not only in the inches, but in the sixteenths and thirty-seconds of an inch."[28]

There is no mention of widths to cut the uprights to. There is a standardization in them; but it appears that the basketmakers used what looked good to their eye, and sometimes substituted a couple of narrow uprights to adjust the body to fit a mold correctly.

Fig.178 The elements you see in this fruit basket you see in almost all the fancy baskets that came out of Mt. Lebanon's system:
* single lashing (on some larger baskets, the lashing may be double)
* double notch
* turndowns only on the inside, with alternate uprights trimmed at the rim
* absence of tool marks, knife marks, little gouges in bentwood parts (excepting the marks on tails)
* absence of hair on uprights or weavers (Indian baskets will have a satin look on the outside, a scraped look on the inside. They were usually made of split ash which wasn't polished like the Shakers'.)
* signature rims with the Mt. Lebanon half-round/oval
* signature handle (This is the same handle, on a smaller scale, as those used in the classic utility baskets—a lovely rendering of flats melting into rounds.)
* molded profile

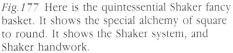

Fig.177 Here is the quintessential Shaker fancy basket. It shows the special alchemy of square to round. It shows the Shaker system, and Shaker handwork.

The "fruit" form, however, is not unique to the Shakers; there are Indian baskets that have the same form (see Fig. 185). What identifies Shaker work is the perfect uniformity, the splint, the tooling in the rims and handles, the precision.

Fig.179 A certain amount of slippage off the fruit mold (depending largely on the angle of the sides of the mold) created the characteristic arch and ears/feet. Over time the shape of the mold was calculated to reduce slippage to a minimum, allowing a basketmaker to achieve the sweeping lines of the basket on the left, with considerably more ease and control.

Fig.180 Shaker eldress with Mt. Lebanon fruit basket. The throat of the basket is fitted with a crocheted or knitted frill.

Figs.181,182 Fruit molds.

Fig.183 Many of the baskets in the sale line were offered "covered" or "uncovered," but lidded examples are now rare. The "captured" lid on this fruit basket slips on the handle. It is woven in a "quadrifoil twill" (resembling a four-leaf clover) which was unique to the Mt. Lebanon Shakers.

Fig.185 The arched bottom and cut-away lines of the cat head—and also the fruit—are attributes a novice collector tends to jump at as "Shaker." Indians, however, were making baskets of the same style, in the same range of sizes; and many more Indian examples have survived because they were still being made past 1900.

Fig.184 Similar to the fruit but smaller, the "cat head" takes its name from the peaked corners of the bottom that form little "cat ears." If you turn it up, you see the flat between the ears also looks like a cat face.

Fig.186 The addition of a domed lid made the cat head more volumetric, and the "quadrifoil" twilling transformed it again into something quite wonderful.

Fig.187 Another typical Mt. Lebanon cat head. The handle is not the usual bonnet type: the simple curve was apparently recognized as nice in itself.

Fig.188 At the rim the handle of Fig. 187 is single notched. A basket this size didn't require a double notch. Note, however, that the tail continues down to the bottom of the basket to offset the single notch, and lashing is double.

108

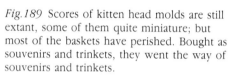

Fig.189 Scores of kitten head molds are still extant, some of them quite miniature; but most of the baskets have perished. Bought as souvenirs and trinkets, they went the way of souvenirs and trinkets.

Fig.190 The "kitten head" is a diminutive version of the cat head.

Fig.191 The "knife" basket was the most popular style in the Shaker fancy line. More knife baskets were sold, and more have survived.

All knife baskets have rectangular bottoms, straight sides and rectangular tops (some of them with rounded ends, and some with straight ends). The sides may rise perpendicular to the bottom or they may flare out a little. Handles are either overhead (both bonnets and hoops) or ear.

In this example, the wire where rim and handle join indicates that this basket once had a lid (see Figs. 194 and 196).

Figs.192,193 Here is the standard the knife baskets were made to. Originally all their lines were this crisp and nice.

111

Fig.196 A modified quadrifoil twill is incorporated in all of the knife lids, and a sawtooth twist (for technical description, see *Chapter Five*) finishes the edge, making it flexible and durable as well as pretty.

Fig.196 A modified quadrifoil twill is incorporated in all of the knife lids, and a sawtooth twist (for technical description, see *Chapter Five*) finishes the edge, making it flexible and durable as well as pretty.

The hinge at the center of the lid is nicely engineered. The stretcher is mortised and tenoned into the handle. Four holes are drilled in the stretcher, and copper wire threaded through then forms a hinge. This wire continues around the outside of the handles and then ties off at the center, keeping tension on the mortise and tenon. Where the lids attach, a wooden bar is tapered from the center to the outside, creating a round edge where the splint ribs wrap around, then bevelling to a point where the weavers start in.

(The stretcher on this basket is inscribed: "Penelope P. Andrews Providence R.I. Aug. 1847." "Bought at the Shakers near Lebanon Springs" is added in pencil.)

Fig.194 The lidded knife is one of the icons of Mt. Lebanon basketry. When you see this material, this technique, these lines, you see Shaker.

Several lidded examples are known. On the bottom of one of them "P.M. 1857" is written in pencil. Philinda Minor (1817–99) came to Canterbury in 1826. In 1852 she was appointed Eldress at the North Family in Enfield, New Hampshire. This basket was probably a gift to her from Daniel Boler who, by 1857, was not only the lead basketmaker but also the lead elder at Mt. Lebanon. It was customary for the New York ministry to make gifts to the ministry in other communities, which helps to account for many prize Mt. Lebanon baskets turning up outside New York.

Fig.195 Although the fancy baskets were made as a sale line, they were also used by the Shakers themselves. It is not unusual to see them in photographs of the sisters. In this example, from Canterbury, a lidded knife is visible on the sewing desk in the right foreground.

(Despite the furniture with classic Shaker lines, the typical peg strip around the walls, and the old-fashioned dresses the sisters wear, a certain Victorianism is evident in this picture. The fact that the sister in the left foreground is playing a concertina indicates that the old severity of Shaker life had been lightened.)

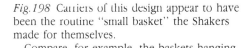

Fig.198 Carriers of this design appear to have been the routine "small basket" the Shakers made for themselves.

Compare, for example, the baskets hanging from pegs in this watercolor sketch of an herb room (1856) with sale carriers offered in the Church Family store (Fig 154, top center). They are the same.

Fig.197 The close correspondence between baskets made "for home use" and "for sale" is seen in a group of carriers which step up in size from the smaller knife basket.

The same series of molds was used to make a range of baskets—some of them so light they seem almost fragile, and others comparatively coarse and heavy. The basketmakers scaled materials up and down to answer the purpose for which a basket was made. Sale baskets matched other fancy baskets in weight; whereas baskets made for "home use" were sometimes of the same material that went into standard apple baskets. (On these, rims and handles were similarly made heavier.)

Fig.199 One of these carriers was lined with woven straw (such as Shaker bonnets were made of), covered on the outside with cloth and trimmed along the inside rim with a straw braid. To see what's underneath, look at the beautiful sweep of the handle, the finesse of the ash splint where it's legible through the cloth, and the nice contour of the outer rim.

Fig.200 The double lashing at the rims and the reinforcing at the bottom indicate this carrier was made for sustained use. Note also that handles and rims are meatier than those in fancy applications.

Fig.201 As in this example, these heavier carriers often have strips reminiscent of those on typical apple baskets applied to the bottom. Split out and dressed with a drawshave, they were nailed on from the outside, and the tails were tucked up the sides.

Fig.202 A similar carrier has strips that run the length of the basket. Again, the tails are woven up the sides.

Fig.203 Fitted with a wooden shelf and equipped with a rope to which a handmade wrought iron hook is attached, this basket was possibly a grafting or pruning basket. Although it uses finer splint than the preceding basket, it also was made for hard use (note double lashing, and turndowns on the outside and the inside).

Fig.204 The bottom of this basket is very close in concept to an apple basket bottom.

Fig.205 This basket (marked ''G.S.'' on the handle, for Girls' Shop) shows considerable wear, and its appearance has been further altered by heavy scrubbing. Weavers were scraped, which left more of the weight in them than planing would have. They were also cut wider than ''fancy'' splint. The uprights were additionally turned down on the outside and the inside to strengthen the basket.

115

Fig.206 This squared-bottom, squared-top lidded basket is probably what the Shakers called a "box" basket. This style, both oblong and square, was also made by the Indians. Shape itself carries no clue as to origin. In Indian work, however, there is likely to be a split upright which is absent in Shaker work, and colored splint (more often detectable on the inside where color hasn't faded). In some Indian examples, wide bands of splint are additionally interspersed in the weaving.

Shaker-make box baskets will usually have the distinctive Mt. Lebanon rims on both the "box" and the lid; the round rims serve to clip the lid to the body. In this example, the outer rim of the lid is flat.

Fig.207 Another Shaker "box," oblong in shape. This basket originally had a pair of loop handles similar to the wrapped handle on the poplar "drawer box" in Fig. 239.

Fig.208 An Indian box basket. The box style is one of the hardest to distinquish between Shaker and Indian. The strongest clues to attribution are in splint preparation and weaving technique, which are discussed in *Chapter Five.*

Fig.209 The "spoon" basket is one of two known Mt. Lebanon fancy styles with an intended oval form. Knife baskets have a square body even though their tops are not always squared; but the body of the spoon is oval as well as the top of it.

Although records indicate that spoon baskets sold well, no examples seem to survive. There are, however, two molds—with sides cupped like a bowl of a spoon—which help to describe what the spoon basket was.

This is our idea of what the spoon looked like—based on our interpretation of the molds, the Shaker system and formulas in the basket-makers' manuscript journal. Keeping in our eye an understanding of Shaker scale, we made the uprights and weavers a size to accommodate the flare of the body; then, because of the tendency of too-light material to collapse at the corners, we gave them some weight. Rims were a given; they were standard. Double lashing reflects a contemporary preference; Mt. Lebanon more often used single lashing on baskets of this size. As to handle, the shape of the body virtually requires little ears, because an overhead handle would have to have more bow than the Shakers liked. A "bail" [wrapped hoop] handle was an alternative (see, for example, Figs. 186, 226, 346) but ears would have been preferred. Some Mt. Lebanon spoon baskets were, however, apparently offered with "bail" handles (see Fig. 240).

Fig.210 Round bottom, round top baskets—which the Mt. Lebanon basketmakers had not previously made for their own use—were introduced in the fancy line. They were especially favored for sewing, knitting, handwork and dressing table use. Along with low-sided fruits, these were collectively referred to as "round work" baskets. Individually, those with straight angled sides were called "tubs"; and others, with a rounding tumblehome, were called "saucers." Of the several types, those that had handles had ears; but many, which were lidded, were made without handles.

Two diminutive round top baskets—one of them a saucer, and the other a cat head stopped low—suggest the form if not the size of round work types. The loop handles on the cat head are unusual. Bent in a teardrop shape, they were extruded through a piece of metal. Their contour is laid to the outside. (A round was usually laid to the inside.) The tails lap on top of each other below the rim, and are notched sideways to the rim. Limited in use to late years at Mt. Lebanon, these handles were substitutes for the classic carved handles in an era when the sisters had to make do.

Fig.211 Another square-to-round fancy basket with the same loop ears is in the collections of the Western Reserve Historical Society. It is fairly described in early accession records as "very small and dainty" (Fig. 212).

Bodies of this design often had cushions inserted in them. An example can be seen on the counter in a photograph of the Mt. Lebanon shop (see Fig. 155a).

Fig.212

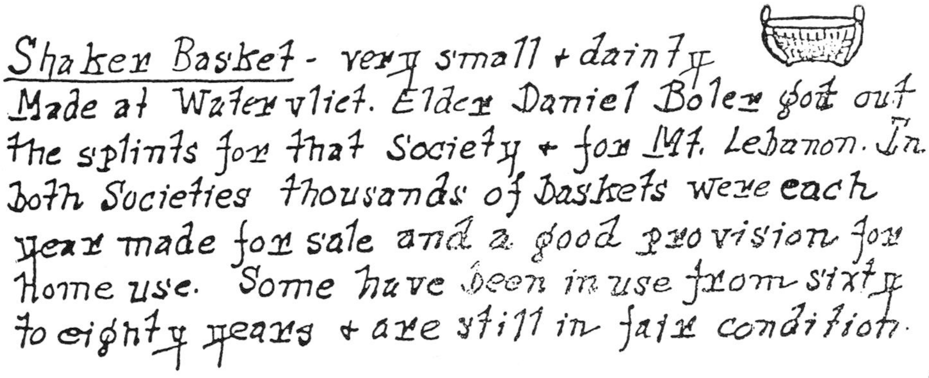

Shaker Basket - very small + dainty Made at Watervliet. Elder Daniel Boler got out the splints for that Society + for Mt. Lebanon. In both Societies thousands of baskets were each year made for sale and a good provision for Home use. Some have been in use from sixty to eighty years + are still in fair condition.

Fig.213 This work basket "furnished" with needle case and wax originally had similar loop handles that didn't survive. It is evident that this is what they were, as there isn't the usual stretching in the weavers left by conventional tails, or any displacement of the lashing caused by a typical handle. Instead, it appears that the basket was lashed and finished and then the handles were simply slipped in.

Fig.214 Ear detail.

Fig.215 Like this straight-sided "tub," all Mt. Lebanon round *bottom* baskets (except those with "hexagon" starts; see Fig. 342) have a quadrifoil center, making them signature baskets. You do not see the quadrifoil outside Shaker work.

Fig.216 Many of the round work baskets were probably "saucers." The saucer form was also easily and handsomely adapted to serve as a lid for round topped baskets (see Fig. 186).

Fig.217 Another tub, on the original weaving stand. The pattern in this basket has been modified by crossing two wide uprights at the center.

Pinholes in the mold follow the pattern of the quadrifoil, indicating that it was used over and over and over again.

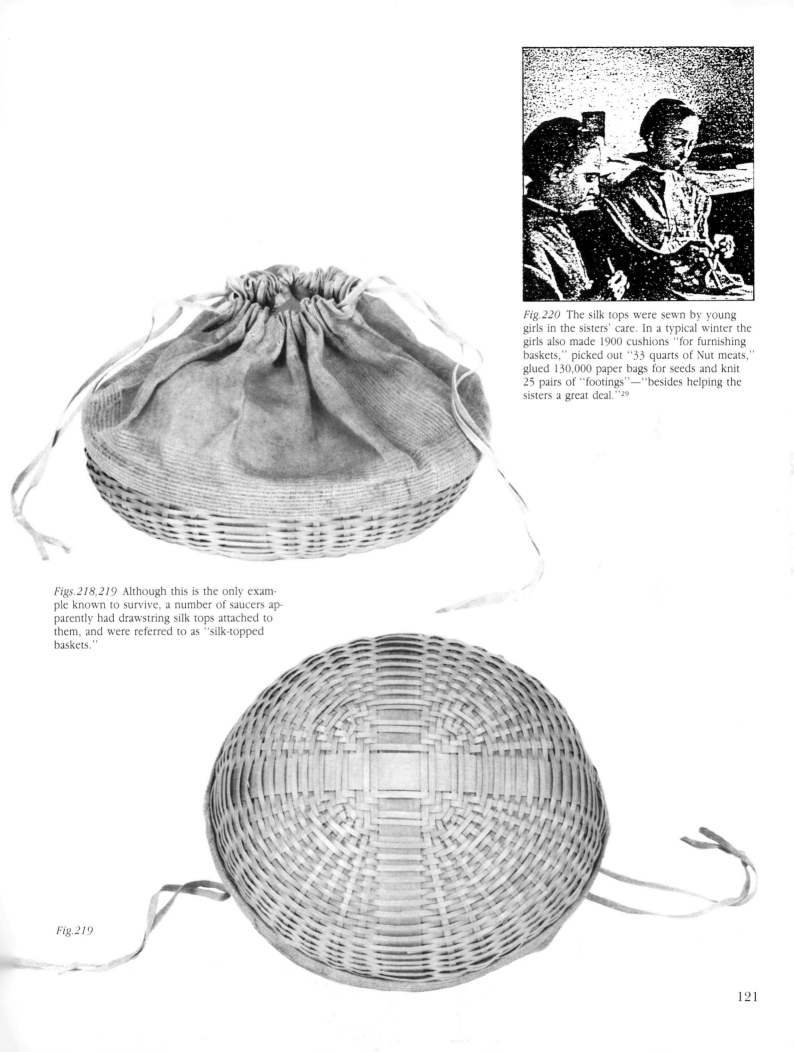

Fig.220 The silk tops were sewn by young girls in the sisters' care. In a typical winter the girls also made 1900 cushions "for furnishing baskets," picked out "33 quarts of Nut meats," glued 130,000 paper bags for seeds and knit 25 pairs of "footings"—"besides helping the sisters a great deal."[29]

Figs.218,219 Although this is the only example known to survive, a number of saucers apparently had drawstring silk tops attached to them, and were referred to as "silk-topped baskets."

Fig.219

Fig.221 "Hexagon" weave—which is just a dressy application of cheese basket weave—was incorporated in a number of toilet and work baskets. These were loosley referred to as "hexagon," "wove Fancylace" and "Fancy plaid." The form may appear to be hexagonal as well (because the weave pattern produced a six-sided base) but these are typically finished as rounds and ovals.

Hexagon is a practical weave, as all the material in a basket is cut the same size, and it is fast. It is also economical, as part of the area is "filled" with holes.

Indians made similar baskets, in great numbers. Because the Shakers finished theirs with splint rims about as often as with tooled rims, it can be difficult to identify Shaker work. If the rims don't tell, the only clue is in the material.

Fig.222 The relation between hexagon and round is seen clearly in this pair of molds used in making the lidded basket to the left. Note that a strip of kid was tacked on the lid mold to make it the right circumference to fit the body.

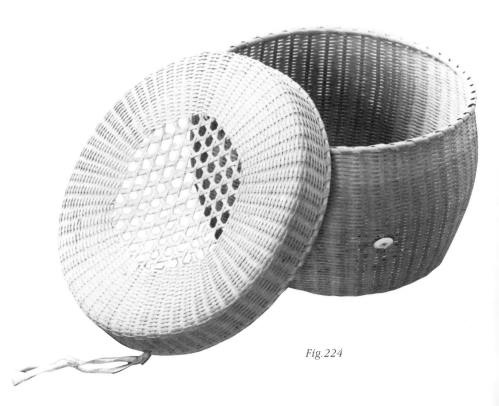

Fig.223 A lidded "hexagon."

122

Fig.224

Figs.224,225 In many examples of the hexagon type, the entire body is openweave; in some examples, however, the bottom is partially open and the sides are solid. An idea unique to the Shakers, this gave a quick and easy way to get a round bottom basket that was also "fancy" looking.

The basket shown here has a partially open bottom corresponding to the lid. Referred to variously as "ball basket," "crochet basket," "covered knitting," "demijon" and "crocha demijon," baskets like this one were designed for holding yarn or thread.

Fig.226 The sister in the foreground is holding a "ball" or "crochet" basket matching the one in Figs. 227–29. The photograph is inscribed on the back: "October 1886 / Samantha, Barbara, Ellie, Samboo / Niskeyuna Shakers."

Fig.227 Among the Shakers basketmaking had initially been men's work; men designed the baskets, and made them. You see their hand, their eye, in the utility work. But a feminine aesthetic informs the fancy baskets, and it culminates in this later work. Only the Shaker sisters and the Indians thought of using ash splint in this way, conceiving these forms and these demonstrations of basketry knowledge. Here was a marked difference from the mindset a factory operator or a country basketmaker brought to his work.

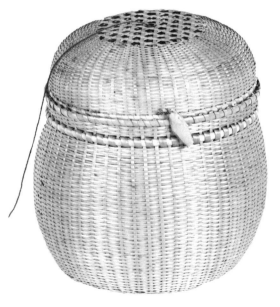

124

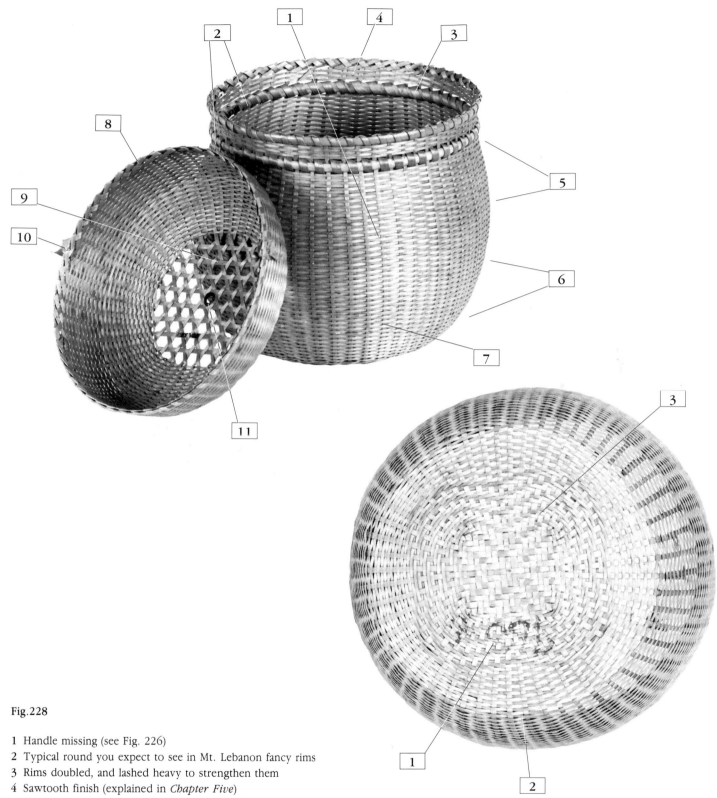

Fig.228

1 Handle missing (see Fig. 226)

2 Typical round you expect to see in Mt. Lebanon fancy rims

3 Rims doubled, and lashed heavy to strengthen them

4 Sawtooth finish (explained in *Chapter Five*)

5 Tumblehome returns at rim; basket was made on a breakdown mold

6 Fat and bulbous tumblehome

7 Nice, nice material; narrow uprights, fine weavers

8 Sawtooth finish allowed lid to fit snugly and to slip easily over throat of basket

9 Hexagon weave

10 Ribbon used for hinges and clasp

11 Brass grommet for pulling thread through; grommet protected both yarn and splint from abrasion

Fig.229

1 "1886": this may be the basket in the accompanying photograph (Fig. 226)

2 Nice, crisp upward turn

3 Quadrifoil start (explained in *Chapter Five*)

Fig.230 This low-sided fruit has been abused by time; but it serves to illustrate how boats were attached to "furnished" baskets.

Fig.231 Another low-sided fruit used as a
work or toilet basket.

Fig.232 Almost any of the larger baskets in
the sale line were offered "furnished" and
"unfurnished." Furnishings typically included
a variety of boats and cushions, along with an
emery, needlecase and sewing wax.

   The tiny baskets shown here were made for
holding thimbles. Absence of rims suggests
that these examples were left unfinished.

Fig.233 Small baskets in hexagon weave were
made in great numbers as accessories for work
and toiletry baskets. The most common of
these were ovoid "boats."

   Indians also made boats, and very similar
work and toiletry baskets with boats attached.
If a boat remains joined to a basket, certain
signatures in the larger basket—rims, handles,
splint, weaving technique—will usually reveal
whether the basket and the boat(s) are Indian
or Shaker. But if a boat is loose by itself, attribution requires close examination.

   If a very small hexagon-weave basket, ovoid
or round, was made by the New York Shakers,
the rims — even though not "typical" New
York rims — will have some contour in them
where they were shaped with a scraper. Indian
rims will be ordinary splint. Material from
which an Indian basket is woven will be irregular in width and thickness. Ovoid boats
and small round baskets woven entirely in
hexagon weave were also made by Shakers
outside New York. These, lacking the scraped
rims used in New York, may be very hard to
tell from Indian examples, unless the material
in them has the exactness of Mt. Lebanon
splint.

   Finally, Shaker boats — at Mt. Lebanon and
elsewhere — were also commonly woven of
palm leaf, because it was suitable for this type
and size of basket (see *Chapter Four,* Note 1).

127

Figs.235–38 Quite often cushions were inserted in woven splint bottoms, ranging from kitten heads to low fruits to saucers. These were then referred to as "cushion baskets" or (in the case of the kitten heads) "kitten cushions."

In some of these the splint is held in place by a strip of kid (cut from skiver) binding the top edge. In others, the uprights are trimmed to a scallop or a point, and left to extend decoratively above a narrow ribbon of kid glued around the top row of weavers, holding them in place. In other examples, the uprights are bent over and locked in a sawtooth edge. And in others, the edge is bound with ribbon.

Fig.238 This badly-frayed basket had a twined edge in place of rims. The velvet cushion was stuffed with scraps of cloth and sawdust. On the bottom the basket is inscribed, "For Miss Carson / Loudonville / Aug 14, 1888 / A souvenir of the Mt. Lebanon Shakers."

Fig.239 An ash splint furnishing basket, bound at the rim with a strip of skiver, is attached to the top of this "drawer basket," which was made of poplar cloth stiffened with cardboard and lined with silk. The handle is cane tightly wrapped with ash lashing.

Fancy goods of this type sold especially well to a Victorian clientele. While this box would appear to be a "work basket," an advertisement from about 1900 indicates that it was also sold as a "jewel case." In the foreground are two "tomato" cushions, wrapped with poplar and bound with kid.

Mount Lebanon, N. Y., August 4th 1874

Friend Sister Mary Whitcher

Bought of Sarah A Lewis & Co.,

DEALERS IN

Baskets, Fans, Spool Tables, Cushions, and a variety of Fancy Articles.

STORE OPPOSITE THE CHURCH.

1	Work stand at 2,00, 1, at 2.53	2	50	
2	Ovel shape, at 3.00, 1, at 2.00	5	00	
2	Heart shape 1.30	1	30	
3	Square furnish 1.00 each	3	00	
3	Coverd Spoon baskets at 3.00	3	00	Various Sizes
3	Spoon with bails 1.50	1	50	.. ..
3	Spoon with Ears 1.50	1	50	.. ..
3	Round Box baskets 2.75	2	75	..
3	Saucer shape 2.75	2	75	..
4	Tub Shape 4.25	4	25	..
6	Cat head shape at 35¢ each	2	10	
6	Kitten heads shape at 25¢ each	1	50	
	$	33	15	
	Less 12½%	4	15	
		29	00	
4	Pendant 3.75 $	3	75	
		32	75	

Fig.240 What was happening at Canterbury during the fancy basket period isn't really known. Several sources—notations of visitors who stopped there—indicate that some baskets were sold. One Canterbury history cites thirty-two baskets made for sale in 1843, but no other record of production has surfaced. Tradition credits Zillah Randlett (1800–69), a Canterbury sister, with making "nice fancy baskets" for sale during her spare time, and identifies Lucy Williams (1776–1863) as making baskets in her "off turns."[30] The rest of the history, except what is carried in the baskets themselves, has been lost.

This invoice from Mt. Lebanon suggests that the Church Family was supplying the Canterbury shop with sale baskets.

Fig.241 The Mt. Lebanon idea is evident in Canterbury fancy types but the work is not as sophisticated; it didn't come out of a system as coherent as Mt. Lebanon's. Rims on many of the baskets are made of cane and typically are single lashed. Notches are also single. Handle design has fewer subtleties.

The basket forms are more straightforward in their contours, and the weave usually has a different look. Uprights alternate wide-narrow, as in this example; or the uprights are wide and the weavers very narrow (Fig. 244), giving a ratio sometimes as high as 6:1.

Fig.241

1 Handle is not contoured like Mt. Lebanon's
2 Rise of handle is closer to body than in Mt. Lebanon work
3 Single lashing
4 Single notch
5 Cane substituted for ash rims, a common practice at Canterbury
6 Mt. Lebanon splint provided by Daniel Boler
7 Alternating wide and narrow uprights, characteristic of many but not all Canterbury fancy baskets
8 Narrow weavers

131

Fig.242 Part of the Canterbury look derives from a different scaling of materials. In the bottom of some baskets, where narrow uprights alternate with wider uprights, as in this detail of Fig. 241, this translates to a "windowpane" effect. The original price remains on the basket: "17 cts."

Fig.244 Another typical Canterbury cathead, with wider uprights all-of-a-size and very fine weavers. This example is double lashed; the notch is single.

Fig.245 A Canterbury kitten head. The body is palm leaf, the rims are cane, the handle is ash, and the lashing (which has been repaired) was ash.

As good ash became harder to come by, it appears that for a while Canterbury got splint from Daniel Boler and then went to using palm leaf in place of splint—even for uprights, as well as weavers and eventually lashing. A weaker material, palm leaf tended to wrinkle; but it worked well enough in small baskets. Its yellow color and lateral ridges identify it.

The use of palm leaf was not unorthodox. Mt. Lebanon's fancy baskets may initially have been made of palm leaf; certainly palm leaf baskets were being made in New York at the same time that splint fancy types are first mentioned. Ash, however, was the preferred material. Once the ash fancy business got going, there is little reference to palm leaf baskets at Mt. Lebanon.

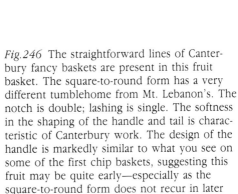

Fig.246 The straightforward lines of Canterbury fancy baskets are present in this fruit basket. The square-to-round form has a very different tumblehome from Mt. Lebanon's. The notch is double; lashing is single. The softness in the shaping of the handle and tail is characteristic of Canterbury work. The design of the handle is markedly similar to what you see on some of the first chip baskets, suggesting this fruit may be quite early—especially as the square-to-round form does not recur in later Canterbury work.

Fig.243 The long thin tail of the handle in Fig. 241 was necessary to offset the shifting inherent in the single notch. This is a recurring attribute in Canterbury fancy basketwork.

Fig.247 In this handle (detail of Fig. 244) note the characteristic flatness of the wood as compared with Mt. Lebanon's tooled contour. Because Canterbury handle stock was thinner to begin with—so it could be bent freehand instead of with a mold—the notch and blocking and tail were not as thick as Mt. Lebanon's, and there was less meat to put a contoured edge on. A similar method and aesthetic were incorporated in Canterbury utility baskets (see Fig. 118).

Fig.248 A squared-bottom, straight-sided fancy basket of extremely fine weave, with a handle running longways like the handles on Canterbury chip baskets. This handle was not formed on a mold; it was just carved out and bent to shape. Tails go down into the bottom and curve around to offset the single notch.

A tag on the basket reads "No. 10 / 1960 / Property of Alice Howland" (a Canterbury sister).

Fig.249 Of similar design to Fig. 248, this basket has a considerably different look. The sides are splayed because the cane rims didn't have the strength to hold the shape. Handle, body, rims—almost everything about this basket seems thin.

The cane foot lashed to the bottom appears to be a later addition; there were originally little button feet at the corners.

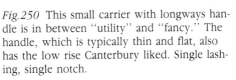

Fig.250 This small carrier with longways handle is in between "utility" and "fancy." The handle, which is typically thin and flat, also has the low rise Canterbury liked. Single lashing, single notch.

Fig.251 In this carrier a Canterbury maker attempted to get the look of Mt. Lebanon shopwork but came out with a different, vertical, look because of the narrow weavers. The handle is wide and thin like Canterbury handles, and has a characteristically rounded tail.

Because Canterbury makers didn't shape their handles on molds, they made them thin so they would bend more easily by hand. As a consequence they tend to spread (whereas Mt. Lebanon handles "took" their shape on the mold).

Fig.252 Sometime prior to 1900 basketmaking at Canterbury had come to an end. A view of the shop reveals a variety of handmade merchandise, but no baskets. Poplar items are, however, prominent in the photograph.

Fig.253a The store at Sabbathday Lake.

Fig.253 For decades Maine baskets were consistently the least like New York's, and it appeared that fancy styles were not even attempted there. So we were shocked when the family at Sabbathday Lake showed us their private collection which they had kept behind doors. There had been nothing, and then suddenly: these. Here were baskets attributed to Alfred that looked just like New York's. [Only the two baskets at the back are not Maine baskets.]

The mystery was explained when we discovered that Harriet Goodwin (1823–1903), an eldress at Mt. Lebanon who served in the parent ministry with Daniel Boler and was among the first sisters identified as basketmakers in 1835 (see Figs. 82-84), was transferred to Alfred in 1879. These baskets indicate that she brought Mt. Lebanon standards with her; and manuscript records reveal that Boler was "shipping splint to Alfred, Maine" after she went to reside there.[31]

Fig.254

1 Classic knife form

2 Handle is a little heavy but still the classic Mt. Lebanon bonnet

3 Double notch; ribbon is attempt to secure the handle at the notch
where the lashing failed to bind it

4 Single lashing

5 Mt. Lebanon material, and typical ratio of weavers to uprights; chase-woven
in a technique unique to the Shakers (explained in *Chapter Five*).

Fig.259 A classic Mt. Lebanon cat head made in Maine.

Figs.255,256 Two colors of horsehair are used as weavers in this whimsical cat head. The basket is attributed to Ada Cummings (1862–1926) who was a Maine Shaker all her life. According to tradition she introduced new poplar box styles and was the first to accent poplarwork with sweet grass, which Indians in Maine used in their baskets. (There are no ash splint baskets known incorporating sweet grass that can be attributed to the Shakers.)

Figs.257,258 This unusual Maine cat head, with three double rows of blue splint decorating the body of the basket, is very similar in concept to the horsehair basket; probably it was made by the same sister. Like the horsehair example, in some ways it doesn't look Shaker at all; and the use of color would initially suggest it was Indian. Material, however, is Shaker and the start (explained in *Chapter Five*) is typical of a Shaker cat head. Rims are classic Mt. Lebanon rims. The ear loop, however, is simply a thick growth ring, hand-shaped and bent.

Fig.261 A lidded "hexagon" weave basket made of palm leaf.

Fig.260 A typical furnishing basket as made at Mt. Lebanon, with a handle attached with ribbon. The rim is finished with a sawtooth edge.

Despite Harriet Goodwin's attempt to transfer Mt. Lebanon's art to Alfred, traditional handles and rims had to be modified in the Alfred work; and the small size of the baskets suggests that splint was limited. The sisters did what they could with what they had, but they needed assistance—and a supply—that was not available.

Fig.262 The palm leaf is easily identifiable in this closer view.

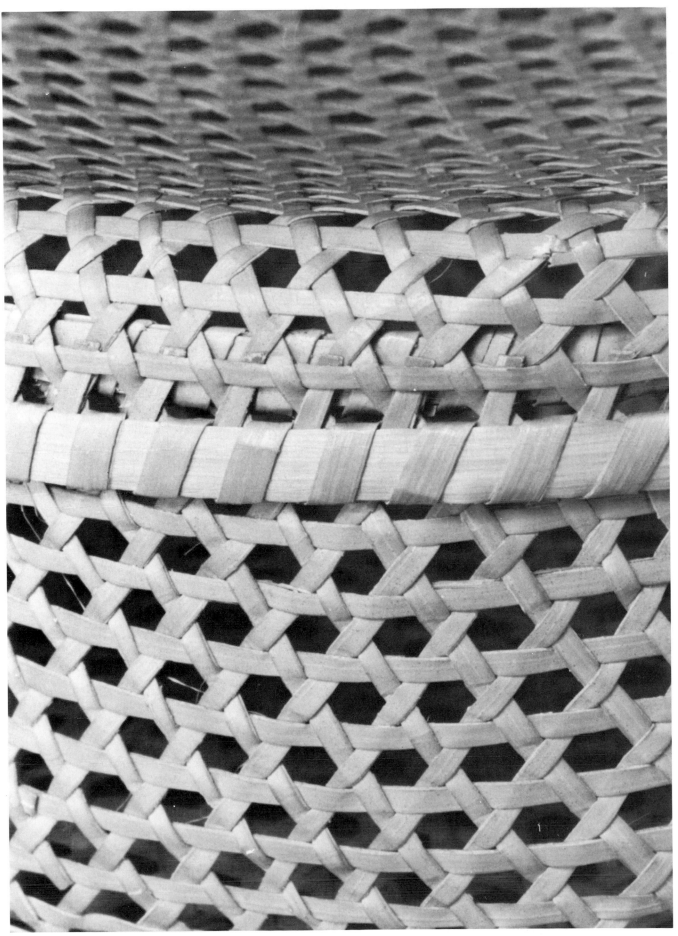

Fig.263 In 1869 a brother at Mt. Lebanon remarks that "good timber of the kind used for manufacturing baskets is getting to be very scarce indeed.[32]

Black/brown ash had never been as plentiful as most other woods; but by 1870 it was precious stuff. Then in 1875 a fire destroyed the Mt. Lebanon shop—molds, tools, inventory, splint. The business never recovered despite a few attempts. It appears that some of the sisters tried to make do by weaving smaller and smaller baskets, while others concentrated on complicated work that gave a better return for time and splint invested. But production was clearly limited, and in 1897 the business closed. After 1900 a few sisters made a few baskets, but the basket industry was at an end.

Fig.264 This photograph of "Sisters Cutting Out Cloaks" was published in the 1936 Darrow School yearbook. Three of the sisters—Ann Maria Graves, Augusta Stone and Harriet Bullard—were veteran basketmakers.

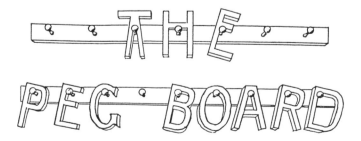

Fig.265

Figs.265,266 In 1932 the Mt. Lebanon property became the site of the Lebanon (subsequently Darrow) School. This advertisement was placed in the 1936 yearbook, which was called The Peg Board (Fig. 265). The "work baskets" were probably not made of ash splint; more likely they were poplar. By this time the basket business at Mt. Lebanon had long since come to an end—even though a film from the 1950s, in the collections of the New York State Museum, features a Shaker sister showing "things they make for sale," including an Indian-type basket typical of the era.[33]

140

THE COTTAGE

We invite the visitors to
The Lebanon School to
inspect hand-made work
baskets and other sou-
venirs at the Cottage.

The Church Family Shakers

Fig.267 The fact that a basket came from a Shaker community doesn't make it "Shaker."

Of the several baskets in use in a Shaker laundry when this photograph was made around 1930, only the basket in the far left corner (a Mt. Lebanon square-to-round shop type) looks for sure to be Shaker. In the left foreground, the upturned basket may be Indian; it may have been bought from a local basketmaker. The two wash baskets behind it are wicker, which is not a Shaker material. The basket in the right middle ground, where the stovewood is stacked, is a typical factory product.

142

"Here are pretty little baskets . . ."

From a Shaker song, 1846[1]

There is something inherent in the idea of Shaker—something implying perfect craft, perfect form—that makes Shaker attribution *nice*. A lot of baskets get called Shaker because they have good lines. But as the preceding chapters show, Shaker is more subtle than this. And because it is subtle, it is also elusive.

Not all Shaker baskets are beautiful, or perfect. Some have lost their original lines or have been weakened by being used for a purpose other than the purpose they were designed for. In some, there was simply a lack of sophistication in the construction of the basket to begin with. Baskets have broken or collapsed because the maker had a poor understanding of stress points and how to relieve them, or design was forced on materials beyond their capacity to hold that shape, or weavers and uprights were allowed to spread apart or jam.

These imperfect baskets, however, didn't come out of a highly-developed system like Mt. Lebanon's; they were the work of novice basketmakers, novice shops. The best baskets *are* extraordinary, combining "right use of material," "right" line, "right" form. You can see a systematic concept and method in them, as well as art. They all look the same; and when you begin to carry that look in your eye, they will jump out at you. (Go back to the photograph that is Fig. 4 and you will easily see the basket is a Mt. Lebanon apple.)

But what about the baskets where a signature is not so pronounced? How do you know if possibly they're Shaker, or just generic American or Indian?

Some of them you can't tell; they pass for country baskets. Those, however, don't have in them the art you're looking for, anyway. The only justification for attributing a basket to the Shakers lies in matching it to other basketwork that can be traced to a Shaker shop. Keep in mind that Shaker aesthetic and sense of order aspired to alikeness; and system, even elementary system, usually produced baskets (and basket parts) that look alike. Study what you know is Shaker. Question any exception. What you're looking for is what was characteristic.

First, you want to look at the material—is it ash? If it's not, a Shaker attribution is unlikely. Excepting some baskets made of palm leaf, there is no eastern Shaker work known that is not ash. There are a few, a very few, examples of oak and willow baskets associated with the western Shakers; but they represent a different tradition, a different concept *(1)*.

So the material is ash? Examine the texture and finish of the splint—is it scraped? split/satin? pounded or filler cut? Are weavers, uprights, rims, handle(s) and lashing all ash, or is other material or fiber mixed in?

Next look at the rims. Rims eliminate a great percentage of baskets. If only one rim is carved or dressed and the other "rim" is a piece of splint, you're probably looking

1. What is most significant about materials the Shakers substituted for ash is that they were "like" ash. The basketmakers didn't have to learn how to work with a new kind of material; they didn't have to tool up differently for it, or revamp their forms or systems or change their concepts, as they would have in order to use material that wasn't ash or wasn't "like" it.

Because it is flat and thin, palm leaf was to some degree interchangeable with ash. Furthermore, the sisters already understood palm leaf, because they were making their bonnets from it. Palm leaf baskets didn't have the same integrity as splint baskets, but palm leaf served its purpose pretty well. Many of the early fancy baskets were made of palm leaf in their entirety. In later baskets, palm leaf was generally used only when suitable ash wasn't available: you see palm leaf weavers here, uprights there, or palm leaf lashing (especially in sawtooth edging).

Although the Shakers sometimes used cane for rims, they did not make baskets of cane. Cane is semi-round, flat oval. It has the right shape for their idea of what rims should be, so on small baskets they substituted cane when they couldn't use ash. Cane rims weren't as good as ash rims; but they worked well enough when they were making do. Cane, however, could not be interchanged for ash, as palm leaf could. It has different qualities, different characteristics. Nonetheless, you find cane used for some repairs. When ash wasn't available, cane was, long after ash was gone; so you may see one cane rim, or cane lashing, or a cane ear.

Oak and willow were apparently used to some extent by western Shakers; but there are no Shaker baskets from the northeast made of oak or willow. These were not "like" ash, and could not be substituted for ash.

Fig.268 In the foreground is the typical knife basket Mt. Lebanon made thousands of. You see at a glance the signature rims, handle, splint. The mold shown would have been for this basket.

The smaller basket on the mold has tapered uprights, which are unusual, and the material is exceptionally light. But the rims identify it conclusively as Mt. Lebanon. The basket is, overall, simply suggestive of the odd little things that sometimes turn up, as variants within the norm.

Much more unusual is the knife basket at left. Materials are Shaker but the uprights are more narrow than the rule. The form is atypically flared on all four faces. And handles and rims are not from the usual system. Rims are simple flat growth rings, as is the handle. Note also the skinniness of the handle, compared with a normal one on the knife basket in the foreground. Provenance remains a mystery.

at an Indian basket. This is the way most Indians, and usually only Indians, rimmed off their work. However, all Indian baskets are not so easily distinguishable. There are baskets that are Indian/settler/Shaker that look very much alike, and are differentiated only in their nuances.

If a basket has two "ordinary" rims, look at them again. How are they dressed—with a knife? a drawshave? a file? a spokeshave or plane? a machine tool? What shape are they in section—square? rectangular? round? oval? triangular?

Examine the handle(s). Repairs and replacements can distort original design; but be cautious of crisscrossed handles, swing handles, etc.—anything that doesn't correspond to *usual* Shaker work.

What shape is the handle in section? How is it dressed? (File marks on a utilitarian basket may help to indicate Shaker work; but tool marks of any kind would tend to disqualify a fancy basket as Shaker. Some fancy baskets made outside New York may retain tool marks; but the Mt. Lebanon basketmakers were scrupulous in removing any trace of a mark, except on the tails of handles.)

If the handle is notched to accept the rim, is the notch single or double? What shape is the shelf of the notch? (Watch out for a triangular shelf characteristic of Indian work.) The lashing, is it single-wrapped or double? Are rims nailed to the body instead of, or in addition to, being lashed? At the rims, are the uprights turned down on the outside only? inside only? outside and inside? are some trimmed at the rim?

Is the weave a typical over-under pattern? a twill? a cheese or hexagonal weave? If hexagonal weave is used, is the entire basket done in that pattern, or is part of it hexagonal and part of it solid?

What shape is the body—squared-bottom, squared-top? squared-bottom, round-top? round bottom, round top? squared-bottom, ovoid top? hexagonal bottom, round or oval top? (Be on guard if the top of a basket is truly ovoid and not just misshapen. With the exception of the "spoon" and the hexagonal "boat," the Shakers are not known to have made production baskets with intentionally oval tops.)

Analyze the tumblehome, any deliberate bow of the body as it rises from bottom to top.

Consider additional or unusual elements.

Is there an inscription?

Are there signs of extra caring? extra skill? What sort of temperament did the maker put into this basket? If, for example, the sides are straight, *are* they straight, or do they cave or look pinched? If they are meant to have some roundness, how smooth is their contour? How evenly is the splint matched in weight and width? Is natural color matched? What is the ratio of weavers to uprights? How does the lashing lay on the rim—is it taut and smooth? loose? uneven? Do rims and handles have a straight grain?

Now stand off a little. Look at form, line, proportion, the relation of rounds to squares, the height of the handle to the body, the relation of throat to base. Consider symmetry, uniformity, balance, weight.

Then appraise patina and condition. Consider what you're selecting for. A broken-up basket has valuable information in it; you can look at it or take it apart and learn from it. But a single break in an otherwise pristine basket can reduce its market value radically. The age of a basket shows somewhat in its patina because patina develops with time. A darkening that occurs from exposure to sunlight, it is also affected by water and dirt and natural oils transmitted in handling. Be careful not to confuse patina with varnish or some other sealant. Varnish is not something you want on a basket. It tends to take away the splint's natural pliability and leave it brittle. Furniture waxes and polishes are also destructive, as they leave a sticky coating that attracts dirt, which accelerates deterioration. Keep in mind that the Shakers themselves did not varnish or paint their baskets.

Can you assign a date to the basket? Traditional baskets are hard to date. Factory baskets can be dated with some accuracy by the technology in them, and sometimes by matching them up with company catalogues. But with traditional baskets, what was made in 1750 was made virtually the same way in 1850 and in 1950. Patina may appear to date a basket: in most cases, the darker the patina, the earlier it is. But patina can be misleading. Hard use, dirt and water will darken splint, as will exposure to light; conversely, baskets protected from light may appear whiter, newer, than actually they are. Most traditional baskets, therefore, elude dating. With Shaker baskets, however, rough date at least is implicit in them. Few of them were made before 1820, and few were made after 1900. Production periods vary from community to community; but most utilitarian baskets were made prior to 1860, and most fancy types were made between 1835–75. For dates within these ranges, clues are carried by form, material, tooling and method.

So, your basket, is it Shaker? Assess what you have. Are there other baskets it can be matched to? Shaker baskets? In what ways?

When you see some characteristics, right off you see "Mt. Lebanon" or "Canterbury" or "Maine." You learn what the rims look like, you learn what the handles look like, you learn what the splint looks like; you learn what some of the styles look like; you learn what they did. Then you can identify anything that came out of that system.

But there are ambiguities in some baskets, in which all the attributes don't add up cleanly.

Consider a basket that looks New York (Fig. 276) but is wrong in some respects. This basket has been associated with Watervliet; it is said to have been made by Morrill Baker (1775–1850), who "officiated" for a while "in the Deacons Order" there.[2] One other has turned up like it. There is evidence that baskets were made at Watervliet (see Notes *Two/10*) but little else is known. Because Mt. Lebanon and Watervliet were closely related, and the ministry (several of whom were the lead basketmakers) resided alternately at each village, it would seem that whatever Watervliet made would be close to identical to what Mt. Lebanon made, but not as doctrinaire. And that is what is demonstrated by this basket. It is a round-bottom, round-top with string used in place of splint to start the bottom. This form and this technique are something you don't see at Mt. Lebanon. But the basket is otherwise so "New York"—rims, handle, splint—it could pass for Mt. Lebanon if the legend attached to it didn't clarify its differences. The system is in this basket in the points that count, and the system validates its loose Watervliet attribution.

The obverse is illustrated by a basket attributed to David Terry (1750–1821) at Enfield, Conn. Stripped of its association, this basket (Fig. 280) would not be one you'd think was Shaker. It is a square-form carrier, but it is crude work. It has no Shaker amenity. Nor is there as yet any documentation that any baskets were made at Enfield, although some very Shaker-looking baskets turn up in photographs made there prior to 1930.[3] Another David Terry (1778–1864) is listed as a cabinetmaker at Hancock[4];

but the basket in question does not look like the work of someone who understood how to work wood. If the basket was made by Enfield's David Terry, certainly it has the look of someone early on working very hard to get a square-form basket. But it doesn't illuminate much. Although they may prove to be correct, attributions like this should be questioned unless there is evidence in a basket to confirm them. Sometimes an object is tagged with a name, and a story develops around it. Before accepting an attribution, look for internal information to corroborate it. All this basket has going for it is its square form and the fact that several others in Shaker collections match it.

An enigma of another dimension is presented by a group of white ash baskets made for heavy use. By the time their membership peaked around 1840–50, the Shakers themselves had little call for additional baskets "for home use," and habits of thrift persuaded them to mend their old ones *(2)*. Some utility baskets were still made, but only a few. Even at Mt. Lebanon Elisha Blakeman notes in 1872 that he has made fourteen bushel and four half-bushel baskets for the year, against twenty-five "old baskets" he has mended.[5]

An exception to this trend may be a basket that may have been made at Enfield, New Hampshire. The basket (Figs. 285-90) expresses a number of attributes that could make it Shaker; but there is no proof that it is. A round-bottom, round-top made of white ash, it is uniquely identified by a basswood disk or plate which forms the bottom and is additionally secured by crosspieces of ash that form a "spider." Two variants turn up again and again: bushel and two-bushel sizes with ear handles, and a swing-handle about one-third bushel size. The splint is heavy, almost strapping-like but it is not filling cut such as would appear in most factory-made baskets; it is pounded. In most cases the splint is high quality; but there appears to have been a period in which poor material was used—it is thin and hairy and is being pushed. Overall, the basket is late-looking, suggesting the use of machinery on a larger scale than at Mt. Lebanon; but it is more quality than most mass-produced baskets made in "the world." It has not been possible to link it to any basket factory.

Enfield had a significant industry in tubs, measures and pails; but there is almost no documentation of basketmaking there. Only a few entries in a journal kept by Seth T. Bradford *(3)* allude to basketwork: "Rimmed a square basket . . . splitting out basket rims . . . turning basket handles . . . turning down baskets . . . turned two baskets . . . nailed strips onto the bottoms of square baskets . . . put wooden bottoms to 7 baskets."[6] Bradford's mention of putting on "wooden bottoms" arouses some interest, as the basket in question has a wooden bottom that's nailed on.

This plated, or plank, bottom basket is not dissimilar to Canterbury work. Rims match the Canterbury rims taken from simple blanks. The ear handles also match up to Canterbury's handles from this same era; the swing handle, if the basket is Shaker, is the only Shaker production swing handle known. There are baskets attributable to Canterbury that have spider bottoms, which are otherwise unique to this plank-bottom basket; spiders do not appear in other splint basketry. The spiders are made of rejected or broken rims—evidence of a frugal system such as the Shakers followed. Typical of factory work, the rims of this basket are nailed on. There are, however, Canterbury baskets with rims nailed on after being lashed. (Lashing was usually the first thing to go in a basket, and nailing rims was a better method.) The tumblehome in Canterbury's white ash baskets is similar to, if not the same as, the tumblehome in the plank-

2. *"Levi and I began to mend old baskets and chairs," Henry DeWitt opens his journal on January 1, 1828. On the 12th he confides, "It was rather a broken time with us. . . . we mended 18 baskets and 3 chairs." On the 14th he almost sighs, "We finished mending old baskets and glad was I."[1]*
It is interesting to note that DeWitt writes just at the time utility production was in full swing: even when they were making hundreds of new baskets, the Shakers were mending old ones that had some use left in them. This discipline became even more important as the years went by. It is especially telling that during the last year of his life, Daniel Boler—the great basketmaker and the top elder—is observed "mending baskets."[2]

3. *Bradford was born in Barnard, Vermont. He joined the Shakers at Enfield in 1835, when he was eleven, and "made his first basket" in 1840 (as he notes in his journal, on May 1). For a period of years Bradford worked at basketmaking during the winter months and "horticulture" in the warmer months. In his journal he mentions also working in leather, making measures and tubs, making brooms, printing and pasting up paper seed bags, doing rough and finish carpentry, and eventually becoming caretaker of the boys. In 1852 he was appointed deacon in the Church Family. In 1856 he left the Shakers.*

Fig.269 Attribution becomes less and less easy when a basket is in someways like, and someways not like, usual Shaker work.

Considering the number of communities there were, the number where nothing is known about basketmaking, and the number of stages any shop went through, it is not surprising to come on anomalous baskets. Some of the odd baskets may be transitional. Others may be the work of a displaced basketmaker attempting to follow his craft in a community that didn't have the experience to back him up. Others may be learner baskets. Anomalies, however, must be accounted for in order to call a basket Shaker.

This large carrier is reminiscent of early Mt. Lebanon shop baskets and carriers, but it doesn't match up entirely. It was clearly made in a shop where tasks were divided. Its sophistication is in the body; the deficiencies are in the rims and handles. Whoever made them did not have the expertise the weaver had.

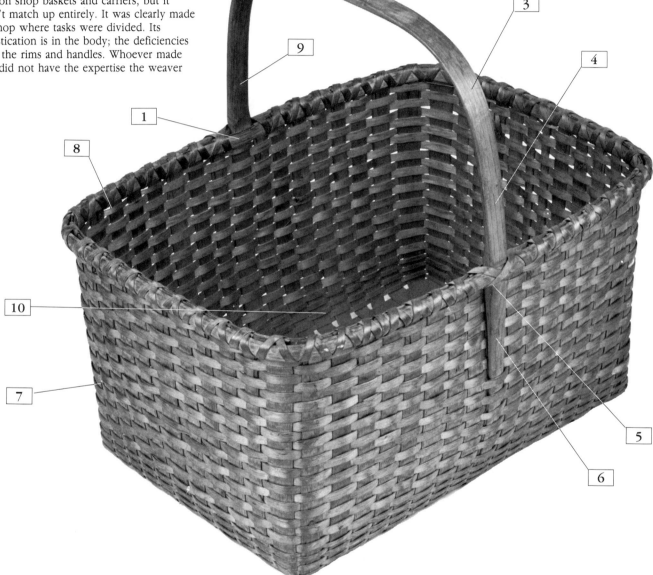

1 Tail runs down outside, which puts most of stress on outside rim and on handle at the notch, where it would want to break; not as good design as when on inside. This in itself helps to date the basket before the classic Mt. Lebanon carriers, made when the basketshop had matured.

2 Chunky in center of grip, with ordinary "country" edge

3 Heavier, more board-like handle. Drawshaven; doesn't have the controlled round.

4 Grain is funny; sign of a more naive basketmaker

5 Little or no blocking

6 Visible hacking here, not a nice clean cut

7 Made on a mold; has good square Shaker form

8 Note lack of contour on inside rim

9 No taper here

10 Starter weavers are narrow; unusual in Shaker work except in round bottoms

148

bottom basket. The use of white ash is also significant: Canterbury used white ash.

There is strong evidence for Canterbury association, but *is* the basket Shaker? Many baskets of this type have been found in Shaker communities. They have been, and still are, found all over New Hampshire; and they're called "New Hampshire baskets" by collectors. All of this suggests they were made somewhere in New Hampshire: and here at Enfield is a basketmaker putting wooden bottoms to baskets. It is not unlikely that Enfield, which had advanced expertise in coopering, adapted a Canterbury idea and made this basket theirs. But if the basket is Enfield's, why is there no machinery around? why no documentation or written record of production? why no molds or jigs? why no local memory of the baskets? why is quality so poor in some examples of the type? how did "seven" bottoms Bradford cites expand into thousands? Bradford, interestingly, left Enfield and left the Shakers in 1856, when he was 32. It is not implausible that he took the idea with him and went into business on his own. Where he went when he left is not known; the answer may lie there.

Figs. 270, 271 A very similar basket is marked "M.S." (Medicine Shop). It is lined with leather; and, as is typical in leather-lined Shaker baskets, the leather is patched out instead of being cut from a whole skin.

The Shaker attitude against artisans marking the work of their hands *(4)* seems, initially, a handicap in attributing Shaker basketwork. If, however, you look at other baskets, you will see that even traditional basketmakers rarely put their name on their work. *Owners* signed their baskets but not makers. Their signature was instead in details of construction, in the way they expressed their idea of how to make a basket. The difference with the Shakers was that their signature usually was of a system rather than of an individual.

Some Shaker baskets, however, are marked in a telling way. These markings are not to identify who made them but to indicate where—and later, to whom—they belonged.

Most commonly the face of a basket was coded with bold letters, usually painted on in black or red, which the members of a community understood to indicate a building ("L" for Laundry) or a use ("X", at Canterbury, for orchard) or users ("MX" for Ministry, "DXX" for Deaconesses). Numbers were sometimes appended to a letter to signify a particular drawer or shelf or room within a building. Codes differed somewhat from community to community; however, "CHH" for Church Family and the coupling of "X" with another letter to indicate brethren and "XX" to indicate sisters was consistent.

4. Recognition of joint interest and collective effort is implicit in the Shaker practice of not marking objects with the name of a maker: "No one should write or print his name on any article of manufacture, that others may hereafter know the work of his hands."³ Although similarly instructed not to "stamp, write or mark" their name on objects they might make specifically for another brother or sister or for common use, members of the community did occasionally indulge that satisfaction.⁴ No baskets, however, are known to be thus inscribed — possibly because the system that was in them was so clearly a collective system.

Because this code is unique to the Shakers, it can appear to be an easy means of identifying Shaker baskets. Be careful, however, of baskets the Shakers bought for their own use, and coded like the others. An example is a round oak basket (in fact, a Taghkanic; see below) marked "CHH OFFICE." Be wary, too, of non-Shaker baskets painted with "typical" letters meant to deceive. Always keep in mind that some attributes of Shaker work are attributes you won't see in other baskets; and if you don't see them where you expect them, be suspicious.

In addition to the baskets that have letters painted on them, some—later—baskets are marked with cloth or paper tags or paper labels, and some are inscribed with ink or pencil. Usually these markings are personal initials—again, not those of a maker but of the owner. Sometimes a name is written out in full. Other tags indicate, instead, location: "Girls Shop," for example. Some refer to use: "Fancy Work. As you please." If using a label or tag to date a basket, keep in mind that, after 1850, members of a community often appropriated older baskets for their particular use, and put their initials on them. A basket may be earlier than the dates of the person who initialled it would suggest, and may have been made at a community different from the one where that person was residing.

Many baskets found in Shaker communities and assimilated as "Shaker" are baskets the Shakers bought for their own use or for resale in their shops. The misattributions are legion, but a few of them can be singled out.

Not far from Mt. Lebanon, several families of basketmakers lived in the hills above Taghkanic, New York, where for generations and generations they made excellent baskets, which they sold to the Shakers and to other farmers in the area. Their signature basket (Fig. 303) was a swing-handle of unique design. A round-bottom, round-top, it was a sturdy basket ideal for use in field and orchard, for picking and sorting. Several characteristics make it special, but what identifies it is the handle. Flat in section and bent in a simple arch, the handle has a hole drilled at either end of it for an ear (which attaches it to the body) to pass through; the ear is turned crossways to fit over, not parallel to, the rims of the basket. No one but the Taghkanics made a swing handle just this way.

The ratio of weavers to uprights in a Taghkanic basket is similar to a Shaker ratio. The baskets express the integrity that Shaker work expresses. They embody an idea of utility. They are not showy. They last. But they differ in other respects. The splint in them is much heavier than splint the Shakers used, and it is always the same weight, whatever the style or size of a basket. The material is a mix of ash and oak and sometimes maple. Rims and handles are split out, cleaned with a drawshave or pocketknife, and that's it: the Taghkanics weren't after perfection. Details the Shakers would have fussed over are left as is. Compared to Shaker work, these baskets have a chunky look, a country look. But they are excellent utility baskets, and the Shakers apparently recognized this.

Around 1920 the Taghkanic basketmakers were "discovered" by the city press, who wrote sensational stories with sensational leads. ("Strange People Populate Taghkanic Hills. They Have no Religion, no Morals, no Education and Run Like Rabbits at the Approach of Strangers—Eke Out Scanty Existence by Making Baskets."[7]) A stigma developed around the basketmakers, which resulted in their history being suppressed; and in time their name was lost. About the same time, "Shaker" was being discovered; and the Taghkanic baskets—which were found in Shaker storerooms and were common in Shaker "territory"—began to pass for Shaker. When we began researching Shaker basketry, we kept coming across these unusually well-made baskets which people told us were Shaker. Even then we knew they weren't, but we didn't know who *had* made them. Finally we tracked them back to Taghkanic, and published *Legend of the Bushwhacker Basket* to set their story straight.

Another extensive group of baskets that have been claimed as Shaker are white willow hampers (Figs. 308-10) which the Shakers imported from Germany[8] and sold in their shops. The form of these baskets, the material and the techniques in them derive from a different type of basketry; they should not be confused with Shaker.

Still another German basket[9] has, in very recent years, been appearing as "Shaker." This is a diminutive basket, toy-like, woven of straw (Fig. 311). Round-bottom, round-top with flaring sides, most examples have a tall loop of a handle, formed of two strands of straw (often vari-colored) twined around each other. There is nothing about these baskets that is Shaker; but collectors have paid $600 for them at Shaker auctions, at a time when legitimate Shaker baskets have gone for significantly less.

If you know what makes a basket Shaker, you won't often mistake non-Shaker. And the way to know is to drill yourself on Shaker attributes, to look at the baskets in the museums, and to appraise honestly the "maybe" basket you have in your collection or may come across. Think system. Think material. Think method. Think form, and tooling. Think Shaker. And beware of exceptions.

Figs.272,273 These two oval carriers, made of oak with ash rims and ash lashing, initially appeared to be unique in Shaker basketry. Our hypothesis was that they had been made by a western Shaker not fully familiar with Mt. Lebanon method.

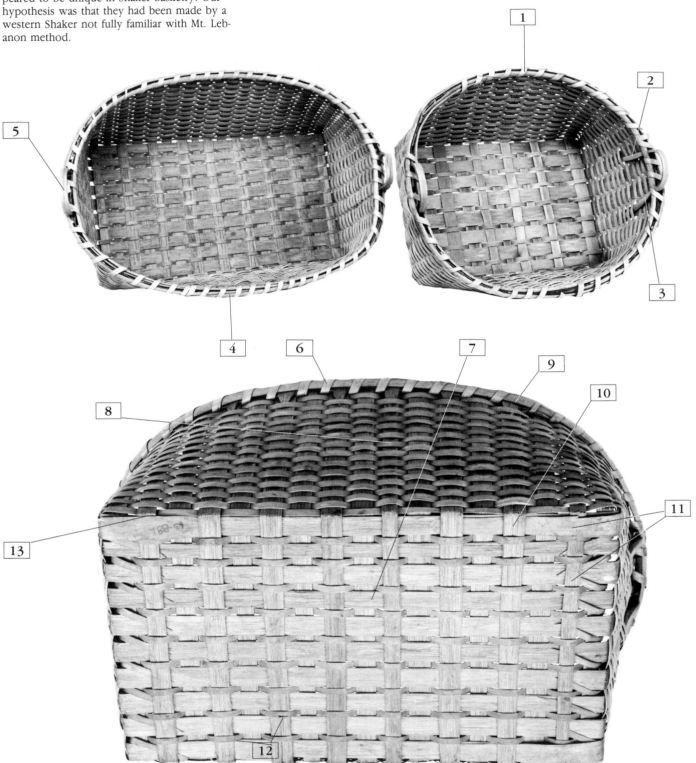

1 Oval

2 Naive carving

3 Handle spread to fit the basket

4 Poor overlaps; this basketmaker wasn't used to working with these rims

5 Handles are different on this basket

6 Single lashed, with ash

7 Body is oak; note grain in bottom

8 Material doesn't lay down

9 Rims appear to have been shaped with Mt. Lebanon knives, possibly leftover rims made for a smaller, lighter basket

10 Sharp turn cause oak to crack; there is tension between the design and the material

11 Oak uprights too stiff to weave smoothly, so bottom was laid up and then bound with narrow strips of filler.

12 Split upright

13 Unusual start for Shaker work: weaver laid in beside upright

Fig.274 At So. Union (Kentucky) we were later shown a collection of five baskets attributed to that community, which are not dissimilar to the two baskets in Fig. 272. They are, additionally, closely identical among themselves.

All of them are woven entirely of oak splint—uprights, weavers and lashing. All have squared corners. All have contoured double rims, with a spline between the rims. The rims are drawshaven, with a uniformity that almost looks planed. All are double lashed, and all have an upright slashed horizontally to make a space for the lashing to pass through. Four of the baskets have identical drawshaven overhead handles; one has ear handles. All handles are double notched, to the inside, and lashing is crossed double (making an ''x'') at the notch. All are turned down alternately on the inside and the outside. All have a spiralling splint filler shaped like a pigtail that travels horizontally along the bottom of the rims to compensate for any shrinkage of the body from the rim. All have a split upright at one corner. All have a filled bottom of some variety. Two have a wide starter weaver.

Fig.275 Daniel Boler, who became lead elder and the lead basketmaker at Mt. Lebanon, was born at So. Union, Kentucky. It is understandable that he would have retained a special affection for the believers at So. Union and, on his official visits there,[34] would have taken pains to instruct them in the art of basketry, as far as Mt. Lebanon form and method could be applicable to oak.

These baskets could be the result of his tutelage. Together with the preceding oval carriers, they suggest that there may be a legacy of western Shaker baskets to be uncovered still.

153

Figs.276–78 If it were not a round bottom, there would be almost nothing to suggest this basket wasn't Mt. Lebanon work. It is straight New York in terms of handles and rims, splint and balance of material. The string bottom (Fig. 279) and tapered uprights, however, are something Mt. Lebanon would have wanted to avoid. Just for efficiency, Mt. Lebanon's square-to-round fruit was more practical to make: cutting the tapered uprights in this basket was a time-consuming job. And the string bottom was a kind of shortcutting Mt. Lebanon's basketmakers wouldn't have sanctioned for themselves.

This basket has long been attributed to Morrill Baker (1775–1850), who "officiated" for a while "in the Deacons Order" at Watervliet; and the details in it substantiate the attribution. It is like Mt. Lebanon work in ways you would expect and different in ways you can accept.

Fig.279 String was used in place of splint to start the weaving in the bottom. The purpose of the string was to crush the uneven uprights into a more perfect circle before the weaving began. But this was a poor way of doing things, and it is not seen in other basketry.

In this view of the bottom of the basket, note the pin hole at the center where the uprights were aligned on the mold.

Fig.280 Tradition has credited this basket to David Terry (1750–1821), a brother at Enfield, Connecticut; and several carriers matching it have turned up in Shaker collections. The weaving, however, is bulky and uneven; the lashing is uneven; the material has knots and flaws throughout. The handle design is unusual—the outer face is sliced off vertically above the rim and trimmed to a single outside notch. The several baskets that are known all have the same signature in them, and all show someone was working hard to make a square-form basket. The squareness is something associated with Shaker; but in these baskets there is nothing more to go on.

Figs.281,282 Another group of very square and early baskets appear in several Shaker collections, and some are also associated with David Terry. Woven in a herringbone twill, these baskets look as if they should be Indian. But herringbone is not unknown in Shaker work (see Fig. 325); and other characteristics give some additional basis for Shaker attribution.

All of the baskets—of which these are representative—are square and straight and made on a mold. All of them have nicely rounded rims (a little heavier than most Shaker). All handles and rims and tails have the same soft contour, and there are file marks on them. All bodies are the same weight material, with uprights and weavers of the same ratios. All are single lashed.

Here again is a signature that eludes identification. Shaker can't be ruled out; but it can't be proven either.

156

Figs.283,284 This basket is one of several that are known with matching characteristics. The quality of the material in the basket is exceptional, and the weaving is very beautiful. It is the kind of basket you want to call Shaker.

In some ways this basket appears to be a lowcut version of the Canterbury white ash round bottoms (Figs. 116,117). But the double bottom is extremely unusual in its structure and design. The uprights taper in width toward the bottom and then continue with no additional taper across the bottom. There is a definite signature in the way the bottom is laid up and woven with the legs of the "spider" showing, instead of being covered up. But this signature doesn't occur in any documentable Shaker work.

Lashing is single, as on many Canterbury round bottoms; but the rims are Indian-like, made from a growth ring instead of a riven blank. Furthermore, rims are oak, which is very odd (although there is a Canterbury basket with oak rims). Handles are thin, and different from similar known Shaker work.

Here are many of the cliches the collector is faced by. The fineness of the splint looks Shaker. The single lashing is "like" Canterbury lashing. The dealer who sold it, who is known to be reputable, called it Shaker. You want it to be Shaker. A matching basket exists at Canterbury. But none of the information is conclusive.

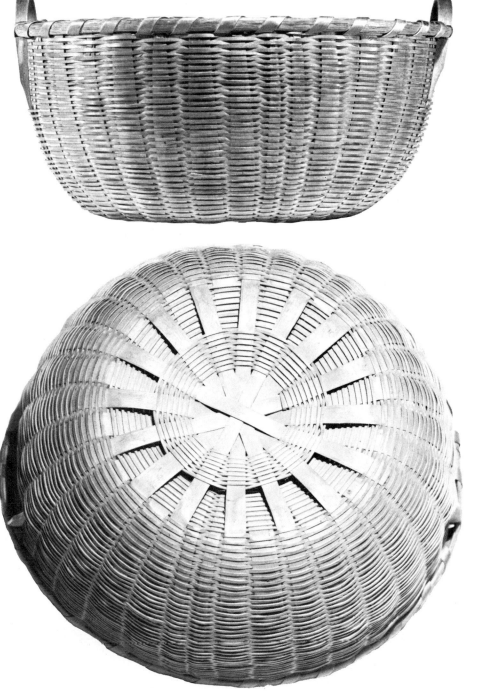

Fig.285 Handles and rims on this plank bottom basket are identical to those on the late apple baskets used by the gross at Canterbury (Figs. 123–28).

Two variants of plank bottom baskets—which have been known among collectors as "New Hampshire baskets"—turn up again and again: big storage or gathering baskets with ear handles, in one and two bushel sizes (Fig. 286); and a swing-handle picking type, about one-third bushel (Figs. 287, 290).

A host of factors link these round-bottom, round-top baskets with Canterbury Shaker work. But there is no proof that they are Shaker. Their tumblehomes match Canterbury tumblehomes. Their rims and handles are made from cubey blanks, matching Canterbury again. The spider on the bottom is found only on these baskets and some at Canterbury. The material is pounded white ash, which the Canterbury Shakers used in their similar round baskets. And uprights on these and Canterbury's are bevelled.

It would appear that the design of these baskets evolved from Canterbury's white-ash round bottoms. But the expertise in the baskets is a cooper's expertise. For this and other reasons, it seems a Canterbury idea may have been shared with Enfield, where the manufacture of tubs and pails was a major industry. There is too much "Shaker" in these baskets that cannot otherwise be explained, and it has not been possible to trace them to any of the known basket factories. Seth T. Bradford, a sometime basketmaker and cooper who mentioned in a diary "put[ting] wooden bottoms" on baskets, left the Enfield Shakers in 1856. It is possible that he developed the prototypes and took them with him, setting up business somewhere else.

Fig.286

Fig.287 The basket in the left foreground of this photograph of Canterbury sisters is the swing-handle mate of the earred basket shown in Fig. 286. The basket in the right foreground is a factory product (see Fig. 147).

158

Fig.288 The large basket on the laundry lift at Canterbury, which is very similar to these production baskets, has a typical Canterbury tumblehome, typical cubey handles and a spider, but not a plank bottom. (Additional strips of splint are applied to the bottom to protect it against wear, and the tails are woven in partway up the sides.)

Fig.289 A basswood plate forms the bottom of the baskets; and a groove around its circumference secures the uprights in position. On the outside the plate is additionally reinforced with a spider. This is a nice bit of joinery that required sophisticated tooling; a channel is routed out to receive the cross members of the spider, which are then also nailed on.

Fig.290 If the white-ash plank bottom baskets are Shaker, the swing-handles are the only production Shaker examples known. Many other swing-handles have been attributed to the Shakers; but none of those made in any volume match up to anything that came out of the Shaker systems.

159

To indicate their intended use, and to facilitate their return to their right location, most Shaker baskets were marked in one way or another. Bold letters painted in black or red designate a building, users or use. Codes differed somewhat in the various communities, but some abbreviations appear to have been common in all: "CHH" for Church Family, "MX" for Ministry, "EX" for Elders, "EXX" for Eldresses, "DX" for Deacons, "DXX" for Deaconesses.

Fig.292

Fig.293

Fig.291

Fig.294 There is some crossover as the years go by. A Canterbury basket coded "SXX" for "Sisters' Shop" was put to good service, in a later period, gathering up sweaters which the sisters knit on machines for sale. "SXX" became "sweaters."

Fig.295

Fig.296.

Fig.297 The Shakers conscientiously observed the dictum: "a place for everything, and everything in its place." Doors, drawers, cupboards and shelves were numbered; and baskets were often coded to correspond.

Fig.298 The idea of "right use" and "right order" was so strong among the Shakers that almost everything that could be labelled was. Many baskets still have cloth or paper tags or paper labels attached to them. These may indicate the location to return the basket to; in other cases, they may indicate the contents of the basket, or carry some instruction relating to the contents.

Fig.299 Although no baskets, it appears, were signed by a maker, Mt. Lebanon baskets marked "Ministry" were probably made by basketmakers in the ministry.

Figs.300,301 Only infrequently do you find a date on a Shaker basket. More often, date is inferred by style, technique or material. Patina also gives some idea of age; but patina can be misleading. A basket that had hard use or was exposed to strong light may appear darker/ older than it is; and a basket protected from light or use may read whiter/newer.

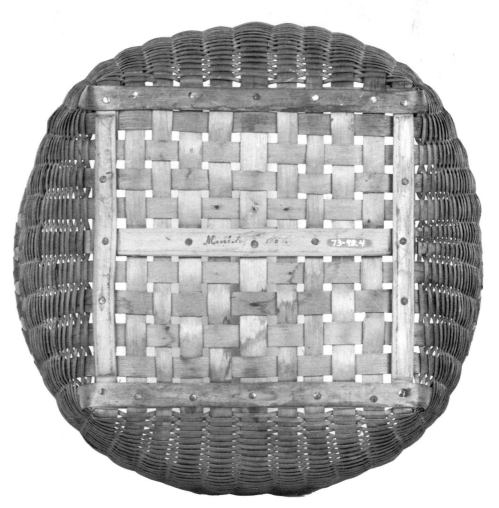

Fig.302 One of the original principles of the Shaker experiment was communal property. There came a time, however, when the idea of individual possession was, to a degree, acknowledged. Consequently, quite a number of baskets are inscribed in ink or pencil with the initials of the person who used/owned that basket. Sometimes names are written out in full. No marks indicating a maker are known.

A basket may be earlier than the dates of the person who initialed it would suggest, and may have been made at a community different from the one where that person was residing.

Fig.303 Because these baskets are made so simply and solidly, and because they turn up where Shaker baskets turn up, they have been incorrectly attributed to the Shakers.

They were made close by Mt. Lebanon, at Taghkanic, New York—where, for uncertain generations, a group of families made their living making baskets (and two members still make them today). These baskets have a sturdy, honest look associated with "Shaker." They aren't flimsy; they were made for use. Their ratio of weavers to uprights is similar to a Shaker ratio. However, the splint in them is much heavier than splint the Shakers used, and it is always the same weight, whatever the style or size of a basket. The material is a mix of ash and oak and sometimes maple. Rims and handles are dressed only with a drawshave or a pocketknife; they're not tooled. The weave has a ridgy texture.

These baskets obviously come from a different aesthetic. But after Shaker began to be collected, they began to be called Shaker. Their own history was lost from them. They are not Shaker; but they are excellent baskets that deserve to be respected in their own right.

The classic Taghkanic basket is a round bottom, round top swing-handle. Many thousands of these were made; and because they were *good* baskets, many are still around.

No better basket for use in field and orchard, for picking and sorting is known. One of the reasons the Mt. Lebanon Shakers didn't make round bottoms or swing handles is that the Taghkanics did. These baskets were so well designed for their use and so well made—and so inexpensive—there was no need for them to duplicate what they could buy.

Figs.305,306 Although their signature was the swing handle, the Taghkanics offered several basket styles, which are simple and straightforward variants of round bottom, round top; square bottom, round top; and rectangular bottom, oval top.

Fig.304 The swing handle you see on a Taghkanic basket is a handle you won't see on any other basket. It is flat in section and is bent in a simple arch. A hole is drilled at either end for an ear to pass through, which attaches the handle to the body of the basket. This ear is turned crossways to fit *over,* not parallel to, the rims of the basket. (The blocking above the drilled hole is relieved in one of two ways. A shoulder is cut away square with a saw kerf, as in this example, or is just tapered out, as in some in Fig. 303).

Fig.307 Like other farmers in the area, the Shakers bought Taghkanic baskets. This round bottom Taghkanic with ear handles marked ''CHH. OFFICE'' was at Mt. Lebanon.

Fig.308 A cache of "Shaker" baskets turn out
to be imported German hampers.

Fig.309 German hampers woven of white willow have been confused with Shaker. These baskets were popular in America in the nineteenth century. The Shakers, and numerous other purveyors, imported them for resale in their shops; but they did not make them.

These willow hampers represent a different concept of basketry. Technique is different, material is different, and the characteristic forms are different.

Fig.310 View of North Family store, Mt. Lebanon. Even in this murky photograph, the distinctive form and weave of imported willow hampers can be recognized (lower left shelf, behind the glass case).

Fig.311 Another German basket that has "become" Shaker, shown actual size.

Round-bottom, round-top with straight flaring sides, these small to tiny baskets are woven from straw. Most of them have a tall loop of a handle, formed of two strands of straw (often vari-colored) twined around each other. There is nothing about these baskets except their size and their "fancy" look that is even suggestive of Shaker work.

167

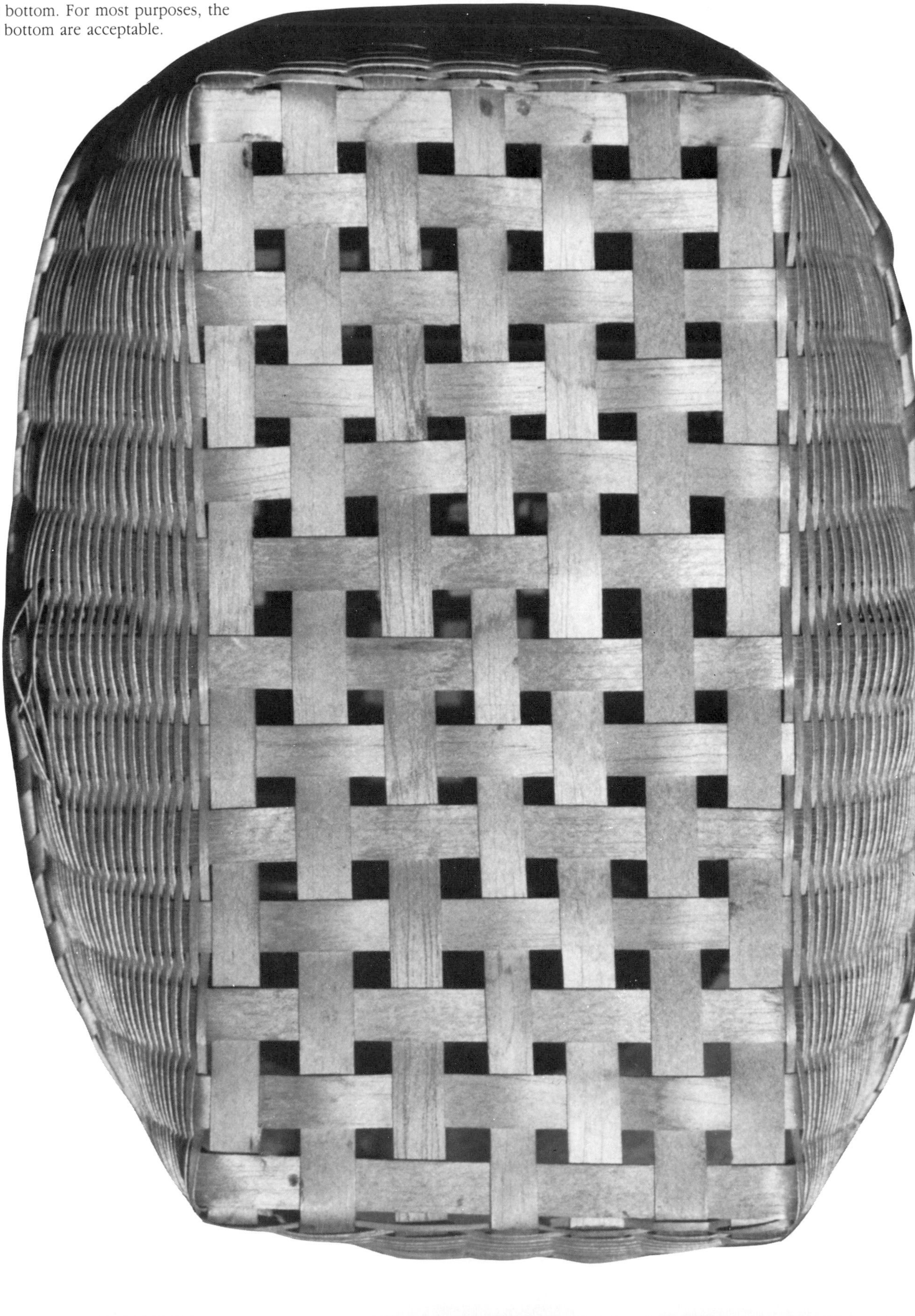

Fig.312 The majority of splint baskets, including the majority of Shaker baskets, have a "loose" bottom. Gaps are left between the strips of splint that are laid across each other to make the bottom. For most purposes, the holes in the bottom are acceptable.

"This is Right. Depend upon it."
From a Shaker pattern book, 1855.[1]

Certain differences in Shaker technique provide additional explication of how the Shakers thought a basket should be made. It is possible to see a great basket is good without examining structural details; but if you want to be a basket connoisseur, you will want to understand these subtleties.

Starting at the bottom, one of the first things to notice about a basket is whether the bottom is "loose" or "tight"—whether you see gaps left in the weave, or you don't. The majority of splint baskets made in the northeast, including the majority of Shaker baskets, have loose bottoms. They are typically laid in a "plain" weave, where opposed crosspieces (which become the uprights) pass over-one, under-one in succession, creating a checkerboard pattern. In this weave the strips of splint won't normally go tight against each other because of resistance in the thickness of the material; as a consequence, gaps are left in the bottom. Loose bottoms take less time to set up, they use less material and they result in fewer uprights to weave around when forming the body. And for most purposes, the holes in the bottom are acceptable.

But there are some uses (or designs) where a "tight" bottom is required. Because the point where the crosspieces "stop" is factored by the thickness of the splint, a bottom can be woven tighter if the edges of the splint are bevelled or if the material is thinned—or both. A bottom can also be woven loose and the gaps filled afterwards, with additional strips of splint called "filling." Or a herringbone twill can be substituted for the usual plain weave: skipping over-two, under-two, a herringbone weave effects a diagonal pattern that allows the splint to lay tight without bevelling or thinning.

These were the traditional methods for getting a solid bottom; and the same methods account for most of the closed bottoms you see in Shaker utilitarian baskets. In the fancy line, however, you may see something else, which was possibly unique to the Shakers. Already the fancy splint was so light it tended to lay in tight, leaving only small holes in a bottom. But in baskets where larger holes would have resulted, instead of "filling" these bottoms after the baskets were finished, the Shakers filled them as they went. Their method was to lay down one upright and weave in all the opposed crosspieces, then to lay in a filler beside the first upright, spreading the crosspieces until this filler would slide against the first upright. The ends of the filler they turned back and tucked under. Then they laid in a second upright, tight to the first filler and continued in the same way until the bottom was complete. This method has some drawbacks, as it leaves considerable space between the remaining uprights, which translates to a weaker body. However, the bottoms *look* nice, because the number of pieces in them gives them an intricate appearance which is unique to them.

When a bottom is laid up, the type of handle to be applied later has to be considered. Whenever an overhead handle is desired, a basket has to be planned so it will have a center upright for the tail of the handle to be placed on. Rectangular or square bottom baskets, therefore, have to have an uneven number of uprights on the handle sides. Round bottom baskets are usually laid up as two conjoined bottoms, eight-over-eight, giving thirty-two uprights. In theory this works for a handle, because an even number of uprights will center it on a round bottom as there is always an opposite. Most round bottoms, however, have a split upright to facilitate continuous spiral weaving; so some crowding of the uprights is necessary to compensate for the "extra" space introduced by splitting an upright. (Round bottoms are, however, more forgiving—visually—than squares and rectangles, if the handle isn't just right.) Side handles require less pre-planning. On larger baskets the handles may span two uprights between their tails; on smaller baskets they often span only one. With side handles, therefore, the task is usually one of designing the handles for the body rather than the body for the handles.

Once a bottom is completed, the free ends of the splint are then bent up against the mold; weavers are woven in and out around these uprights to form the sides of the basket. Here at the bottom, the way the first weaver is started often helps to identify Shaker work. Most commonly, this weaver was folded in half and slipped over an upright. From that center point, one end of the weaver was woven in and the other end was left hanging. When the first row was completed and the weaver returned to the point at which the weaving started, the hanging end was picked up and woven around, and the first "weaver" was left hanging, to be picked up in turn when the second "weaver" came around. (When the first piece of splint was used up, additional splint was added in, as row built on row.) This method is called "chasing." A variant was to start with two separate weavers; when this was done, you see two weaver-ends stuck into the bottom or up the sides of the basket. But more often, you see the first weaver folded around one of the uprights, with a single twist (so that the good face of the splint was on the outside).

A more unusual method of starting the weave, seldom found in old baskets that aren't Shaker, resulted from "adding" an upright. A weaver was laid in vertically at the top of the basket and run down between the uprights at a corner, then turned horizontally to start the weave. This also added the odd upright necessary for traditional spiral weaving. In lieu of chasing, a single piece of splint was woven around continuously until it gave out and then a new piece was started.

Unless a basket has an odd number of uprights or the weave is chased or laid in one row at a time, stopped and started again, a weaver will always come around and overlap on top of itself. If an upright is added, the weaver then passes on the opposite side of the uprights in each tier, and so "climbs" up the body. The conventional way of getting an odd upright was to split one of the regular ones. But to the Mt. Lebanon eye, this threw off the symmetry of a basket and the matched widths of all the uprights. (In many non-Shaker baskets, uprights are random-width to begin with.) Mt. Lebanon's added-upright method preserved the symmetry but it also created a weak splint which had to be treated with respect, as it was easily pulled out of position and so could throw off the lines of a basket. Outside New York, where Shaker basketmakers were less doctrinaire, a split upright is not uncommon. And even at Mt. Lebanon, in work the size of an apple basket and up, an upright is typically split.

In large baskets a spiral weave became impractical. If a basket is, say, two feet long by one foot wide, it takes a seven foot weaver to go around it, and that's a pretty long weaver. In baskets such as these, weavers were laid in one row at a time, overlapped and then cut off, with the next weaver being started on the opposite side of the basket to prevent a bulge from always occurring in the same place. This nonclimbing weave is fine in utility baskets where a tier of weaving consumes the whole of a long weaver anyway. But in small fancy work, where there would be many tiers comprising the sides of a basket, the repeated overlaps at each tier would create weak points.

All Shaker baskets, like all splint baskets, are "plaited"—woven of flat strips crossing over and under. As a general rule, the tighter the weave, the better—so long as the weaving isn't so tight it looks pinched. One way the Mt. Lebanon makers got a tight weave was by putting tension on the weaver as they worked against the mold, weaving over-under, over-under several uprights, then pulling on the weaver while packing it down into the basket. If a weaver is wrapped around an upright and pushed down, wrapped around the next upright and pushed down, around and down, around and down—which is the traditional way of weaving—the result is a less tight, less tensile basket. By doing it their way, the Mt. Lebanon Shakers ended up with a rigid shell which no other basketmakers using thin splint obtained.

The majority of Shaker baskets are woven "plain weave" (over-one, under-one). But some incorporate different weaves. Most of these are variants of twilling, achieved by passing the splint over-*two*, under-*two*. Twilling can be strictly utilitarian. One of the more elementary examples of it is a herringbone bottom, where the twill weave gives a nice tight bottom. Another simple but intentionally decorative example is a twilled chain used in some Mt. Lebanon fancy baskets (and—a Shaker anomaly, some Maine utility baskets). Starting in the bottom, a weaver was laid in so that it skipped over two uprights and then continued normally until it came back around; in each row the weaver naturally skipped two again, making a continuous spiral up and around the basket. More complex patterns were created by doubling back or skipping three uprights.

The most difficult twill was the "quadrifoil," which appears to be unique to the Mt. Lebanon Shakers. Twilling is a technique common to Indian and other baskets; you see it even in the German hampers which have been confused with Shaker. But the "quadrifoil" has not been found in other basketwork. The pattern was begun with a herringbone square. Then an upright was added by starting a weaver in line with the uprights. At the center this weaver was turned horizontally and woven in a twilled pattern around the initial square. When the quadrifoil was complete, the weaving changed from a twill to an ordinary over-under. In some examples the look of the weave was changed by crossing a pair of wide uprights at the center.

The quadrifoil weave was used in the bottoms of all round fancy baskets, such as tubs, saucers and some other round work types. It was also used in the simple mats which the Shakers offered for sale alongside their baskets. (The tablemats look like the bottoms of the baskets; where the sides of a basket would have started up, they are finished with a sawtooth edge.)

Lids for round-topped forms, such as fruits and cat heads, were similarly woven in the quadrifoil pattern; and all known examples of the double hinged lids on knife baskets incorporate a modified quadrifoil. On these, a plain-weave square was woven at the center of the lid so that it interlocked with the pivot bar. At the far ends of the square, the ribs running perpendicular to the bar were fanned out to form two quadrants. As ribs were added in outside the square and perpendicular to the bar, they were turned where the center ribs were splayed to become weavers, continuing back along the square to the bar, wrapping around it and reversing direction. The only twilled portion of the lid is the part that fills the two quadrants, giving the pattern the look of a gothic arch.

One other decorative weave is the "hexagon" weave, which was originally used in making cheese baskets. Unlike the square and round bottoms of other baskets laid in two planes, hexagon bottoms are laid in three: sets of uprights are placed in parallel lines within each plane, with the angle of intersection creating six-sided holes. This pattern produces a hexagon base which can be finished as a round or an ovoid. Strength of the weave is determined by the smallness of the holes where the strips intersect, with smaller holes resulting in a stronger basket. Indians also made fancy baskets with hexagon weave; but only the Shakers combined partial hexagon bottoms and solid sides. The switch to solid weaving was accomplished by adding an upright and turning it to serve as a weaver and then continuing in the usual way, over-under, over-under, around the free ends of the splint.

Whatever the weave pattern, Shaker basketmakers liked to thin their overlaps. Where one weaver ended and another was laid in, the splint was pared down to equal, when overlapped, the thickness of one weaver, thus eliminating unsightly bulges or ridges in the weave. This is an extra touch typical of Shaker sensibilities.

Most Shaker baskets are spiral woven, with each row of the body continuously climbing. To level off the top, the Shakers trimmed the last weaver to a gradual taper. In some fancy baskets and some utility ones, they next applied a "binder." When the last weaver was in place, they put above it on the next tier another single (and heavier) band of splint which was the same height as the rims would be. When the inside rim, outside rim and this binder were lashed together, the basket would hang from the binder, relieving stress on the weavers. (Other basketmakers tended to simply lash over three or four rows of weavers, creating a weak spot where splint could sag or crush under stress, because the weight carried by the basket would be transferred to the lashing and, in turn, to the splint.)

After the uprights were trimmed, they were usually turned down. On fancy types, they are almost always turned down only on the inside; every other upright was cut off at the rim, and only those in between were actually turned down. On utility types, uprights are usually turned down alternately on the inside and the outside, although some are turned only to the inside. If you come across a fancy basket, particularly a small one, on which the uprights are turned down on the outside, there's something to question.

Most turndowns are trimmed to a point and tucked down behind several weavers in the body. On a very few baskets, the uprights were folded over and cut off at the bottom of the rim—just snipped off and not run down inside at all. (This, however, is more common in Indian work.) Sometimes the thickness of the splint was relieved where they were folded down, to reduce any bulges between the rims; half the material was peeled away from the tail that turned down.

The majority of Shaker baskets were finished off with carved or tooled inside and outside rims which were lashed together. But there are some baskets, usually small ones and usually those from later years, that do not have conventional rims. In the simplest of these, there is no turndown. The uprights were just cut off in rounded stubs or points, and a piece of kid was glued around to secure the weavers. In similar examples, the uprights were trimmed off flush with the top of the shell, and a strip of kid was folded over to bind the edge. Another variant has a "twined" edge. The uprights were cut to points extending about 1/8" above the top edge and then two strips of splint were held together and twisted alternately under-and-over around the uprights. (This isn't up to usual Shaker standards, and it isn't something you see much of. As the splint wasn't really locked in place, a twined edge was only suitable for baskets that had cushions in them.)

A third method for finishing a basket without lashed rims was a sawtooth edge, which is the most common and the most satisfactory of the several alternatives. A rim or a piece of splint was attached to the outside face of the body, on top of the last weaver. The uprights were cut off about ¼" above the top edge of the shell, then folded down and to the left. A lasher was run in, tying the tip of each bent upright to the inside of the body. This sawtooth edge was used on many lids and on several types of fancy baskets, including hexagon weaves and cushions.

When lashing—tying the two rims and the body together with a strip of splint—the Shakers wrapped the splint either once (single lashing) or twice, from opposite directions (double lashing). They preferred to start and stop lashing on the inside; but they didn't otherwise make a practice of always doing the same thing. The tail of the lashing in some baskets is just cut off under the rim and left there; in others, it's run down inside the basket. Utility baskets at Mt. Lebanon were normally double lashed, and at Canterbury they were more often single lashed; but in all categories there are exceptions. In the fancy baskets, single lashing is most common which is understandable, even though the lashing is the weakest element in a basket, because these baskets didn't receive hard use or carry heavy weight. However, if fancy baskets increased to some size, and thus the weight they might carry was increased, lashing was more apt to be double. On double-lashed baskets, the lashing typically crisscrosses at the handle to stabilize it. Single lashing is seldom double-crossed there.

The shapes of handles and rims, which have been described in preceding chapters, help significantly to identify Shaker work. But the way these are attached is also telling. Most handles are notched into the rims, and the notching is part of a signature. Notches may be single or double. A double notch helps to keep a handle from slipping; but a single notch is acceptable when it's compensated for by a longer tail which continues down to the bottom of the basket.

Whether the tails of a handle go down the outside or inside of the body is determined by the type of handle and by the maker's understanding of stress. It is preferable for an overhead handle to go down the inside; the only time it is necessary that an overhead handle be on the outside is when the body caves toward the throat. If an overhead handle is placed on the outside, when the handle is lifted stress is transferred to the notch, which is the weakest point in the handle; and it tends to break the wood. If an overhead handle is placed on the inside, stress instead compresses the notch to strengthen the union. Side handles are almost always placed on the outside of the body because handles on the inside are inconvenient. Because the grain of the wood in a side handle is turned perpendicular to the rim, and because it's meaty enough to tolerate the cut-away of the notch, the stress that weakens an overhead handle placed on the outside in this case strengthens the notch.

Some fancy handles were attached with ribbon instead of notches. When the sisters were short on material and expertise, they made baskets without normal rims. And the lack of rims meant that the concept of rim and handle had to be adjusted. Usually the top of the body was finished with a sawtooth edge. Where the handle met the body, a hole was drilled in the sawtooth trim and the handle, and ribbon was tied through. At the bottom of the handle, ribbon was looped through the splint body and around the handle and tied off.

Another handle variant is the hoop handle on certain baskets such as box and ball types, where a flexible bow was required. A single piece of cane or splint was looped at either end to form ears, then wrapped with ash lashing. In some examples, ribbon was threaded through the loops and tied to the basket. In other examples, little loops of splint were put through the loops in the handles, and the ends of the splint that made the ears were woven back up into the body.

This hoop handle, which is very similar to some Indian handles (see Fig. 358), was an expediency atypical of Shaker work. The comparative flimsiness is something the Shakers ordinarily avoided. What made their way of doing things different was an idea of perfection that informed it. In basket shape, concept and method, they didn't depart radically from what other basketmakers did; they just subtly made the details better.

Fig. 312a Mt. Lebanon fancy baskets with (fancy lace) bottom, shown with mold on which the baskets were formed. The combination of filled sides and hexagon bottom is a Shaker signature. Molds in background are for cat heads and kitten heads.

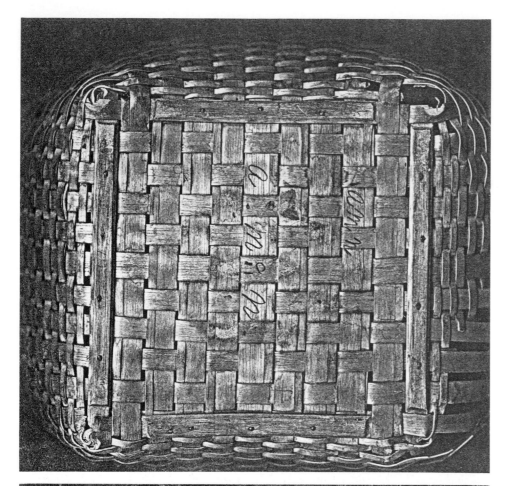

Fig.313 Some uses or designs require a "tight" or solid bottom. The easiest way to get a solid bottom is to make it up "loose" and fill it afterwards. The bottom of this Mt. Lebanon apple basket was filled in this manner after the basket was completed. The additional strips of splint threaded in to fill the narrow gaps throw off the usual alternating pattern of the weave, as two horizontal strips are laid in the same sequence side by side. (The heavier strips around the perimeter have nothing to do with filling; they were applied at a different stage to reinforce the bottom.)

Fig.314 In some baskets the bottom was filled as it was put together, in a method apparently unique to the Shakers. First they laid down one upright and wove in all the opposed crosspieces; then they laid in a filler beside the first upright, spreading the crosspieces until this filler slid tight against the upright. The ends of the filler they turned back and tucked under (as you can see in a couple of places here). Then they laid in a second upright, tight to the first filler, and continued in the same way until the bottom was complete.

Fig.315 The bottom of this carrier was also filled at the start.

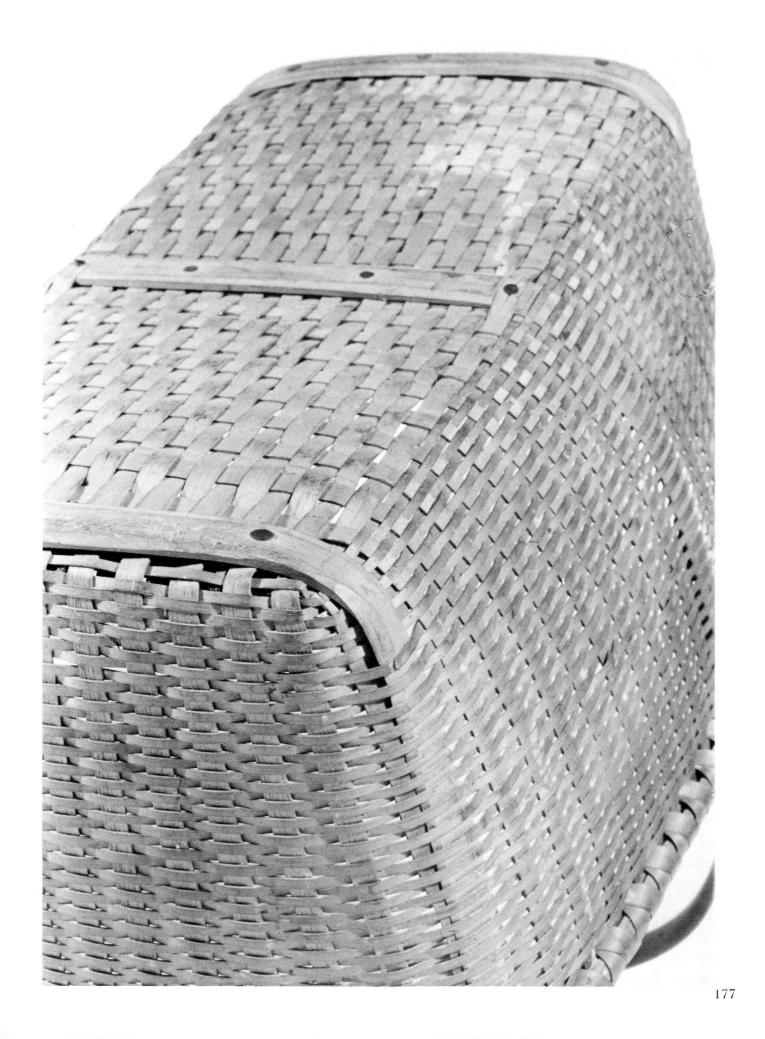

Fig.316 Detail of box lid, showing thinness of the splint and bevels.

Fig.317 Resistance in the thickness of the material is what prevents uprights from laying tight in a bottom. If the thickness of the material is reduced or the edges of the strips are bevelled, a bottom can be woven tighter, making even a light basket strong and solid. This is demonstrated in the lid of a Mt. Lebanon box basket.

Fig.318 When a bottom was forced tight by bevelling the splint, a little notch was often clipped out of the uprights where they turned up to form the sides and their width was shaved above. Otherwise, the uprights were so tight, there was too little room for the weavers to be laid in smoothly.

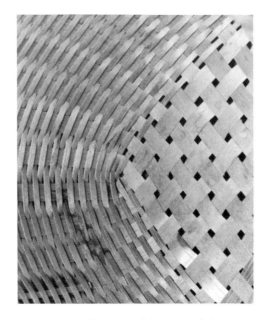

Figs.319,320 The start of the weave helps to identify Shaker work.

Many Shaker baskets are "chase" woven. At the bottom of the basket the first weaver was folded in half and slipped over an upright. From that center point, one end of the weaver was woven in and the other end was left hanging. When the first row was completed and the weaver returned to the point at which the weaving started, the hanging end was picked up and woven around, and the first "weaver" was left hanging, to be picked up in turn when the second "weaver" came around.

Look for a starter weaver folded around one of the uprights. This detail, however, may have been abraded, especially if the weaver was started at a corner, because the corners receive the severest wear.

A variant of chase weaving was simply to start with two separate weavers, instead of a single folded piece. If this was done, the loose ends of the weavers were tucked in under the bottom or up the sides.

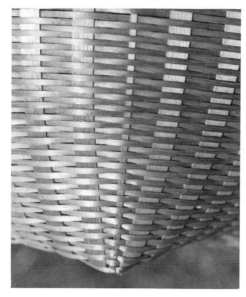

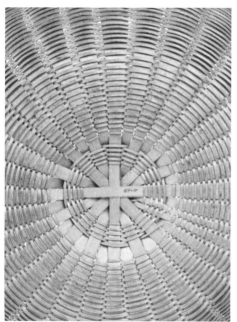

Figs. 322-24 Sometimes the weaving was started by "adding" an upright. As in this example, a weaver was laid in vertically at the top of the basket and run down between the uprights at a corner, then turned horizontally to start the weave. This also added the odd upright necessary for traditional one-strand-at-a-time spiral weaving. (In lieu of chasing, a single piece of splint was woven around continuously until it gave out and than a new piece was started.)

This method is seldom found in old baskets that aren't Shaker. If you see a splint basket with an added upright down one corner, you are very likely looking at a Shaker basket.

Fig. 321 Unless a basket has an odd number of uprights or the weave is laid in one row at a time, stopped and started again, or chased, a weaver will always come around and overlap on top of itself. If an upright is added, the weaver then passes on the opposite side of uprights in each tier, and so "climbs" up the body. The conventional way of getting an odd upright was to split one of the regular ones. However, the Mt. Lebanon Shakers tried to avoid this, as—to their eye—it spoiled the symmetry of a basket and the perfectly matched widths of all the uprights. But outside New York, where Shaker basketmakers were less doctrinaire, a split upright is not uncommon. And even at Mt. Lebanon, in baskets the size of an "apple" and up, an upright (as shown here) may be split.

Figs.326,326a A twill was also used to make a basket showier. In the example of this Mt. Lebanon knife basket, a chain was produced by laying in a weaver so that it slipped over two uprights and then continued normally until it came back around; in each row the weaver naturally skipped two again, making a continuous spiral up and around the body.

Fig.327 In round bottom utility baskets made in Maine, it is not unusual to see a twilled chain that begins in the bottom and continues up and around the sides. If the bottom, as here, is twilled in its entirety, all the uprights but one are split, giving the work an intricate appearance because the number of uprights is doubled.

Fig.325 Shaker baskets, like other splint baskets, were normally woven "plain weave" (over-one, under-one). But in some of the baskets a twill weave (over-two, under-two) was used instead.

Sometimes a twill was used for practical reasons, to get a solid bottom without filling or bevelling or thinning the splint. Creating a herringbone pattern, such as the one here, the twill allowed uprights to slip tight against each other.

Fig.328 A more complex pattern was achieved in this fruit basket by introducing additional chains at each corner, which crossed at mid-point.

Fig.329 The most sophisticated twill is the "quadrifoil," a Shaker pattern unique to Mt. Lebanon, where it was used to start all the fancy round bottom baskets except those with "hexagon" starts.

To achieve the "quadrifoil," a square was woven in a herringbone pattern. Then a weaver was laid in as an added upright. At the center this weaver was turned horizontally and woven in a twilled pattern around the initial square. When the quadrifoil was complete, the weaving changed to an ordinary over-under.

Figs.330,331 An incipient quadrifoil forms the start of this diminutive round bottom; even at this small scale, the signature quadrifoil was utilized.

Fig.332 The double hinged lids on knife baskets were woven in a modified quadrifoil. First a "plain" square was woven at the center of the lid so that it interlocked with the pivot bar. At the far ends of the square, the free ends of the ribs running perpendicular to the bar were fanned out to form two quadrants. As ribs were added in outside the square and perpendicular to the bar, they were turned where the center ribs were splayed to become weavers, continuing back along the square to the bar, wrapping around it and reversing direction. The only twilled portion of the lid is the part that fills the two quadrants, giving the pattern the look of a gothic arch.

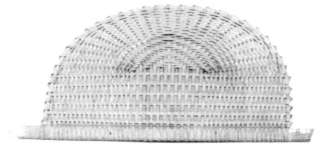

Fig.333 Another weave seen in some Shaker baskets is the "hexagon" weave. Originally used in making cheese baskets, it was later incorporated in a number of fancy types.

Hexagon bottoms are laid in three planes (instead of two): sets of uprights are placed in parallel lines within each plane, with the angle of intersection creating six-sided holes. This pattern produces a hexagon base which can be finished as a round or an ovoid.

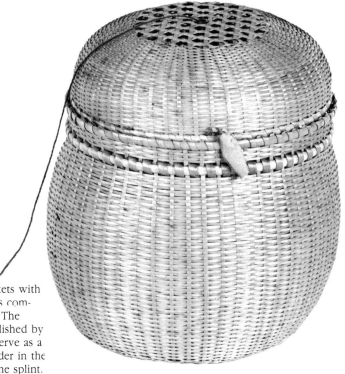

Figs.334,335 Indians also made baskets with hexagon weave; but only the Shakers combined open bottoms and solid sides. The switch to solid weaving was accomplished by adding an upright and turning it to serve as a weaver and then continuing over-under in the usual way, around the free ends of the splint.

Fig.336 After the body of a basket was complete, the uprights were trimmed and usually turned down.

On fancy baskets, uprights were typically turned down only on the inside; the usual procedure was to turn down every other one, and cut off those in between at the rim.

Fig.337 On utility baskets, uprights were normally turned alternately on the inside and the outside; but some were turned only to the inside.

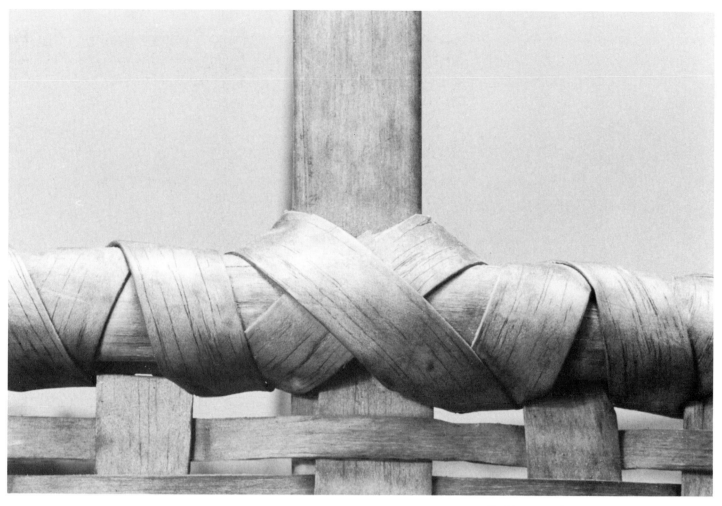

Fig.338 Most Shaker baskets are finished with a carved/tooled inside and outside rim, which are lashed together. Depending on the use the basket was made for, and the system or aesthetic it came from, the lashing is double (wrapped twice, from opposite directions) or single (wrapped once).

Double-lashed baskets are typically criss-crossed at the handle, with the double cross (which helps to anchor the handle) on either the inside or the outside.

Fig.339 Single-lashed baskets are seldom double-crossed at the handle.

189

Figs.340–42 Some baskets, particularly small late ones, were finished without conventional rims. Among these a "sawtooth edge" provided the most satisfactory alternative and was most common. To make a sawtooth edge, one normal rim or a piece of splint was attached to the top on the outside face of the shell. Then the uprights were trimmed about ¼" above the top edge and folded down in a point. A lasher was run in to tie the tip of each bent upright to the inside of the body.

A sawtooth edge was also used on knife basket lids and several lidded bodies.

Fig.345 In some of the late baskets, handles were attached with ribbon instead of notches. In these instances the top of the body was usually finished with a sawtooth edge. Where the handle met the body, a hole was drilled in the sawtooth trim and the handle, and ribbon was tied through. At the bottom of the handle, ribbon was looped through the splint and around the handle and tied off.

Figs.343,344 Most Shaker handles are notched into the rims. This notch may be single (Fig. 343) or double (Fig. 344). A double notch helps to prevent a handle from slipping up and down; but a single notch can be stabilized by a long tail continuing down to the bottom of the basket—as in Fig. 343.

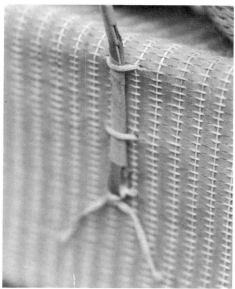

Fig.346 The loop handle made of cane or splint wrapped with ash lashing, used on baskets where a flexible bow was required, was also attached without notches. Sometimes this handle was tied on with ribbons; other times, it was secured with little ears of splint, the tails of which were woven up into the body. A similar handle was used on poplar-work, as shown here.

Fig.347 A Mt. Lebanon basketmaker sits for
the camera with a selection of fancy baskets
showing the system that is in them.

S · I · X

"We find out by trial what is best, and when we have found a good thing we stick to it."

A Mt. Lebanon elder, quoted in *New America,* 1867[1]

Any experienced basketmaker develops system. But the system the Mt. Lebanon Shakers implemented achieved a finesse no one else duplicated. Molds, jigs, machine tooling and divided expertise let them make their baskets "right" over and over and over. In every aspect of their lives, the Shakers were looking for an efficient way to obtain perfection; and in the premise that system promised efficient perfection lay the essence of their basket design and production.

When we began to study Shaker basketry, we were still learning to read the information that is in a basket. But as we came to understand system, we began to make more meaning of what we saw. We learned to recognize certain signatures; and we also learned to ask if those signatures made sense. Work attributed to a shop, we realized, had to match the system that was there.

In time we were able to place almost any Shaker basket we came across, assigning it a community and era. But there was one unusually excellent basket we couldn't explain by the system that was in it. Something about it didn't add up.

This basket (Fig. 348) was given to us by a great collector. First, there was only it. Then, there was another. In the process of surveying museum collections for potential Shaker work, we saw a close mate (Fig. 349) at the Essex Institute in Salem, Massachusetts. And in this one there was a tag, written prior to 1907, indicating that it was "bought at some Shaker settlement in New Hampshire about the year 1816 by Jonathan P. Saunders" *(1)*.

Meanwhile, at the Shaker Museum at Old Chatham, New York, we came across two similar, but not identical, baskets (Figs. 350 and 351).

At Pleasant Hill, in Kentucky, we found another (Fig. 352).

There were characteristics the baskets clearly shared. They all had a dark, dark patina, "black" like the earliest shop baskets at Mt. Lebanon. All were fruits, square-to-round, of the same size, with the same tumblehome; they looked like they came off the same mold. All had excellent lines, and their proportions were striking: bodies were tall in relation to their width, and the handles had a high arc. Rims on all of them were the exact same round. Two of the baskets (Figs. 349 and 352), however, had uprights alternating wide and narrow; the others had uprights all of a size. The bottoms of two baskets (Figs. 348 and 352) were laid in a herringbone pattern, while the others were plain weave—and of those, two (Figs. 350 and 351) were laid tight, and one (Fig. 349) was loose (with the alternating wide and narrow uprights creating a "windowpane" effect). The ratio of weavers to uprights was virtually the same (4:1 or 5:1) in all the baskets. All of the handles excepting one (Fig. 351) were the same hoop design; and four had outside tails with a very unusual contour. At the grip each handle

1. The basket had originally been given to the Peabody Academy of Science (now the Peabody Museum). When the Essex Institute was established in 1907, many domestic items were transferred to the new museum from the Peabody Academy. This basket was one of those items. The name of the donor isn't known, unless it is the "Miss Mack" on whose calling card the tag is written.

was flat on the outside and half-round on the inside—typical for Shaker; but the tails were also half-round—and this was odd. The one bonnet handle (Fig. 351) was, in design, strangely like the one-size-for-all handle on Canterbury's early chip baskets.

Here was a puzzle. The basket at the Essex Institute ("bought at some Shaker settlement in New Hampshire" around 1816) was strongly reminiscent of "our" basket, which we had been told by the original collector was from Canterbury. Were they all Canterbury baskets?

The problem there was that the work in them was much more sophisticated than anything coming out of Canterbury at such an early date. It was also too different in concept. Why hadn't Canterbury continued to develop designs based on these attributes? What had happened to the system that produced these?

Maybe they were from Enfield, the other New Hampshire "settlement"?

We had, however, found no real history of basketmaking at Enfield, certainly nothing that would suggest a shop capable of producing work of this caliber. Maybe, we hypothesized, these uniquely beautiful baskets were the work of a Mt. Lebanon maker who had resided for a brief time at Enfield or Canterbury. That would explain the New Hampshire "origin" of work that looked much more like New York's.

But the hypothesis wasn't satisfactory, and the apparent date of the work (prior to 1835) seemed too early.

Over the years we kept coming back to these baskets, but we couldn't break their mystery. Then, as we were completing copy for final editing, we had a call from Dean Lahikainen, Curator of the Essex Institute. He had uncovered information that suggested two additional baskets in the Ropes Mansion (which is affiliated with the Essex Institute) might be Shaker, and he wanted us to give our opinion on them.

We went and took a look. There was no question that the two baskets (Figs. 353 and 354) were Shaker. There was also no question that they related closely to the five baskets of elusive provenance. They were not identical. (Most noticeably, these had "captured" lids typical of Indian "feather" baskets; and their tumblehomes, also, were slightly different, suggesting they came off a different mold.) But they did match in significant ways. The basic shape of the baskets was the same, the rims were the same, handle details were the same, and the herringbone bottoms of these two were the same as "our" herringbone.

The "new" baskets were two items among the furnishings of a grand house in Salem which had been the residence of Ropes family. Virtually everything this family had acquired in the course of several generations had remained in the house when it was deeded over as a museum in 1907. And the family had kept records providing documentation of virtually every expense. In the summer of 1817, on a trip to upstate New York, the newly-married Sally Ropes and Joseph Orne noted in an account book, "July 12. At Ballston Spa. July 14. By the Shakers for diaper [linen cloth, see p. 83], boxes, baskets. $21.60. July 16. To Saratoga, Lake George and back."[2] These "baskets" they bought in 1817 had to be the two lidded baskets.

The basket we had seen initially at the Essex Institute—which matched ours and the others we had seen—and these two, with lids, carried dates within a year of each other. They were the earliest known documented Shaker baskets, and that explained everything odd about them.

"[A]fter the year 1813," Isaac Youngs had written, the sisters "began by little to make baskets for sale."[3] In 1816 the triphammer was adapted to pound ash logs to ease the labor of obtaining splint, and in the next few years other conveniences were introduced. These baskets came from that period when Mt. Lebanon was just developing a production system. The basket business was in infancy, and design was not yet resolved. The basketmakers understood shape and line; they were putting a perfect contour on their rims and handles; they had nice splint. But technique—the way they got their look—still needed work.

No where else in Shaker basketry is there a group of baskets that are so like and still so different as these. And no where else are there even Shaker baskets that come up to their art. The basketmakers were putting their soul in them. But system was still elementary.

Made "for home use" and "for sale," these baskets were evidently distributed to the other communities, and thus became the models those communities went by. However, basketmakers outside New York couldn't quite copy them, or didn't choose to. (At Canterbury, where baskets of know origin can be compared, even the square-to-round form was dropped, except in cat and kitten heads. All that was specifically retained was the idea of alternating wide and narrow uprights; narrow splint; herringbone bottoms; and "chased" weavers.) At Mt. Lebanon, too, these original designs changed. Later work shows how the basketshop shifted to production, keeping the same aesthetic, the same concerns, but getting finesse efficiently.

To understand system—Shaker system—look at what was carried over from these prototypes and what was altered. Look at how Mt. Lebanon got things "right" and then replicated that. Look at how system made it possible.

Fig.348 An early fruit basket, lined with leather, given to us with a Canterbury attribution. The basket has a double notch, double lashing. A hoop handle comes down on the outside of the body. Turndowns are to the inside. The bottom is laid up in a herringbone weave. A folded start and chase weaving are signs of Shaker provenance, as are the tooled rims. The body was woven on a mold and the splint is refined, like Mt. Lebanon splint.

Fig.349 This similar fruit basket, at the Essex Institute (Salem, Mass.), was tagged prior to 1907: "bought at some Shaker settlement in New Hampshire about the year 1816." It has a single notch, double lashing. A hoop handle comes doen on the inside. Turndowns are to the inside. The bottom is laid up in plain weave, with alternating wide and narrow uprights effecting a windowpane pattern. A drilled start [a hole was drilled in an upright, through which the first weaver was inserted] suggests the basketmaker was experimenting with system. The weaving is chased. As in Figs. 348 and 350–54, the splint has the look of Mt. Lebanon splint, the body was woven on a mold, and the rims are tooled.

Fig.350 A fruit basket of the same era, now at the Shaker Museum (Old Chatham, N.Y.), has double notch, single lashing, a plain-weave bottom laid in tight. The hoop handle comes down on the outside. Turndowns alternate outside, inside. The weaving was begun by adding an upright, in the Shaker method.

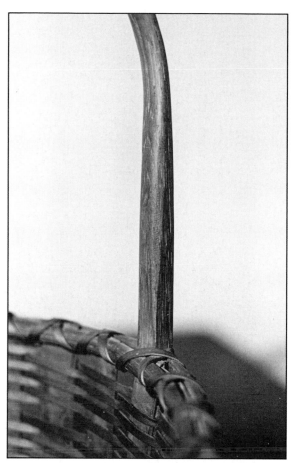

Fig. 351 Another, related fruit basket at the Shaker Museum (Old Chatham). Double notch, double lashing, plain-weave bottom laid in tight. A bonnet handle comes down on the outside.

Fig. 352 Even broken, this basket at Shakertown at Pleasant Hill, Ky. can be matched
readily with these other early fruits. Double
notch, single lashing. Alternating wide and narrow uprights are laid up in a herringbone bottom. A hoop handle comes down on the
outside; turndowns are to the inside.

Fig.353 Apparently purchased at Mt. Lebanon in 1817 and preserved at the Ropes Mansion (Salem, Mass.), this fruit basket—and another, Fig. 354, virtually like it—have "captured" lids. Each of the baskets has a single notch, double lashing, a folded chase start, and herringbone bottom. The hoop handle on each comes down on the inside. The lids are finished with one tooled rim, one splint "rim."

This basket and the two baskets shown in Figs. 354 and 348 are the earliest known datable Shaker baskets. All three are documented as having been purchased around 1816 and 1817.

Fig.353

Fig.354 Companion basket to Fig. 353. Its only difference is in height; Fig. 353 is slightly taller in the body and overall.

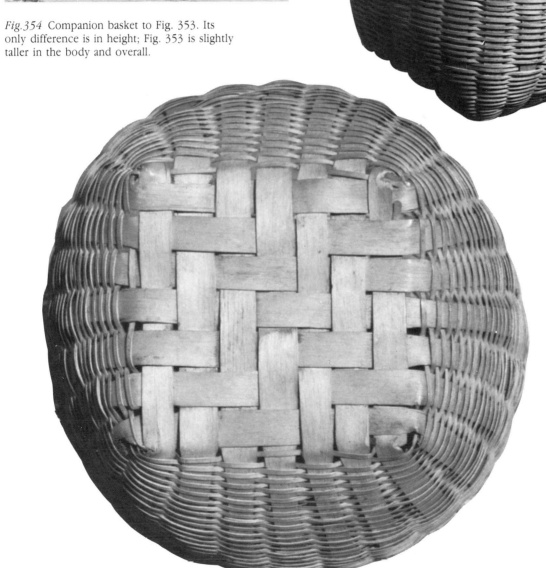

Fig.355 The shape of these first fruit baskets is similar to the shape of Mt. Lebanon's shop baskets of the same era; there is something almost moral in their lines.

Fig.356 Later fruits are less severe. They have a different volume, a fuller line. Control is evident in them, but it doesn't seem so chaste.

Fig.357 Indians also made "free" lids. The handle on this Indian basket is a broad, flexible loop of tightly-wrapped splint attached to the body instead of the rims, to enable the lid to be lifted off. A similar handle occurs in some Shaker work (Figs. 186, 207, 226–28, 239, 346) but it was an imperfect solution which the Shakers didn't condone.

Fig. 358 When the Mt. Lebanon basketmakers
began to make lidded baskets, they borrowed
a captured "feather" lid, which was a common
Indian design (used originally to contain vola-
tile down or feathers in baskets).

Fig.359 The Shakers didn't like just to copy what they felt they could improve on. The feather lid disappears in later work from Mt. Lebanon, replaced by a similar but radically rethought lid: a "captured" quadrifoil.

Fig.360 Because the quadrifoil relieved much of the inefficiency in making a round lid or bottom, the Mt. Lebanon sisters eventually utilized it in every round start—except those done in hexagon weave, which was another idea they developed.

Fig.361 The quadrifoil was emblematic of the Shaker vision of a radiant heavenly sphere; it was a graphic signature. The weave itself was in transition, or translation (a word the Shakers liked), evoking something spiritual. But it was eminently practical, too. Round bottom baskets conventionally required tapered uprights (which were time consuming to prepare) or split uprights (which the Shakers didn't prefer). The quadrifoil used ordinary splint for uprights, the same as weavers, which was a significant benefit in production basketry. Because it began as a square bottom with the uprights spreading to a round, the quadrifoil could additionally be cupped to create feet or ears, or left flat; the uprights beyond the twilling could also be bent downward to form a crown, as was often done when making lids.

The quadrifoil is the embodiment of what made the Shaker system "Shaker." It united system and soul.

210

CHAPTER ONE

Sources cited in text

1. Amelia M. Murray, *Letters from the United States, Cuba and Canada* (New York: G.P. Putnam and Company, 1856), p. 139.

2. E.M. Forster, "Mount Lebanon," *Two Cheers for Democracy* (New York: Harcourt, Brace and Company, 1951), pp. 337–39.

3. William J. Haskett, *Shakerism Unmasked . . .* (Pittsfield: Published by the Author, 1828), p. 223.

4. Edward Deming Andrews and Faith Andrews, *Fruits of the Shaker Tree of Life* (Stockbridge: The Berkshire Traveller Press, 1975), p. 22.

5. Walter A. Dwyer, "The Furniture of the Shakers: A Plea for Its Preservation as Part of Our National Inheritance," *House Beautiful* (May 1929) cited by Flo Morse, *The Shakers and the World's People* (New York: Dodd, Mead and Company, 1980), pp. 270–71.

6. Marguerite Melcher, *The Shaker Adventure* (Princeton: Princeton University Press, 1941; reprint ed., [Cleveland]: Press of Western Reserve University, 1960), pp. 191–92.

7. William Hepworth Dixon, *New America*, 3rd ed. (Philadelphia: J.B. Lippincott and Co., 1867), p. 303.

8. Dwyer, "The Furniture of the Shakers."

Sources cited in notes

1. Wend Fischer, "The functionalism of the Shakers" in [Karl Mang and Wend Fischer], *The Shakers* (Munich: Die Neue Sammlung, 1974), p. 22.

2. Bernard Champigneulle, "Art after the First World War" in *Larousse Encyclopedia of Modern Art* (New York: Prometheus Press, 1965), pp. 293–94.

CHAPTER TWO

Sources cited in text

1. John Kouwenhoven, *Made in America* (Garden City: Doubleday and Company, 1948; reprint ed., *The Arts in Modern American Civilization* (New York: Norton, 1970), pp. 119–20.

2. This and other statements (see Item 6 below and Item 1, Notes to Chapter Three) ascribed variously to Mother Ann and to "the Shakers" have been published in a range of secondary sources. They are taken here from [Mang and Fischer], *The Shakers*, pp. 51–52.

3. "The Covenant of the Church of Christ, in New Lebanon, relating to the Possession and Use of a Joint Interest," Mt. Lebanon, N.Y., 1795. Courtesy, Henry Francis du Pont Winterthur Museum, Winterthur, Delaware, The Edward Deming Andrews Memorial Shaker Collection [hereafter Andrews Shaker Collection, Winterthur], No. SA 742.

4. *The Random House College Dictionary*, rev. ed. (1979), s.v. "economy."

5. Benson J. Lossing, "The Shakers," *Harper's New Monthly Magazine* (July 1857) cited by Flo Morse, *The Shakers and the World's People*, p. 113.

6. [Mang and Fischer], *The Shakers*, p. 51.

7. Henry DeWitt, manuscript journal, Mt. Lebanon, N.Y., 1827–67. Shaker Manuscripts Collection, Western Reserve Historical Society, Cleveland, Ohio.

8. "Millennial Laws" cited by [Mang and Fischer], *The Shakers*, p. 52.

9. Isaac Youngs, "A Concise View of the Church of God and of Christ, on Earth . . . ," Mt. Lebanon, N.Y., 1856–60, p. 236. Andrews Shaker Collection, Winterthur, No. SA 760.

Sources cited in notes

1. Cyrus Bradley, manuscript diary, 1832–37. Manuscripts Collection, New Hampshire Historical Society, Concord, N.H.

2. Sister Jennie Wells, quoted in Berton Roueche, "A Small Family of Seven," *The New Yorker* (Aug. 23, 1947), p. 48.

3. Calvin Green and Seth Y. Wells, *A Brief Exposition of the Established Principles of the United Society of Believers Called Shakers* (New York: Printed by Edward D. Jenkins, 1851), pp. 10–16.

4. Hervey Elkins, *Fifteen Years in the Senior Order of Shakers . . .* (Hanover: Dartmouth Press, 1853), p. 23.

5. "Account of bonnets, baskets etc. made at Watervliet, N.Y.," 1836–57. Papers of the Shakers, Library of Congress, Washington, D.C.

6. Accession Card No. 2249, Western Reserve Historical Society, Cleveland, Ohio. (See Fig. 212)

7. William Dean Howells, "A Shaker Village," *The Atlantic Monthly* (June 1876), p. 705.

8. Daniel W. Patterson, *The Shaker Spiritual* (Princeton: Princeton University Press, 1979), p. 20.

9. *Half-Hull Modeling*, second ed. (Bath, Me.: Apprenticeshop of the Maine Maritime Museum, 1980), p. 23.

10. *The Shaker Manifesto* (August 1882), p. 173. Published at Canterbury, N.H.

11. "Sidney Gage & Co. Baskets," catalogue and pricelist, Bellows Falls, Vt., c. 1900.

12. Ronald Jackson, interview, Center Ossipee, N.H., 1981.

CHAPTER THREE

Sources cited in text

1. Memoranda book kept by John DeWitt, Jr. and by an unidentified sister, Mt. Lebanon, N.Y., 1824–25; 1835–36. Shaker Manuscripts, Western Reserve Historical Society.

2. Attributed to Shaker elder Joseph Meacham, c. 1795; quoted in [Mang and Fischer], *The Shakers*, p. 52.

3. Sister Jennie Wells, quoted in Roueche, "A Small Family of Seven," p. 47.

4. "Diary of a Trip to the White Mountains from Boston," 1834. Manuscripts Collection, N.H. Historical Society.

5. *A Dictionary of American English* (Chicago: University of Chicago, 1938), s.v. "fancy."

6. "Records Kept by Order of the Church, Volume III," Church Family, Mt. Lebanon, N.Y., 1856–71. Courtesy, The Shaker Museum, Old Chatham, N.Y. [hereafter Shaker Museum, Old Chatham], No. 10,342.

7. "Journal of Expenses and Incomes Kept by the Sisters," Church Family, Mt. Lebanon, N.Y., 1864–75. Shaker Manuscripts Collection, Williams College Library, Williamstown, Mass.

8. "Records Kept by Order of the Church, Volume III." Shaker Museum, Old Chatham.

9. Andrew Fortier, manuscript diary, Church Family, Mt. Lebanon, N.Y., 1860–1878. Shaker Museum, Old Chatham, No. 19,213.

10. Youngs, "A Concise View," p. 266. Winterthur.

11. "A Memorandum of Baskets etc Kept by the Basket Makers. Also directions for weaving twilling and proceeding with the work. Recorded from 1855," Mt. Lebanon, N.Y., 1855–75. Andrews Shaker Collection, Winterthur, No. SA 995.

12. A[manda] B. Harris, "Among the Shakers," *Granite Monthly* (April 1877), p. 23.

13. "A Memorandum of Baskets." Winterthur.

14. Ibid.

15. Fortier diary. Shaker Museum, Old Chatham.

16. Elisha Blakeman, "A Daily Journal, or Diary, work. etc. performed by the Boys and their Caretaker; in the First Order, [Church Family], New Lebanon, Columbia Co., N.Y.," 1867–73. Shaker Museum, Old Chatham, No. 7212.

17. Fortier diary. Shaker Museum, Old Chatham.

18. "A Memorandum of Baskets." Winterthur.

19. Benjamin Lyon, "A Journal of Domestic Events Kept by Benjamin Lyon, 18, Begun Dec. 21st, 1838," Mt. Lebanon, N.Y., 1838–78. Andrews Shaker Collection, Winterthur, No. SA 1031.

20. Betsey Bates, manuscript journal, 1833–35. Western Reserve Historical Society.

21. Isaac N. Youngs, "Domestic Journal of Daily Occurrences," Mt. Lebanon, N.Y., 1834–46. Special Collections, New York State Library, Albany.

22. Diary kept by Sisters, Church Family, 1862–75. Shaker Museum, Old Chatham, No. 13,619.

23. Giles Avery, manuscript diary, 1873. Western Reserve Historical Society.

24. Avery, manuscript diary, 1881. Western Reserve Historical Society.

25. Manuscript diary, 1890–92. Western Reserve Historical Society.

26. Fortier diary. Shaker Museum, Old Chatham.

27. Charles Nordhoff, *The Communistic Societies of the United States* (New York: Harper and Brothers, 1875), p. 139.

28. "[Second] Family Record," Hancock, Mass., 1829–71. Andrews Shaker Collection, Winterthur; quoted in June Sprigg, *Shaker Design* (New York: Whitney Museum of American Art, 1986), p. 23.

29. Marguerite Frost to Daniel Patterson, May 25, 1965, p. 3. University of North Carolina, Folklore Archives, "Daniel W. Patterson Collection"; quoted in Patterson, *The Shaker Spiritual*, p. 13.

30. Edward Deming Andrews, *The People Called Shakers* (New York: Oxford University Press, 1953; enlarged ed., New York: Dover Publications, Inc., 1963), p. 152.

31. Patterson, *The Shaker Spiritual*; also, *Gift Drawing and Gift Song* (Sabbathday Lake: The United Society of Shakers, 1983).

32. Youngs, "A Concise View," pp. 132–33. Winterthur.

33. Gift song attributed to Gloucester, Me., 1846; transcribed by Patterson in *The Shaker Spiritual*, p. 325.

34. "A Memorandum of Baskets." Winterthur.

35. Isaac Youngs, manuscript journal, Mt. Lebanon, N.Y., 1856, cited by Andrews, *The People Called Shakers*, pp. 225–26.

36. "Notes by the way, while on a journey to the State of Kentucky in the Year 1873. By Henry C. Blinn, Canterbury, N.H. 1873." Shaker Museum, Old Chatham, No. 12,791.

37. Avery, manuscript diary, 1880. Western Reserve Historical Society.

38. Fortier diary. Shaker Museum, Old Chatham.

39. "Journal," Church Family, Mt. Lebanon, N.Y., 1886–92. Shaker Museum, Old Chatham, No. 8853.

40. "A Journal Kept by the Deaconesses, Church Family, Mount Lebanon, N.Y.," 1893–97. Shaker Museum, Old Chatham, No. 8856.

41. Accession Card No. 10,600, Shaker Museum, Old Chatham, N.Y. Because the basket was "not quite perfect," Mary Dahm asked—when she gave the basket to the museum in 1958—that it not be shown.

Sources cited in notes

1. [Mang and Fischer], *The Shakers*, p. 52.

2. Dixon, *New America*, pp. 304–305.

3. Edward Deming Andrews, *Community Industries of the Shakers* (Albany: University of the State of New York, 1933; reprint ed., Charlestown, Mass.: Emporium Publications, 1971), p. 166.

4. "Records Kept by Order of the Church at New Lebanon, N.Y., Volume IV," 1871–1904. Shaker Museum, Old Chatham, No. 10,343.

5. Youngs, "A Concise View," p. 266. Winterthur.

6. *Berkshire Evening Eagle* (Feb. 11, 1875) quoted in "The Great Fire at Mount Lebanon," *The Peg Board* (New Lebanon, N.Y.: Darrow School, 1936), pp. 53–54.

7. Ibid., p. 55.

8. Ibid.

9. *The Manifesto* (February 1893). Published at Canterbury, N.H.

10. Theodore E. Johnson, "The 'Millennial Laws' of 1821," *The Shaker Quarterly* (Summer 1967), pp. 35–58; "Rules and Orders for the Church of Christ's Second Appearing," *The Shaker Quarterly* (Winter 1971), pp. 139–65.

11. J.S. Buckingham, *America: Historical, Statistic and Descriptive* (London: Fisher, Son and Co., 1841), Vol. II, p. 305.

12. Howells, "A Shaker Village," p. 699.

13. *A Dictionary of American English*, s.v. "shaker."

14. Constance Fenimore Woolson, "Anne," Chapter X, *Harper's New Monthly Magazine* (May 1881), p. 854.

15. "Millennial Laws," 1845; cited in Andrews, *The People Called Shakers*, p. 257.

16. Patterson, *Gift Drawing and Gift Song*, p. 71.

17. Beverly Gordon, *Shaker Textile Arts* (Hanover: University Press of New England, 1980), p. 4.

18. Bates journal. Western Reserve Historical Society.

19. Youngs journal. New York State Library.

20. "Journal of Daily Occurrences," Church Family, Mt. Lebanon, N.Y., 1788–1877; Vol. 1847–55. Western Reserve Historical Society.

21. Ibid.

22. "Journal of Daily Occurrences," Vol. 1856–77. Western Reserve Historical Society.

23. Henry DeWitt journal. Western Reserve Historical Society.

24. Youngs journal. New York State Library.

25. Account of funeral service published with Giles Avery, *Autobiography* (East Canterbury, N.H.: United Societies, 1891).

26. Avery, *Autobiography*.

27. "Journal of Domestic Events Kept by Deaconesses of the Church Second Order," Mt. Lebanon, N.Y. Shaker Museum, Old Chatham.

28. "A Large Square by Father James," undated manuscript, Sabbathday Lake, Me.; cited by Virginia Weiss, "Every Good and Simple Gift," Part I, *The Shaker Quarterly* (Fall 1973), p. 90.

29. Patterson, *Gift Drawing*. Additional drawings are reproduced in Edward Deming Andrews and Faith Andrews, *Visions of the Heavenly Sphere* (Charlottesville: Published for the Henry Francis du Pont Winterthur Museum by the University Press of Virginia, 1969).

30. Patterson, *The Shaker Spiritual*, p. 419.

31. Patterson, *Gift Drawing*, p. 79.

32. Obituary clipping quoted in Patterson, *Gift Drawing*, p. 78.

33. Patterson, *Gift Drawing*, Plate I.

34. Elkins, p. 38.

35. "Journal of Expenses and Incomes." Williams College.

36. "Journal kept by the Deaconesses at the [Church] Office," Mt. Lebanon, N.Y., 1830–71. Andrews Shaker Collection, Winterthur, No. SA 894.3.

37. "A Diary Kept by the Sisters for the year 1883," Harvard, Mass. Special Collections, New York State Library.

CHAPTER FOUR

Sources cited in text

1. Patterson, *The Shaker Spiritual*, p. 325.

2. "Records of the Church at Watervliet, N.Y.," 1788–1851. Western Reserve Historical Society.

3. See, for example, Elmer R. Pearson and Julia Neal, *The Shaker Image* (Boston: New York Graphic Society, 1974), Fig. 50.

4. Edward Deming Andrews, *Shaker Furniture* (New Haven: Yale University Press, 1937), p. 48.

5. Blakeman diary. Shaker Museum, Old Chatham.

6. Seth T. Bradford, "A Diary or Memorandum Kept by Seth T. Bradford Born June 11, 1826 Stockbridge, Winsor, Vt. Mostly while acting in the horticultural line of Employ It having been most 14 yrs. And leave that and become caretaker of boys. Copied and Written Nov. 1850," Enfield, N.H., 1834–49. Private Collection of Viola and Wendell Hess.

7. Chatham (N.Y.) *Courier* (Feb. 16, 1922).

8. Christoph Will, *International Basketry for Weavers and Collectors* (Munich: Georg D.W. Callway, 1978; reprint ed., Exton, Penna.: Schiffer Publishing Ltd., 1985). See, for example, Fig. 281.

9. Ibid., Fig. 407.

Sources cited in notes

1. Henry DeWitt journal. Western Reserve Historical Society.

2. Manuscript journal, 1892. Western Reserve Historical Society.

3. "Millennial Laws," 1845; cited by Andrews, *The People Called Shakers*, pp. 273–74.

4. See June Sprigg, *Shaker*, catalogue of an exhibit at the Katonah Gallery, Katonah, N.Y., Nov. 20, 1983 through Jan. 8, 1984.

CHAPTER FIVE

Sources cited in text

1. "A Memorandum of Baskets." Winterthur.

CHAPTER SIX

Sources cited in text

1. Dixon, *New America*, p. 311.

2. Ropes Family account book, Salem, Mass., [1817]. Courtesy, Ropes Mansion, Salem, Mass.

3. Youngs, "A Concise View," p. 266. Winterthur.

Sources cited in captions

1. Joseph Meacham, *A Concise Statement of the Principles of the Only True Church of Christ . . .* (Bennington: Haswell and Russell, 1790; reprinted 1847), p. 9.

2. Edward Deming Andrews, *The Gift to be Simple* (New York: J.J. Augustin, 1940; reprint ed., New York: Dover Publications, Inc., 1962), p. 103.

3. Robley E. Whitson (ed.), *The Shakers: Two Centuries of Spiritual Reflection* (New York: Paulist Press, 1983), pp. 1, 43.

4. Artemus Ward [Charles Farrar Browne], *His Book* (New York: Carleton, 1862), pp. 31–33. Published originally as "The Shakers" in *Vanity Fair* (Feb. 23, 1861).

5. *New Hampshire Sunday News* (Feb. 22, 1981), pp. 1B, 9B.

6. Roueche, "A Small Family of Seven," pp. 42–43.

7. J.P. Maclean, *Shakers of Ohio* (1907) quoted in Flo Morse, *The Shakers and the World's People*, p. 112.

8. [Amanda] Harris, "Among the Shakers," *Granite Monthly* (April 1877), p. 21.

9. Bradley diary. N.H. Historical Society.

10. Youngs, "A Concise View," p. 236. Winterthur.

11. *Nile's Weekly Register* (1821) quoted in Edward Deming Andrews and Faith Andrews, *Work and Worship* (Greenwich: New York Graphic Society, 1974; reprint ed., New York: Dover Publications, Inc., 1982), p. 153.

12. Isaac Youngs, "Narrative of Various Events," Mt. Lebanon, N.Y., 1815–23. Papers of the Shakers, Library of Congress.

13. Henry DeWitt journal. Western Reserve Historical Society.

14. Blakeman diary. Shaker Museum, Old Chatham.

15. Blinn diary. Shaker Museum, Old Chatham.

16. Blakeman diary. Shaker Museum, Old Chatham.

17. [Mang and Fischer], *The Shakers*, p. 52.

18. *Columbia Hall, Lebanon Springs, N.Y.* (1902), advertising brochure quoted in Cynthia Rubin, "Shaker Industries," *The Clarion* (Fall 1979) published by the Museum of American Folk Art, p. 54.

19. "Sketches Among the Shakers," *The Illustrated News* (Oct. 29, 1853).

20. "Editor's Easy Chair," *Harper's* (April 1860), p. 701.

21. Sister Jennie Wells, quoted by Roueche, "A Small Family of Seven," p. 45.

22. "Journal Kept by the Deaconesses at the [Church] Office." Winterthur.

23. Blakeman diary. Shaker Museum, Old Chatham.

24. "A Memorandum of Baskets." Winterthur.

25. "Journal of Daily Occurrences," Vol. 1847–55. Western Reserve Historical Society.

26. Andrews, *The People Called Shakers*, p. 254.

27. Youngs, "Narrative of Various Events"; quoted by Patterson, *The Shaker Spiritual*, p. 261.

28. Andrews, *Shaker Furniture*, p. 17.

29. "Journal Kept by the Deaconesses." Winterthur.

30. Exhibit files, "Blessed in our Basket," Shaker Village, Inc., Canterbury, N.H., 1985.

31. Avery, manuscript diary, 1873. Western Reserve Historical Society.

32. Fortier diary. Shaker Museum, Old Chatham.

33. Historical and Anthropological Services, New York State Museum, Albany.

34. For more information about Boler's trips "home," see: Bro. Thomas Whitaker, "Daniel Boler: Mt. Lebanon and South Union," *Shaker Messenger* (Spring 1987), p. 11.

Figure sources and credits

1. Herb room, Hancock Shaker Village, Pittsfield, Massachusetts. Photograph by Nathan Taylor.

2. Baskets made at the Martha Wetherbee Basket Shop. Photograph by James Kittle at the Basket Shop, Sanbornton, New Hampshire.

3. Photograph by William F. Winter, published as Plate 13 in Edward Deming Andrews, *Shaker Furniture,* 1937.

4. Photograph by Armin Landeck, n.d. Courtesy, Henry Francis du Pont Winterthur Museum, The Edward Deming Andrews Memorial Shaker Collection, Winterthur, Delaware.

5. "The March: Shaker Worship, Lebanon," Aug. 16, 1856, watercolor by Benson J. Lossing. Courtesy, Henry E. Huntington Library, San Marino, California.

6. "The Whirling Gift," woodcut published in David R. Lamson, *Two Years' Experience Among the Shakers,* 1848.

7. Shaker gift drawing, "Mother Ann's Word to her little child Elizabeth Cantrell," Aug. 14, 1848. Courtesy, Hancock Shaker Village, Inc.

8. Arthur Corliss, basketmaker, at Sandwich, N.H., c. 1940. Courtesy, League of New Hampshire Craftsmen, Concord, New Hampshire.

9. Black ash swamp. Photograph by Martha Wetherbee.

10. Photograph by Bill Finney at Martha Wetherbee Basket Shop, Sanbornton, N.H.

11. Photograph by Richard Starr at Martha Wetherbee Basket Shop.

12. Wetherbee/Taylor Collection. Photograph by Martha Wetherbee.

13. Wetherbee/Taylor Collection. Photograph by Martha Wetherbee.

14. K. Scott Collection. Photograph by Martha Wetherbee.

15. Wetherbee/Taylor Collection. Photograph by Martha Wetherbee.

16. Wetherbee/Taylor Collection. Photograph by Nathan Taylor

17. Private Collection. Photograph by Martha Wetherbee.

18. Private Collection. Photograph by Martha Wetherbee.

19. Private Collection. Photograph by Martha Wetherbee.

20. K. Scott Collection. Photograph by Martha Wetherbee.

21. Same

22. Private Collection. Photograph by Martha Wetherbee.

23. Wetherbee/Taylor Collection. Photograph by Nathan Taylor. L 12½" W 8½" H 6¼" OH 7⅛"

24. Collection of Jeanne d'Arc Rheault. Photograph courtesy of Bob Raiche.

25. Same

28. Arthur Corliss, c. 1940. Courtesy, League of N.H. Craftsmen.

29. Private Collection. Photograph by Martha Wetherbee.

30. Wetherbee/Taylor Collection. Photograph by Nathan Taylor.

31. Private Collection. Photograph by Martha Wetherbee.

32. Lee Diamond Collection. Photograph by Nathan Taylor.

33. Wetherbee/Taylor Collection. Photograph by Martha Wetherbee.

34. Private Collection. Photograph by Martha Wetherbee. D 15" H 9" OH 16"

35. Private Collection. Photograph by Martha Wetherbee.

36. Warna Brickner Collection. Photography by Martha Wetherbee.

37. Wetherbee/Taylor Collection. Photograph by John Adams. D 7⅝" H 6¼" OH 8¾"

38. Photograph by Chansonetta Stanley Emmons at Kingfield, Maine, c. 1901. Courtesy, Marius Peladeau.

39. Shaker brother Daniel Crosman, Church Family, Mt. Lebanon, New York, c. 1860. Courtesy, Charles "Bud" Thompson.

40. Detail of Shaker gift drawing (see Fig. 169). Courtesy, Hancock Shaker Village, Inc.

40a. Detail, Shaker basket label (see Fig. 299). Collection of Robert Wilkins and Suzanne Courcier. Photograph by Hugh McMillan 3rd.

41. Photograph, Church Family, n.d. Archives, Shaker Village, Inc. Canterbury, N.H.

41a. Joshua H. Bussell, "A Plan of Alfred Maine," 1845. Library of Congress.

42. From the collections of The Shaker Museum, Old Chatham, N.Y. Photograph by Nathan Taylor. D 30" OH 23"

43. Photograph, Chair Shop, Mt. Lebanon, N.Y., c. 1930. Courtesy, New York State Museum, Albany, N.Y.

44. From the collections of Hancock Shaker Village. Photograph by Nathan Taylor.

45. From the collections of The Shaker Museum, Old Chatham. Photograph by Nathan Taylor.

46. From the collections of The Shaker Museum, Old Chatham. Photograph by Nathan Taylor.

47. Basket at top from the collections of the New York State Museum. Basket at bottom from the Wetherbee/Taylor Collection. Photograph by Hugh McMillan 3rd. Both baskets: L 22" W 22½" H 13" OH 15½"

48. Ironing room, Mt. Lebanon, N.Y. Photograph by J.E. West, c. 1875. Courtesy, Hancock Shaker Village, Inc.

49. From the collections of Hancock Shaker Village. Photograph by Nathan Taylor.

50. Sewing room, Mt. Lebanon, N.Y. Photograph by J.E. West, c. 1875. Archives, Shaker Village, Inc., Canterbury, N.H.

51. Courtesy, New York State Museum.

52. Photograph by Bill Finney at Martha Wetherbee Basket Shop.

53. Wetherbee/Taylor Collection. Photograph by Nathan Taylor.

54. Same

55. From the collections of Hancock Shaker Village. Photograph by Hugh McMillan 3rd.

56. Wetherbee/Taylor Collection. Photograph by Nathan Taylor

57. Private collection.

58. Photograph by Martha Wetherbee at Martha Wetherbee Basket Shop.

59. Photograph by Bill Finney at Martha Wetherbee Basket Shop.

60. From the collections of Hancock Shaker Village. Photograph by Hugh McMillan 3rd.

61. From the collections of Hancock Shaker Village. Photograph by Hugh McMillan 3rd. L 18½" W 10" OH 17⅛"

62. Ed Clerk Collection. Photograph by Hugh McMillan 3rd.

63. From the collections of The Shaker Museum, Old Chatham. Photograph by Nathan Taylor.

64. Wetherbee/Taylor Collection. Photograph by Martha Wetherbee.

65. Same

66. Private Collection. Photograph by Martha Wetherbee.

67. Wetherbee/Taylor Collection. Photograph by Martha Wetherbee.

68. Same

69. From the collections of Hancock Shaker Village. Photograph by Hugh McMillan 3rd.

70. Same

71. Same

72. From the collections of The Shaker Museum, Old Chatham. Photograph by Hugh McMillan 3rd. L 22½" W 18¾" H 9½" OH 18"

73. From the collections of the New York State Museum. Photograph by Hugh McMillan 3rd. L 22½" W 19" H 8" OH 15"

74. From the collections of Hancock Shaker Village. Photograph by Hugh McMillan 3rd. L 26½" W 14¼" H 8½" OH 16"

75. From the collections of The Shaker Museum, Old Chatham. Photograph by Hugh McMillan 3rd. L 21½" W 16" H 8½" OH 16"

76. View of bottom. Photograph by Paul Rocheleau.

77. From the collections of Hancock Shaker Village. Photograph by Nathan Taylor.

215

78. Same

79. Mt. Lebanon carrier and apple basket. From the collections of The Shaker Museum, Old Chatham. Photograph by Paul Rocheleau.

80. From the collections of Hancock Shaker Village. Photograph by Hugh McMillan 3rd. Top right: D 13″ H 8″ OH 14⅝″; bottom center: D 14½″ H 9″ OH 15″

81. Same

82. Private Collection. Photograph by Hugh McMillan 3rd. D 14½″ H 9″ OH 15″

83. Same

84. Same

85. From the collections of Hancock Shaker Village. Photograph by Hugh McMillan 3rd. Top: D 14¼″ OH 6¼″; bottom: D 15″ H 9″ OH 16″

86. From the collections of the New York State Museum. Photograph by Hugh McMillan 3rd. D 21″ H 12″ OH 14″

87. Bernice Hunter Collection. Photograph by Peter Britton.

88. From the collections of Hancock Shaker Village. Photograph by Hugh McMillan 3rd.

89. From the collections of the New York State Museum. Photograph by Hugh McMillan 3rd. D 13¾″ H 9″ OH 17½″

90. Wetherbee/Taylor Collection. Photograph by Hugh McMillan 3rd.

91. Same

92. From the collections of Hancock Shaker Village. Photograph by Nathan Taylor.

93. From the collections of Hancock Shaker Village. Photograph by Hugh McMillan 3rd.

94. From the collections of Hancock Shaker Village. Photograph by Nathan Taylor.

95. From the collections of The Shaker Museum, Old Cahtnam. Photograph by Hugh McMillan 3rd. D 26½″ H 8½″

96. From the collections of Hancock Shaker Village. Photograph by Hugh McMillan 3rd.

97. Ed Clerk Collection. Photograph by Hugh McMillan 3rd. L 22″ W 15½″ H 10½″ OH 17½″

98. Wetherbee/Taylor Collection. Photograph by Paul Rocheleau. L 17″ W 13″ H 9¾″ OH 12½″

99. Ed Clerk Collection. Photograph by Hugh McMillan 3rd. L 21¾″ W 17¼″ H 9¾″ OH 11½″

100. Wetherbee/Taylor Collection. Photograph by Martha Wetherbee. L 15″ W 12″ H 8¼″ OH 12¼″

101. "Brethren's Retiring Room," engraving from *Frank Leslie's Popular Monthly*, December 1885.

102. Nellie Ptaszek Collection. Photograph by Peter Blakely.

103. From the collections of Shaker Village, Inc., Canterbury, N.H. Photograph by Todd Smith. L 16½″ W 21″ H 10¾″ OH 16″

104. Same

105. From the collections of Shaker Village, Inc., Canterbury, N.H. Photograph by Todd Smith. L 18″ (bottom) 17½″ (top) W 13″ (bottom) 12″ (top) H 10¾″ OH 16″

106. Same

107. From the collections of Shaker Village, Inc., Canterbury, N.H. Photograph by Todd Smith. L 21¼″ W 16¼″ H 10¾″ OH 17″

108. Same

109. From the collections of Shaker Village, Inc., Canterbury, N.H. Photograph by Todd Smith. L 21½″ W 15″ H 11″ OH 13½″

110. Same

111. From the collections of Shaker Village, Inc., Canterbury, N.H. Photograph by Todd Smith. L 20″ W 15″ H 10½″, OH 17¼″

112. Same

113. Shaker sisters making dusters, c. 1920. Archives, Shaker Village, Inc., Canterbury, N.H.

114. Photograph by Nathan Taylor.

115. From the collections of Shaker Village, Inc. Photograph by Paul Rocheleau.

116. From the collections of Hancock Shaker Village. Photograph by Hugh McMillan 3rd. Upper: D 13¾″ H 9¾″ OH 14½″; lower: D 17⅛″ H 12½″ OH 14½″

117. View of bottom (basket with overhead handle). Photograph by Hugh McMillan 3rd.

118. Handle detail. Photograph by Hugh McMillan 3rd.

119. From the collections of United Society of Shakers, Sabbathday Lake, Me. Photograph by Nathan Taylor.

120. Same

121. Private collection. Photograph by Nathan Taylor. D 15″ H 7″

122. From the collections of Shaker Village, Inc., Canterbury, N.H. Photograph by Todd Smith. D 22½″ H 8¼″ OH 10″

123. Wetherbee/Taylor Collection. Photograph by Nathan Taylor.

124. Archives, Shaker Village, Inc., Canterbury, N.H.

125. -128. Same

129. From the collections of Shaker Village, Inc., Canterbury, N.H. Photograph by Todd Smith.

130. Detail from Shaker gift drawing, "A Present for Holy Mother to Brother John C. Brot by her little Dove," 1848. Courtesy, Western Reserve Historical Society.

131. From the collections of United Society of Shakers, Sabbathday Lake, Me. Photograph by Nathan Taylor.

132. -135. Same

136. From the collections of Hancock Shaker Village. Photograph by Nathan Taylor.

137. Archives, Shaker Village, Inc., Canterbury, N.H.

138. From the collections of United Society of Shakers, Sabbathday Lake, Me. Photograph by Nathan Taylor.

139. -141. Same

142. Photograph by Chansonetta Stanley Emmons at Kingsfield, Me., c. 1901. Courtesy, Marius Peladeau.

143. Peterboro Basket Co., c. 1900. Courtesy, Peterborough Historical Society, Peterborough, N.H.

144. Same

145. Same

146. Photograph published in Manchester (N.H.) *Union Leader*, n.d.

147. Pricelist, Peterboro Basket Co. Wetherbee/Taylor Collection.

148. Pricelist, Sidney Gage & Co. Wetherbee/Taylor Collection.

149. Same

150. Same

151. Needham Basket Co. Courtesy, Peterborough (N.H.) Historical Society.

152. Same

153. Same

154. Church Family store, Mt. Lebanon, N.Y., c. 1875. Courtesy, Charles "Bud" Thompson.

155a. Church Family store, Mt. Lebanon, N.Y., c. 1875. Private collection.

155b. Postcard, n.d. Private collection.

155c. *Ladies' Home Journal*, December 1908. Courtesy, Gloria Lynch.

156. View of commercial square, Bristol, N.H., late 19th century. Courtesy, Bristol (N.H.) Historical Society.

157. Wetherbee/Taylor Collection. Photograph by Martha Wetherbee.

158. Pricelist, Church Family Shakers, Mt. Lebanon, N.Y., n.d. Private collection.

159. Photograph, c. 1920. Private collection.

160. Photograph, Mt. Lebanon (N.Y.) Shakers, n.d. Private collection.

161. Photograph, Church Family, Mt. Lebanon, N.Y., n.d. Private collection.

162. Sample entry, "A Memorandum of Baskets . . . ," 1855–75. Courtesy, Henry Francis du Pont Winterthur Museum, The Edward Deming Andrews Memorial Shaker Collection, No. SA 995.

163. Photograph, Church Family, Mt. Lebanon, N.Y., n.d. Private collection.

164. Henry C. Blinn, "View of N. Lebanon Columbia County, N.Y." (detail), 1842–48. Courtesy, The Sherman Collection.

165. Shaker gift drawing, "A Heart of Blessing for Daniel Boler," 1844. Courtesy, Western Reserve Historical Society.

166. Shaker gift drawing, "A word of comfort from Holy Mother to Daniel Boler," 1846. Courtesy, Western Reserve Historical Society.

167. "Circular March," Mt. Lebanon, N.Y., from *Frank Leslie's Popular Monthly,* December 1885.

168. Instructions for a Shaker march, 1858. Courtesy, Henry Francis du Pont Winterthur Museum, The Edward Deming Andrews Memorial Shaker Collection, No. SA 1328.

169. Shaker gift drawing, "An Emblem of the Heavenly Sphere," 1854. Courtesy, Hancock Shaker Village.

170. Wetherbee/Taylor Collection. Photograph by Hugh McMillan 3rd.

171. Photograph by Sandy May for Land's End Direct Merchants, Dodgeville, Wisconsin, "Martha Wetherbee and the (almost) lost art of the Shaker Basket," February 1988.

172. From the collections of the New York State Museum. Photograph by Martha Wetherbee.

173. From the collections of The Shaker Museum, Old Chatham. Photograph by Nathan Taylor.

174. Detail of Fig. 179.

175. From the collections of The Shaker Museum, Old Chatham. Photograph by Nathan Taylor.

176. Entry, "A Memorandum of Baskets...." Courtesy, Henry Francis du Pont Winterthur Museum, The Edward Deming Andrews Memorial Shaker Collection, No. SA 995.

177. From the collections of Fruitlands Museum, Harvard, Mass. Photograph by Nathan Taylor. D 9½″ H 5½″ OH 11″

178. Fruit basket. Ed Clerk Collection. Photograph by Hugh McMillan 3rd.

179. Ed Clerk Collection. Photograph by Hugh McMillan 3rd. D 8¾″ H 5¼″ OH 11″

180. Portrait of Anna White, church family, Mt. Lebanon, N.Y., nd. Photograph by J. West. Courtesy of The Shaker Museum, Old Chatham.

181. From the collections of the New York State Museum. Photograph by Hugh McMillan 3rd. D 8¾″ H 5½″; inscribed in pencil "#1 Fruit"

182. From the collections of the New York State Museum. Photograph by Hugh McMillan 3rd. D 9″ H 7″

183. Wetherbee/Taylor Collection. Photograph by Martha Wetherbee. D 9½″ H 5½″ OH 10″

184. Private Collection. Photograph by Martha Wetherbee at Willis Henry Auction. D 3½″ H 2¼″ OH 3¾″

185. Private Collection. Photograph by Martha Wetherbee.

186. Courtesy, Henry Francis du Pont Winterthur Museum, 70.203, Gift of Mrs. Edward Deming Andrews.

187. Frederick and Anne Tolman Collection. Photograph by Nathan Taylor.

188. Detail, Fig. 187.

189. From the collections of the New York State Museum. Photograph by Hugh McMillan 3rd. From the left: D 4⅞″ H 4″; D 4″ H 3″; D 2¾″ H 2⅛″; D 2½″ H 1¼″; D 1⅞″ H 1½″

190. Frederick and Anne Tolman Collection. Photograph by Nathan Taylor.

191. Ed Clerk Collection. Photograph by Hugh McMillan 3rd. L 6½″ W 3½″ H 2⅜″ OH 5¼″

192. From the collections of United Society of Shakers, Sabbathday Lake, Me. Photograph by Nathan Taylor.

193. Detail, Fig. 192.

194. From the collections of The Shaker Museum, Old Chatham. Photograph by Nathan Taylor.

195. Courtesy, New Hampshire Historical Society, Concord, N.H.

196. Wetherbee/Taylor Collection. Photograph by Nathan Taylor. L 8″ W 5″ H 3⅛″ OH 6½″

197. From the collections of the New York State Museum. Photograph by Hugh McMillan 3rd. From upper left: L 14⅛″ W 7″ II 6″ OH 11½″; L 14″ W 6¾″ H 5½″; L 11¾″ W 5½″ H 5¾″; L 9¾″ W 2¾″ H 3⅝″; L 8¾″ W 3¾″ H 3¾″ marked "#3 Knife"; L 8½″ W 3⅝″ H 4¼″

198. "Finish Shop, Labelling," Aug. 18, 1856, watercolor by Benson J. Lossing. Courtesy, Henry E. Huntington Library.

199. From the collections of the New York State Museum. Photograph by Hugh McMillan 3rd. L 11″ W 7½″ H 5¼″ OH 10¼″

200. Nellie Ptaszek Collection. Photograph by Peter Blakely.

201. Detail, Fig. 200.

202. Private Collection. Photograph by Nathan Taylor.

203. From the collections of the New York State Museum. Photograph by Hugh McMillan 3rd. L 18″ W 10½″ H 6″ OH 11½″

204. Detail, Fig. 203.

205. From the collections of the New York State Museum. Photograph by Hugh McMillan 3rd. L 20½″ W 15″ H 8″ OH 16″

206. Courtesy, Marius Peladeau.

207. Wetherbee/Taylor Collection. Photograph by Martha Wetherbee. L 7¾″ W 2⅞″ H 4″ OH 4¼″

208. Wetherbee/Taylor Collection. Photograph by Martha Wetherbee. L 5″ W 2¼″ OH 2½″

209. Wetherbee/Taylor Collection. Photograph by Martha Wetherbee. L 6″ W 3″ H 3″ OH 3½″

210. From the collections of Fruitlands Museum. Photograph by Nathan Taylor.

211. From the collections of Western Reserve Historical Society. Photograph by Martha Wetherbee. D 5″ H 2¾″ OH 3″

212. Accession card, Western Reserve Historical Society.

213. Wetherbee/Taylor Collection. Photograph by Martha Wetherbee. D 4⅛″ H 1½″ OH 2¼″

214. Detail, Fig. 211.

215. From the Fruitlands Museum. Photograph by Nathan Taylor. D 9½″ H 3″

216. From the collections of Fruitlands Museum. Photograph by Nathan Taylor.

217. From the collections of The Shaker Museum, Old Chatham. Photograph by Nathan Taylor.

218. From the collections of the New York State Museum. Photograph by Hugh McMillan 3rd. D 3½″ H (basket) 1″

219. Same

220. Photograph, n.d. Courtesy, New York State Museum.

221. From the collections of The Shaker Museum, Old Chatham. Photograph by Nathan Taylor.

222. Same

223. Same D 3⅝″ OH 3″

224. Wetherbee/Taylor Collection. Photograph by Nathan Taylor. D 6¼″ H 4″ OH 4⅛″

225. Same

226. Photograph, 1886. Courtesy, New York State Museum.

227. From the collections of the New York State Museum. Photograph by Hugh McMillan 3rd. D 4¾″ H 4¾″ OH 6″

228. Same

229. Same

230. From the collections of Shakertown at Pleasant Hill, Kentucky. Photograph by Linda Butler. D 10″ OH 4¼″

231. From the collections of Hancock Shaker Village. Photograph by Hugh McMillan 3rd. L 4″ W 2″ OH 1⅝″ (basket)

232. Bargar Collection. Photograph by Nathan Taylor. D 8⅛″ H 2¾″ OH 3½″

233. From the collections of The Shaker Museum, Old Chatham. Photograph by Nathan Taylor. D ⅞″ H ¾″

234. Private Collection. Photograph by Nathan Taylor, courtesy of Willis Henry Auctions, Inc. Left: D 2¼″ H 1″; right: D 3½″ H 1¼″ OH 3¾″

235. Wetherbee/Taylor Collection. Photograph by Nathan Taylor. W 2″ H 2″

236. Wetherbee/Taylor Collection. Photograph by Nathan Taylor. D 2½″ OH 2½″

237. Wetherbee/Taylor Collection. Photograph by Nathan Taylor. D 2″ H 1⅞″

238. Wetherbee/Taylor Collection. Photograph by Nathan Taylor. D 2¾" OH 2⅛"

239. Wetherbee/Taylor Collection. Photograph by John Adams. Poplar box: L 6¼" W 3¼" H 3" OH 7"; splint furnishing basket: D 2¾" H 1¼"

240. Invoice from Church Family Store at Mt. Lebanon, N.Y. to Church Family Store at Canterbury, N.H., 1874. Courtesy, Miller Collection.

241. Wetherbee/Taylor Collection. Photograph by Todd Smith. D 4⁵/₁₆" H 3" OH 5"

242. Detail, Fig. 241. Photograph by Todd Smith.

243. Same

244. Same

245. Private Collection. Photograph by Nathan Taylor. D 2¾" OH 3½"

246. From the collections of The Shaker Museum, Old Chatham. Photograph by Nathan Taylor.

247. Detail, Fig. 244.

248. Ed Clerk Collection. Photograph by Hugh McMillan 3rd. L 12" W 9" H 4¼" OH 9¼"

249. Dabrowski Collection. Photograph by Hugh McMillan 3rd. L 15" W 9" H 6½" OH 11"

250. From the collections of United Society of Shakers, Sabbathday Lake, Me. Photograph by Martha Wetherbee. L 15" W 9" H 6½" OH 11"

251. From the collections of The Shaker Museum, Old Chatham. Photograph by Nathan Taylor. L 14½" W 12¼" OH 7"

252. Photograph, c. 1900. Wetherbee/Taylor Collection.

253. From the collections of United Society of Shakers, Sabbathday Lake, Me. Photograph by Nathan Taylor.

253a. Photograph, c. 1925. Courtesy, United Society of Shakers, Sabbathday Lake, Me.

254. From the collections of United Society of Shakers, Sabbathday Lake, Me. L 7¾" W 5½" H 2¾" OH 5⅞"

255. From the collections of United Society of Shakers, Sabbathday Lake, Me. Photograph by Nathan Taylor. D 2" H 1¼"

256. Same

257. From the collections of United Society of Shakers, Sabbathday Lake, Me. Photograph by Nathan Taylor. D 5" H 2" OH 2¾"

258. Same

259. From the collections of United Society of Shakers, Sabbathday Lake, Me. Photograph by Nathan Taylor. D 3¾" H 2" OH 2¼"

260. From the collections of United Society of Shakers, Sabbathday Lake, Me. Photograph by Nathan Taylor.

261. From the collections of United Society of Shakers, Sabbathday Lake, Me. Photograph by Nathan Taylor. D 4¾" OH 2½"

262. Detail, Fig. 261.

263. Courtesy, Henry Francis du Pont Winterthur Museum, The Edward Deming Andrews Memorial Shaker Collection, SA 1427.

264. Photograph published in *The Peg Board* (Darrow School), 1936.

265. Advertisement published in *The Peg Board,* 1936.

266. Masthead from *The Peg Board,* 1936.

267. Courtesy, Henry Francis du Pont Winterthur Museum, The Edward Deming Andrews Memorial Shaker Collection, SA 474.

268. From the collections of The Shaker Museum, Old Chatham. Photograph by Nathan Taylor. Right rear: L 4½" W 3" H 1¾"; left rear: L 6¼" W 4¹/₁₆" H 2½"

269. From the collections of Hancock Shaker Village. Photograph by Hugh McMillan 3rd.

270. From the collections of the New York State Museum. Photograph by Hugh McMillan 3rd. L 17½" W 15½" H 9½" OH 15½"

271. Same

272. From the collections of the New York State Museum. Photograph by Hugh McMillan 3rd. Left: L 22½" W 20" H 9" OH 11"; right: L 28" W 20½" H 9½" OH 11"

273. View of bottom (basket at left).

274. From the collections of Shakertown at South Union, Ky. Photograph by Martha Wetherbee. Carrier, far right: L 19" W 15" H 8½" OH 10"

275. From the collections of Shakertown at South Union, Ky. Photograph by Martha Wetherbee. L 14" W 10" H 6½" OH 11"

276. Charles "Bud" Thompson Collection. Photograph by Martha Wetherbee. D 8" H 6" OH 10"

277. -279. Same

280. From the collections of the New York State Museum. Photograph by Hugh McMillan 3rd. L 11½" W 8¼" H 5¼" OH 8½"

281. From the collections of the Western Reserve Historical Society. Photograph by Nathan Taylor. Left: L 6¾" W 4½" H 4"; right: L 14" W 8" H 5¾" OH 6⅜"

282. Detail, similar basket in private collection. Photograph by Nathan Taylor.

283. Wetherbee/Taylor Collection. Photograph by Steve Grivois. D 13¾" H 6¼" OH 7¼"

284. Same

285. Wetherbee/Taylor Collection. Photograph by Nathan Taylor. D 20½" H 14¾" OH 17"

286. Same

287. Archives, Shaker Village, Inc., Canterbury, N.H.

288. Laundry, Canterbury Shaker Village. Photograph by Todd Smith.

289. Wetherbee/Taylor Collection. Photograph by Martha Wetherbee. D 12¼" H 8½" OH 13½"

290. Same

291. Mt. Lebanon carrier in private collection. Photograph by Nathan Taylor.

292. Canterbury chip basket, Wetherbee/Taylor Collection. Photograph by Martha Wetherbee.

293. Canterbury carrier, Frost Collection. Photograph by Martha Wetherbee. L 18½" W 15½" H 10¾" OH 18½"

294. Canterbury round bottom from the collections of The Shaker Museum, Old Chatham. Photograph by Nathan Taylor. D 20⅛" H 11" OH 13⅝"

295. New York State Museum. Photograph by Hugh McMillan 3rd.

296. Maine Shaker round bottom from the collections of United Society of Shakers, Sabbathday Lake, Me. Photograph by Nathan Taylor.

297. Mt. Lebanon shop basket from the collections of The Shaker Museum, Old Chatham. Photograph by Nathan Taylor. L 22½" W 23¼" H 11¼"

298. Mt. Lebanon carrier from the collections of The Shaker Museum, Old Chatham. Photograph by Hugh McMillan 3rd.

299. Handle detail, Canterbury chip basket, Wilkins and Courcier Collection. Photograph by Hugh McMillan 3rd.

300. Mt. Lebanon carrier with date "1838" incised in handle, from the collections of Fruitlands Museum. Photograph by Nathan Taylor.

301. Mt. Lebanon apple basket dated "1858," from the collections of Hancock Shaker Village. Photograph by Hugh McMillan 3rd.

302. Detail, Mt. Lebanon apple basket (see Fig. 313).

303. Nellie Ptaszek Collection. Photograph by Peter Blakely.

304. Detail, Taghkanic swing handle. Private collection. Photograph by Peter Blakely.

305. Taghkanic square-to-round swing handle baskets, Nellie Ptaszek Collection. Photograph by Peter Blakely.

306. Taghkanic fruit baskets, Nellie Ptaszek Collection. Photograph by Peter Blakely.

307. From the collections of The Shaker Museum, Old Chatham. Photograph by Nathan Taylor.

308. German willow hampers, Nellie Ptaszek Collection. Photograph by Peter Blakely.

309. White willow hamper, made by Rachel Nash Law, c. 1980. Courtesy of the artist.

310. Photograph, late 19th century, Mt. Lebanon, N.Y. Private collection.

311. German straw basket, 19th century. Courtesy, Willis Henry Auctions, Inc.

312. Knife basket, Bill Allen Collection. Photograph by Nathan Taylor.

313. Mt. Lebanon apple basket, Wetherbee/Taylor Collection. Photograph by Nathan Taylor.

314. Mt. Lebanon apple basket, Wetherbee/Taylor Collection. Photograph by Nathan Taylor.

315. Mt. Lebanon carrier, Nellie Ptaszek Collection. Photograph by Peter Blakely.

316. Mt. Lebanon box basket, lid detail, Wetherbee/Taylor Collection. Photograph by Peter Blakely.

317. Courtesy, Marius Peladeau.

318. Wetherbee/Taylor Collection. Photograph by Nathan Taylor.

319. Mt. Lebanon fruit basket, Wetherbee/Taylor Collection. Photograph by Nathan Taylor.

320. Same

321. Canterbury round bottom, Wetherbee/Taylor Collection. Photograph by Nathan Taylor.

322. Mt. Lebanon fruit basket, Wetherbee/Taylor Collection. Photograph by Nathan Taylor.

323. Same

324. Same

325. Mt. Lebanon fruit basket (detail of Fig. 348), Wetherbee/Taylor Collection. Photograph by Nathan Taylor.

326. Mt. Lebanon knife basket. Bargar Collection. Photograph by Nathan Taylor.

326a. Detail of Fig. 326.

327. Maine Shaker round bottom, Miller Collection. Photograph by Martha Wetherbee.

328. Mt. Lebanon fruit basket, Wetherbee/Taylor Collection. Photograph by Steve Grivois. D 11″ H 6⅛″ OH 12″

329. Mt. Lebanon tub, Wetherbee/Taylor Collection. Photograph by Nathan Taylor.

330. Mt. Lebanon-influenced round bottom. Courtesy, Hood Museum of Art, Dartmouth College, Hanover, N.H. D 2½″ H 1¾″ OH 3¹/₁₆″

331. Same

332. Lid, Mt. Lebanon knife basket, from the collections of the New York State Museum. Photograph by Hugh McMillan 3rd.

333. Private collection. Photograph by Nathan Taylor.

334. Ball basket, Wetherbee/Taylor Collection. Photograph by Hugh McMillan 3rd.

335. Detail, Fig. 260.

336. Mt. Lebanon knife basket, Wetherbee/Taylor Collection. Photograph by Martha Wetherbee.

337. Canterbury carrier, Wetherbee/Taylor Collection. Photograph by Martha Wetherbee.

338. Photograph by Bill Finney at Martha Wetherbee Basket Shop.

339. Canterbury chip basket, Wetherbee/Taylor Collection. Photograph by Nathan Taylor.

340. Alfred fancy basket, from the collections of United Society of Shakers, Sabbathday Lake, Me. Photograph by Nathan Taylor. D 3¾″ H 2″

341. Same

342. Same

343. Canterbury cat head, Wetherbee/Taylor Collection. Photograph by Todd Smith.

344. Mt. Lebanon apple basket, Wetherbee/Taylor Collection. Photograph by Martha Wetherbee.

345. Alfred fancy basket, from the collections of United Society of Shakers, Sabbathday Lake, Me. Photograph by Nathan Taylor.

346. Poplar drawer box, Wetherbee/Taylor Collection. Photograph by Martha Wetherbee.

347. Church Family sister, Mt. Lebanon, N.Y., with sale baskets, late 19th century. Courtesy, Fruitlands Museum, Clara Endicott Sears Collection.

348. Wetherbee/Taylor Collection (ex. Andrews Collection). Photographs by Nathan Taylor. D 7¼″ H 6⅛″ OH 10¾″

349. From the collections of the Essex Institute, Salem, Mass. Photographs by Nathan Taylor. D 7½″ H 6″ OH 10″

350. From the collections of The Shaker Museum, Old Chatham. Photographs by Nathan Taylor.

351. From the collections of The Shaker Museum, Old Chatham. Photographs by Nathan Taylor. D 7½″ H 6″ OH 11″

352. From the collections of Shakertown at Pleasant Hill, Ky. Photograph by Linda Butler.

353. From the collections of the Ropes Mansion, Salem, Mass. Photographs by Martha Wetherbee. D 7″ H 5⅛″ OH 9″

354. From the collections of the Ropes Mansion. Photographs by Martha Wetherbee. D 6½″ H 4½″ OH 8″

355. Detail, Fig. 348.

356. Detail, private collection and Figure 328.

357. Indian fruit-style basket, Ed Clerk Collection. Photograph by Hugh McMillan 3rd.

358. Detail, Fig. 353.

359. Mt. Lebanon lidded cathead. Courtesy, Henry Francis du Pont Winterthur Museum, 70.203, Gift of Mrs. Edward Deming Andrews.

360. Mt. Lebanon saucer from the collections of Fruitlands Museum. Photograph by Nathan Taylor.

361. Detail, Mt. Lebanon tub from the collections of Fruitlands Museum. Photograph by Nathan Taylor.

Martha Wetherbee and Nathan Taylor are preeminent basketmakers who have studied traditional American basketry for fifteen years. Their interests lie not only in the making of baskets but also in uncovering and documenting the lost history of the basketmaker's art. Their knowledge of how baskets are made allows them to "read" basket history from a unique perspective.

Recognized as the authorities in their field, Martha Wetherbee and Nathan Taylor are best known for the Shaker baskets which they reproduce at the basketshop adjoining their home in a hillside clearing in Sanbornton, New Hampshire. In recent years they have been touring the United States as lecturers and teachers, sharing their knowledge of the Shaker basket system and other "signature" styles. Their baskets are exhibited internationally, and have been featured in magazines such as *Americana, Country Living, Country Home* and *Fine Woodworking*.

Shaker Baskets is their second major publication, following *Legend of the Bushwhacker Basket* published by Martha Wetherbee Books, 1986. The authors may be reached by mail at Star Route, Box 116, Sanbornton, NH 03269.